Me & My Shadow

Move from Fear and Control

to Love and Freedom

Diana Rose Iannarone

Change Your Mind; Change Your Life, LLC

Getting People Out of Their Own Way!™

www.standingup.us

ISBN: 0988950103

ISBN-13: 978-0-9889501-0-8

Wading River, New York

For Ashleigh, for her unending love,

which always carried me through.

For Finn, for personifying the end of the cycle of abuse.

Preface

Wake Up, Stand Up, Live Free

Given something drew you to open this book, I am going to suggest that at some level, though perhaps a purely unconscious one, you know that you are diligently working to ignore some reality in your life. At a deep level you know something is hiding in the *shadows,* something just isn't right. It just seems easier to remain asleep to that darkness, to deny its existence, rather than awakening to the truth about yourself and the true conditions of your life.

It really is possible to spend your whole life reading self-help books while remaining "asleep" in your own life. In fact, after scouring the self-help section of book stores for decades, I now know that there was an important book missing from those shelves. That is the book that I have attempted to write.

Perhaps you have heard that age-old expression, "Teachers teach what they most need to learn?" Despicably true I am afraid. Teaching can be an avoidance technique. We focus on others instead of ourselves. We try and fix "them" instead of putting our energy into our own lives.

I spent much of my life as the classic teacher, assisting others in freeing themselves from negative perceptions and beliefs while still being unconsciously entrenched in my own. It is only now that I am writing to you as the one who has learned, though my path to this knowledge has not been an easy one. My journey spans nearly three decades, many miles, and uncounted tears. I am hoping that with this guide, your path to freedom may be less arduous than my own.

In order to *wake up*, the first thing we have to be willing to do is recognize and acknowledge that we are asleep. In our asleep state, we are choosing to be unaware of the entirety of ourselves and our circumstance. Not being aware of our own thoughts and feelings allows us to deny truths that are right in front of our eyes. We often believe the authority in our lives, the controller of our circumstance, is outside of ourselves. What if this is false? We must consider that allowing anything outside of ourselves to designate our path may not lead us to where we claim we want to go. Once we choose to begin to awaken to our reality, we are still in a groggy state, and it can take time to decipher what is real and what is a dream, what is good and what is bad. Full wakefulness takes courage and empowerment to then Stand Up in our truth to all that is in the shadows, and finally Live Free.

All the great authors and prophets talk about awareness being the key to all the wonders of living a happy and full life, and I wholeheartedly agree. Except it begs the question, if we are not aware, or awake to the reality of our life, how can we possibly know we are unaware, or as I often reference it, "asleep"? And if we are not aware, what can we do to become aware? To be aware we need to wake up fully, our eyes must be wide open to the truth, first in our individual world and then in the world at large. In this book I intend to lead you there.

Remaining asleep can sometimes feel very natural, but on a long enough timeline it will become very difficult to ignore those red flags waving in front of your face. Red flags are promptings that are trying to warn us that some aspect of our life, be it our spiritual, financial, emotional, physical, or mental self, is teetering on the edge of utter despair. This book can change your life by empowering you to Wake Up to the potentially harsh realities of your current situation and give you the tools you need to change that situation. Waking up may be hard to do; however it is the first step on the path to freedom and happiness. Waking up begins to free you from delusion and deception allowing you to enjoy the vibrancy and emotional fullness of living life wide awake.

I am awake. One might usually pinch themselves to be sure. I, on the other hand, am aware that for the first time in my life I am not being pinched, criticized, diminished, deceived, controlled, neglected, violated, or abandoned. Simply put, I have no abuse in my life, not even my own views or words to myself, about myself. I am free from addictions, compulsions, and worry. Today the full power within me is alive and well.

Prior to awakening, I managed to build a façade so impenetrable that even I was unaware of the pain in my existence. If you could see behind that façade, it would surely frighten you. It might frighten you to hear of the suffering I allowed in my life in an effort to accomplish what I had believed was my purpose; to understand and heal the heart of the abuser. I believed this to be my greatest task in life, or my "soul purpose." I say "soul purpose" and not sole purpose because my purpose seemed so clear to me. It was a given. I thought it was my reason for being. I suppose now when I look at it, ultimately I believed it would lead to my feeling loved, feeling more important or worthy in some way. Perhaps it would make me feel I was enough, I was loveable. As parts of my story are revealed to you it might frighten you because it may be incomprehensible to you that someone would allow such abuse, or it might frighten you because my story will sound strikingly familiar, and in those moments where it resonates, you will know that you too, may be asleep.

Freedom does exist and it is not just in fairy tales. It is a decision. Make the decision to unleash the truth of who you truly are and be courageous enough to live it. Be awake to all the realities around you. Live free. It can happen to you.

As you travel with me to my arrival at freedom, assess where you are on that path, and start your journey from there. It is time to Wake Up, Stand Up and Live Free!

"None are more hopelessly enslaved than those who falsely believe they are free."
Johann Wolfgang von Goethe
(1749-1832)

4

Sleeping

You have likely heard the expression we don't know what we don't know. Consider that it is also true that the more we know, the more we realize how much we don't know. So the question becomes how willing are we to investigate what we don't know? How willing are we to look at ourselves to discover how much of the beliefs we are living by are truly our own?

What if at the deepest level of our soul we always know what is right for our highest, greatest good even if that truth seems concealed from us? What if your inner knowing is prompting you to remember your truths, the ones you buried long ago? And what if given that at our deepest core we know, when we operate against it, we also know? The reason this is critical is if there is a *misalignment* between our beliefs at our soul level and what we are experiencing in our life, then an *incongruence* is created. That incongruence creates an inner prompting, a small voice that raises a red flag to say, "Something isn't right, Wake Up!" It is telling us we moved our eye off the ball, which is love. Amazingly though, while asleep, we ignore that voice because while we are asleep we are living unconsciously devoted to proving our false beliefs true. This is not because that decision is for our highest, greatest good. No, it is because we refuse to look at ourselves to discover the misalignment between what is for our highest, greatest good and how we are living. Instead, we continue to live with our suffering, not just live in it, but exacerbate it.

Being asleep is simply being in denial of the reality of our circumstance by unconscious choice, often because we choose to make those outside of ourselves an authority. We believe *them* over our inner *knowing*. That incongruence is telling us there is a misalignment. All we need do is remember or rediscover the truth about what we know, and recognize every action by yourself or another that is out of alignment with that truth. It is wholeness we seek and finding our wholeness is simply getting in alignment with ourselves, and nothing or no one else. While being incongruent we may treat others in alignment with our soul beliefs of right and wrong while we allow treatment of ourselves based on our false beliefs. The false beliefs are created as a child and held steadfastly to all the days of our life until we choose to examine them, and then have the courage to let them go.

So what makes us ignore our own thoughts and feelings? It starts when we are very young, often before the age of seven. We long for love and acceptance and at first we look to our parents or guardians, our first authority, for that love and acceptance. Through their guidance, good or bad, we become what we perceive we need to be to receive love and acceptance. This created "self" has little to do with who we actually are. Left unchecked, as we grow older, we never find "ourselves" again.

There are many people around us who wish to add to and influence our beliefs about what is required for us to be *good enough* or *deserving enough,* and our lack of understanding of who we really are and what we truly believe makes us candidates for that influence. Every person who wants to influence us has an agenda. Early on your parents had an agenda, consciously or unconsciously. Maybe it was to develop you into the person that could live the life that they wished they had, or maybe it was to control you physically or emotionally so that they could have *power over* or *control of,* something. Or maybe their agenda was to have a well behaved child, or the smartest child or the one that went to the best school or married into the best family. What is important to note is none of those agendas are about love of you, even though the parent or guardian may have believed that it was *only* about love. Instead, some of it may have been about ego, the desire to look good or to be seen as accomplished in the manner of society. We all want to be seen as good to obtain what we often believe is elusive: love and acceptance. Often we long for admiration and validation of our success from those outside of us.

As we get older where do we turn to learn who we need to be to achieve those things? And who do we allow to influence that? And do we consider, really consciously consider, whether or not those wishing to influence us have an agenda of their own? And do we ever assess their agenda against our own agenda, our own soul belief system, to see if it is in alignment? And just what is the consequence if we don't make that assessment? I am suggesting that, if we don't look at the truth in this arena, we remain asleep our whole life, unaware of the many ways in which we are being controlled, influenced or harmed. In essence, we blindly drink the Kool-Aid and, eat the porridge that is being given to us. We accept it as true, while pretending we are happy doing so. Or we accept that we are unhappy, just a victim of circumstance of our sad surroundings and our endless feelings of helplessness. We often believe we have no choice. What if this is simply not true? Wake up!

When others outside of us have an agenda they will look to create evidence to support that agenda. Any agenda is designed to keep you from being a free thinker, or simply free; a person that can discover and experience the greater whole...the all that is. The agenda, if we allow it, puts a narrow box around the possibilities...when in fact they are often boundless. People often use news reporting, textbooks, the Bible or other religious doctrine, and societal concepts and convictions, as the sole basis for their ideologies. Consider that there is often an accompanying view that those resources are all encompassing as if there are no omissions, omissions that may have been made from those resources to lead people to draw conclusions, perhaps to satisfy an agenda. This agenda may not truly be for **our** highest, greatest

7

good, but theirs. I dare make the same claim of history books and other texts...what has been purposefully omitted from those books? Why has that information been left out? Again I state, the more someone chooses to know, the more they will discover how much they don't know. Yet in order to arrive at that place of *knowing* they have to be willing to acknowledge that there are things beyond the scope of their present thinking that they don't know.

If we began to consider that every message from a source outside of ourselves had an agenda and to accommodate that agenda there may be something hidden from us, left in the darkness of the shadows in the hopes we would never see, would the temptation to wake up become compelling or more frightening? If it is compelling, you may already be on your journey to wakefulness or awake. If it is frightening or perhaps terrifying you might be dead asleep. Asleep, utilizing *ignorance is bliss* so that you might experience the illusion of joy, but you simply do not know what you do not know!

In my experience those things that you do not know are normally not found in a text book, Bible or any standard resource alone. Instead, you must not fear looking to resources that perhaps you had never considered looking to. That fear just may have been instilled in you, so that you would never know. That fear was created so that you believe you must stay on this tight rope for your own safety and salvation. Perhaps you will have to open the cover of books or resources outside the grounds of *instilled* thinking, to learn what **you** truly believe, **your** truth. Isn't it true that their breakthroughs, the breakthroughs of outside-the-box thinkers, are often regarded as hogwash? Maybe even by you? Perhaps that label of hogwash is just a safety mechanism to keep you in your illusion, or to maintain a view-point you established at a very young age, that you just don't want to let go of or are unconsciously afraid to let go of. After all, who doesn't like the security blanket of the illusion of knowing? Yet as we step outside the bounds of those thoughts instilled in us and allow ourselves the freedom to discover what truly feels right to us...something magical happens. We begin to see that many free thinkers have drawn the same conclusions, those in complete opposition to some of what we have always been taught to know or believe. And it feels right. And at that moment...*a congruence* is formed. Something that tells you, this is true, this is aligned with my deepest core, my *soul* *knowing*...and then you suddenly realize to speak of these matters you will need courage, because others will go back to their resources to prove to you that you are wrong. You see while their resources may be accurate in the content they have, they may be inaccurate due to the content intentionally left out of those pages. You needn't convince others of your view, just be willing to establish a view that is your own. There is no need to be compelled to convince another that the tight rope they are walking on may be faulty. Only those that wish to see the light of the truth can find it. If they truly wish to find it, they will seek it. And the less you feel that you must persuade another that you are right and they are wrong, it may reflect nothing more than the significant truth that you may have found your wholeness in yourself. You just may be Awake!

Be warned, however, that the commonality that you discover in that small circle of individuals that speak outside the standard instilled beliefs about religion, politics, relationships, human behavior, the world, war, economics, the body, the mind, the spirit, anything at all, does NOT now confirm that **this** truth is the absolute truth and you should look no further. No, it is that once you are willing to go on that path, to venture outside the scope of the beliefs that you have perceived were yours all the days of your life, but have since discovered they were in fact someone else's, that willingness compels you to have an open mind, a broad manner of thinking. In these moments you begin to realize that maybe establishing your own beliefs, becoming your own authority, can keep you safe from guilt and shame that others often would like to put upon you to keep you in line. Your willingness to look inside yourself and venture to any outside resource that you feel guided to allows you to have the benefit of knowing that learning never ends, and that your life is a constant flow of abundant happenings that prove each theory you embrace as you walk through. You begin to watch as you experience your new beliefs creating new realities...and once you arrive where you witness the truths of the new found wisdom and knowing, you will not be moved when someone tries to narrow your focus by referencing a text that has been labeled "bible" or "authority" by some...you see in that, all the wars begin. A command that my way is better, my way is right, as if there are not boundless possibilities of right or better will no longer be acceptable to you. *It is in this text, reference, or book, therefore, it is true* will be overcome by

9

It is in my heart, it is in my knowing, and, therefore, it is true. You needn't agree with me, I have peace in my own knowing, my certainty. And thus, you will finally know, you are Free.

It is not just texts and written data I am referring to. I am also referring to the words that we hear from people that we view as an "authority." These are directives we get from others on how we should behave. There are those that wish to define for us what is proper and right by some standard, perhaps just capitalizing on the knowing that we are uncertain about whom we are and what is good and right for us. We are unclear of what will lead to our feelings of love and acceptance or right and wrong, so we listen. We listen to those outside of ourselves and trust their moral code, without every assessing the depth of morality of our chosen guide. Be clear that this is not to say that any doctrine, text or authority is wrong, and, frankly, who would I be to judge that for you? It is to say rather, regardless of your view of the rightness of any authority, what harm is there in venturing beyond the resources you have always sought? And what could possibly be wrong with turning inward to learn? As if you don't venture beyond where you have been, you cannot know if there is something that would feel more right to you because you will never know the truth, that the more you know, the more you will know you don't know...

So allow me to share with you what I didn't know while asleep to my incongruence.

What I didn't know was that above all else, I decided men were my authority. I believed their words and ignored their actions, I was asleep. My desire for love and acceptance was so great that I allowed them to be my guide. What I didn't know was that I allowed them to have *power over* and *control of* me because I was unaware that I had soul beliefs that were for my highest, greatest good. My soul beliefs were hidden from me, in favor of more damaging beliefs I acquired as a child. I consciously had no understanding of what **my** beliefs were, because I never looked. I was simply living by the beliefs I integrated unknowingly into my life. You will see though, the power of our beliefs create our lives. I assure you it is worth investigating your beliefs, so that you might live free of any controls and free to be precisely who you really truly are, finally living with only love and freedom.

Who is your authority? And is it really true that they are **the** authority or **more** of an authority than you? Is it your spouse, partner, parents, preacher, church, boss, teacher, sibling, work, school, or society as a whole...and do you really want to give them power over or control of you?

Given my goal is to free you from all deception and controls; I want to be upfront. I am not **your** authority and this book **has** an agenda. Uniquely, the agenda is to lead you to discover what your agenda is, and to help you decide that you are free to live in accordance with that. In your quest to live that agenda you must embrace the knowledge, perhaps unnervingly, that you are your own and only authority. Learn how to discover who you have given your power to and learn to reclaim it and all lost parts of you. Discover what your beliefs are at the soul level, rather than those that have been adopted by you due to influences and sources outside of yourself. It is at that time, you will be whole and complete and finally Living Free, no delusion, no control...just love, joy and a feeling of peace.

Diana Rose Iannarone

It may seem that those comments are in conflict. How can I suggest we only focus on ourselves while simultaneously saying we will begin to change the world? It is about changing the world one person at a time. Through our own healing we are more powerful in affecting change outside of ourselves. That first person we must heal is ourselves. That task may seem ominous, yet the effort of clearing the dark clouds leads to such exuberant living, we will never look back.

As you begin to look into yourself, it may be helpful to see an image of the world as a jigsaw puzzle. Now visualize the people of that world each holding their piece of that puzzle over their head. If each person held their own piece of that puzzle, the world would be at peace. In reality each of us observes how another is holding his or her piece and then we often judge them. We decide if they are holding their piece the right way or the wrong way, according to us. Or perhaps we decide that person isn't holding their piece at all, so we may begin our powerful and often disastrous function of trying to hold their piece for them. So what do you think happens as each of us stretches our fingers out far and wide to hold the pieces of those around us, perhaps disregarding the one over our head? We lose our stability. We are no longer steady on our feet, as our strength begins to diminish. The more we try to hold the pieces of those around us, the greater the likelihood that our piece will fall, along with all those pieces that others have let go of given we were willing to carry them. For now, let go of the burden of the responsibilities of others. This is all part of the waking process.

Once we Wake Up in our lives as individuals, we begin to notice when others are asleep; we have a broader, more aware view. Recognizing the large-scale deceptions and controls enables us to also experience their counterpart, the fullness of true and complete freedom.

As we grow stronger we will naturally apply our knowledge on a grander scale. As more of us awaken, we can influence the world by using our power of collective consciousness, our common awareness, to create the reality we desire. Aren't we all longing for the same things—joy, comfort, peace, love, and freedom? If these things are truly our goals, why can they seem so

15

unattainable? I believe we can reach these goals in the world, if we first look within, at our personal world.

I vividly remember the day my foot first fell upon the path to being awake. Another moment where I end the relationship and I evict the man after I endure intolerable pain, and yet, pieces of me want desperately to grab his sleeve and beg him to stay.

"Pieces of me," I say that literally and figuratively. We compartmentalize our lives and ourselves so that we can choose to look at the things we can bear, and avoid or disassociate from the things we are not yet ready to see. Unfortunately though, most of us don't know we are doing this, until we become aware. And when we attain this awareness, it is like watching as a movie unfolds, but this is no movie, it is our life. In this fragmented or wounded state, we cannot feel whole. Although we may be unaware or asleep to this reality, as will be revealed to you, it is our longing for wholeness that creates our journey.

Immediately upon awakening, we begin to see every truth that was hidden before—every deception, every manipulative act of sheer cruelty or even simple unkindness that was unleashed on us. In the past we minimized this hurt and excused these actions because we believed that the person hurting us had been hurt in the past, or in our delusion we completely denied that they harmed us. *They were doing the best they could*, we told ourselves. We couldn't see their acts as evil or cruel. Instead we saw their actions as a testament to their poor and injured soul. The idea that their acts and words were a manipulation with the intent to harm another was preposterous to us. We wanted to be of service in their healing, in the healing of all others, sadly without any consideration for ourselves. You will see this type of harmful self-sacrifice as a recurring theme until Awakened. We may choose to risk our lives or joy to alleviate another's mere discomfort. We will do anything to not be judged as mean or inadequate, fearing that loss of love and acceptance. However, this sacrifice is not an appropriate allocation of our most important resource, ourselves. We are worthy of far better than survival, we are worthy of love, and of freedom.

The Truth May Rest in the Shadows

Conflict and drama. I think it is author Susan Jeffers who refers to it as "living in the horseradish." It sure is a lousy feeling, yet it is often what we know, so we stay there until we absolutely can't bear it anymore.

You may wonder why we are so quick to excuse the cruelty, evil-doings or even simply the meanness of others. This is because we ourselves are unwilling to see our own capacity for evil. We do not even like the word. We shudder to think we could possibly have such a capacity and, as a result, we deny it in ourselves and we deny it in others, even as this truth is displayed boldly before us. We have disowned our capacity for evil long ago, perhaps with no conscious awareness. We close our eyes to it. We deny this *capacity* that is inherent in every human. Yes, every human has the capacity for evil, even us, and even those we love.

I too struggled to understand that people could be bad. In fact, when asked by my therapist what I told my daughter about ending one abusive relationship, I shared with her that I told my daughter, "He was a good man that did some bad things and he wasn't healthy for us to live with anymore."

I was instructed to go home right in that moment, and tell my daughter that I had told her what I believed was the truth, but that now I learned something different, and needed to tell her what was the more accurate truth.

"He was a bad man who did some good things and he wasn't healthy for us to live with anymore."

To help me see this conclusion my therapist asked me if I would do to another the things that were being done to me. My answer was an adamant "no"…but of course my immediate thought was so clear, *no one understood his pain like I did, if they did, they would know he was doing the best he could.* I couldn't see the great assessment tool I was given in that moment, to ask, "What would keep me from doing those acts on another?" I couldn't see that it was because they were mean, cruel, yes, even evil acts. They were too mean for me to do *to* another, yet not too mean for me to accept *from* another. I couldn't see *my* pain through my illusion of *their* pain.

He was a bad man. I had never even opened my mind or heart to that consideration that some people are inherently bad and I wouldn't for quite some time.

He was a bad man who did some good things and he wasn't healthy for us to live with anymore.

My daughter knew from that moment on that some people, men or women, were bad. She was Awake. Her wisdom was greater than mine in this regard.

Our rejection of our capacity for evil or our "shadow side," means we are not willing to embrace all of who we are, and in doing so we remain fragmented and not whole. You cannot disown any parts of yourself and be whole and complete. Until we embrace our own capacity for evil, we deny evil when we see it in others. How can we recognize that which we refuse to see?

To achieve wholeness we must be awakened to and accept *all* parts of ourselves, even those parts of ourselves that we view as imperfect. We will always be an imperfect species. While on our unconscious quest for wholeness, we begin to painfully and unwittingly seek that which we deny in ourselves. We seek to find the missing pieces of ourselves in another.

The fact that we have the capacity for evil or harm does not make us evil. If you prefer, think of it as your dark side, or your shadow; the part of you where the light is hidden from. You would not do evil. It is your sense of ethics that keeps you from acting in evil ways, however, that does not nullify the reality that you have the *capacity*. You cannot awaken until you embrace this truth. All humans have the capacity. To start, consider this; have you ever had an evil thought? Something that you considered but you would never do? Perhaps you have even acted on it. Perhaps you have lied, or manipulated, or stolen. These are all acts of the shadow, but these mere acts do not make you an evil person.

Once you embrace this capacity it may very well give you a lifeline. There are lifelines available for you that would seem unreasonable to grab while you are asleep. In fact, while asleep, you are not even able to see the lifeline. Part of awakening is accepting this side of you, the shadow side. You cannot arrive at your freedom without it.

I know that if you turn on the television and hear about someone going into a school and killing children, you would recognize that as an act of evil. However, you also likely don't believe there is anyone in your life capable of that act, and that may not be true.

If we only live in the innocence, the goodness side of our capacity, and we are unaware of our dark side, then we have an imbalance. This imbalance makes us more susceptible to have evil befall us because we are blind to the potential to fall prey to evildoers. We are unarmed and unarmored and have an unwillingness to truly protect ourselves.

If you ignore your capacity for evil as I did, it just may show up in some monumental way. In my case, it showed up in my tendency to draw into my life people operating from what I call the "shadow side" or "dark side".

19

Whatever label you give to these people is unimportant, what is important to grasp is that they embrace the capacity that we ignore, the capacity for evil—the side of them that justifies doing harm. I was unaware that I was inviting them in as part of an unconscious effort to find my wholeness, seeking the parts of me I had rejected. The parts of me I had disowned.

To acknowledge and embrace your dark side does not mean you operate from it. It means you accept its significance and no longer need to seek it outside of yourself. Those that operate from the shadow have rejected the light of their innocence. To be safe from them we must ignite and embrace our shadow side, not to do harm, but to protect first ourselves and then others from harm. We must stop concluding that protecting ourselves by placing boundaries for our safety makes us mean. We must eliminate the perceived challenge of using the word "no" as a strong and nonnegotiable word to honor ourselves.

In essence in an asleep state, we judge people by our own standard of being because it is all we can see. My experiences have taught me that this can be very dangerous. The reason this is dangerous is if we decide that no person who claims to love us, or even a person we just met, could bestow an act of evil, harm, or deception upon us because we would not do so to another, then even when we catch glimpses of red flags, we discount those warning signs and excuse them away. We can't believe such cruelty exists so we decide it is simply them doing the best they can. They may hurt us, but they don't mean to. We begin to believe we must be crazy to think or feel hurt or concerned. They are good. They must be good…Right?

We decide that the feeling we have that this treatment is wrong must be what is wrong. They love us and would never harm us. They wouldn't intentionally be mean.

The feeling I have that this is wrong
must in fact be what is wrong. My feelings are wrong,
not the act of what is happening to me or being told to me.

I believe this reasoning is often what immobilizes people when they are observing something unthinkable happening, like someone being raped or

20

beaten. It's as if they tell themselves it is not happening and therefore they sit idly by and watch without doing anything to attempt to interfere. We *all* have the capacity for good and evil. What you see and experience is this playing itself out, pay attention. We must own all capacities within ourselves so that we can see them in others.

Look at your life and the relationships in it. Do you see continuous mistreatment of yourself by others? If you back up and look across your life and see a pattern of pain and excuses, then you have been allowing abuse in your life. It is also likely you have not accepted the whole of you, your capacities for both good and evil. You are asleep. The more asleep you are the greater the level of abuse you are willing to tolerate.

So many acts of violence, including murder, are instituted on us by people that claim to love us or people that we think we know. Wake Up! If you think you see signs that demonstrate *incongruence* or conflict between actions and words, don't disregard that inner knowing, presume they are real. Honor that still small voice that knows. Often these abusive relationships are wrought with constant incongruencies. We hear the words "I want help," while the speaker seeks none but that which we ourselves give. We hear the words "I love you," while being beaten down physically, emotionally or mentally. We hear the words "I promise" yet there is nothing ever delivered. Those empty promises that we chose to cling to helped to create our empty lives. Can you see this in the world at large as well? Over and over these patterns repeat, yet another red flag waving proud in front of our blind eyes. At all levels of life, look for this incongruence.

The object here is not to become paranoid and believe that everyone is going to harm us. When you are awake, embracing all parts of you, you are more able and willing to see all parts of others; you become much more aware as you observe people.

Since we are so often followers of established rules, and we are so unlikely to recognize evil, we have a hard time grasping that those in authority may be bad. Those in authority can be anyone, whether it is a parent, boss, sibling, lawyer, police officer, politician, or even a spouse. Anyone who we perceive has power over us, or is more aware of what is best for us, we consider an authority. Our belief that we must honor authority, must respect authority, is often a byproduct of conditioning. We don't evaluate whether or not these individuals we view as authority are worthy of our honor and respect. We blindly honor them as we feel it is our duty. Worse, we perceive that we have to earn the right to be honored by them in return. We long for their compassion and respect, or we simply trust they have our best interests at heart. We often trust them based on position alone. We work harder and do more to achieve the compassion or respect we desire. We get in line to do what is expected of us. Instead, we need to realize that from the moment we were born we deserved to be honored. We need to realize that our loving nature is sacred, and should be held to a high esteem for those that are worthy of the honor of our love, not those that wish to harm. We also need to realize that even those in authority have a shadow side. It is our responsibility to observe and determine if they are operating from the light or the dark. Lastly, we need to realize that we are powerful. We hold a sword. We can use our sword to preserve our honor. We need not hide our power. We must embrace our power.

We must accept that it is not mean to protect ourselves. It is, instead, mean to ourselves not to.

To begin to learn to honor yourself, I ask you to have an image of a small child. I ask you to see that child holding your hand in every experience you encounter. Imagine that the small child endures everything you allow yourself to endure. Realize that it is your job to keep him or her safe and begin to show them by example, what is necessary to take care of themselves. Show them what it means to deeply and completely love themselves. Think of it as your responsibility to help that child see that they do not need to spend their energy defending, instead, they need *you* to create a life where defending themselves is unnecessary. This child is you. The child is in you longing for the *parent* in you to awaken. You need to be the best, most loving parent to yourself until you truly become the self-sufficient adult. Adult, not defined by your age, defined instead by the quality of your life, by your freedom, by your independence from fear and control.

To eliminate abuse in your life you must Wake Up to the denial of your reality and Stand Up so that you can finally embrace the freedom you deserve. Decide there will no longer be abuse in your life, and then you can shine the light to help end abuse on a broader scale, even if only by illumination of your peaceful life.

Wake Up, so that you may Stand Up and Live Free!

Me and My Shadow

Diana Rose Iannarone

The Decision

That day when I began my long arduous journey to waking is etched into my memory because I remember the particular words that echoed through my head like God himself was shaking me to listen. Here I was at 33, speaking to my long-time best friend screaming in despair, "I have kicked him out and he is leaving! He is leaving!" Her response was "Diana, it's not you, let him go." "Diana, it's not you." "Diana, it's not you!" The sound of those words resonated through the very essence of my being. Any good and loyal friend may have given this advice as they witnessed their friend, in this case me, falling victim to abuse. She had always been one of my biggest supporters throughout the years, and she felt that since I was a good person, I must just have horrible luck. However, after hearing those words from my friend year after year, relationship after relationship, I began to wonder. In that moment, I took a pause and simply said, "Of course it is me, or you wouldn't have been telling me that for nearly 15 years." And so my journey toward awakening began, albeit with a distorted perception.

My friend and I often laugh as we think back on that moment from where we sit now. As she now knows, as I now know, of course it was me. Today I see that I was my own worst abuser, for refusing to protect myself. From my perspective, the Universe, Source, or whatever you believe God to be, gives you a message in the way that you can hear it, gently at first. What I needed at that time so I could keep stepping forward was support and acceptance of myself, the person who I was in the world at that particular time. Through her providing me support, I was able to see the truth I needed to embrace. God sends you nothing but angels, and in that moment she was my angel. For the first time I could see a piece of reality I had hidden from before, a piece of reality that until that moment I could not even begin to embrace or accept. It *was* me.

I had started therapy just a few months before this particular day, hoping I could change enough to make the relationship work. I "knew" it was my words and actions that were always upsetting him, and I wanted to learn how to be a better partner to this man I thought I loved. How can I behave better? How can I do better, be better? I had always blamed my *behavior*, believing I was responsible for eliciting the abuse I received. I thought I was the reason for the issues, but I thought I was the reason because I wasn't good enough. The reason I had conjured up, that I had to do better or be better, was what was actually killing me. I had to realize instead that I needed to do better and be better for *me*, not anyone else. I needed to realize I deserved better than the circumstances of my life. I needed to realize I was the creator of the horseradish I was standing in, or more aptly put, sitting in with burning, tearing eyes. I *was* the problem, not because of my behavior, but because I was willing to accept the behavior of my abusers.

I didn't fully understand lies, deception, manipulation, or any form of evil. Since I perceived they weren't in *my* makeup, I assumed they weren't in anyone else's either. I never even looked, not even for a moment, at what was happening to me and being inflicted on me. I was blind to the deception and manipulation because I could only see the good. I would think I saw or felt red flags occasionally. I would experience little inner promptings warning me, but time after time I would choose to ignore these signs. I didn't understand they were warning me that I was incongruent with my soul; the

26

knowing of what was in my highest, greatest good was always present. Instead, at some unconscious level, I decided if I looked, or perhaps feared if I looked at the message of the red flag, my whole world would come crashing down. During that time I was asleep I never stopped to see that my personal world was already a train wreck; a train wreck that could have been salvaged at any time. It was then, and always will be, our choice.

One might presume that enlisting a very bright and talented therapist at my age of 33 would assure a peaceful life in roughly a few years. That would likely be true if I was willing to face the whole truth, and wake up fully to my reality. It would be more than a decade from when I had the inkling that I was the problem, before I Woke Up from my slumber. The precise moment I Woke Up was a moment that I will never forget. A point in time when I knew my life was forever changed. That moment in time literally felt as though a light switch had being flipped. For the first time my reality was illuminated, I could see the parts of my life I would not accept. Eventually, and in perfect timing, I will reveal that moment to you.

What if every person who enters your life is part of a Universal plan to bring you to self-love? What if every moment is a perfectly orchestrated synchronicity giving you the opportunity to honor your human value? What if at any moment we could choose healing over pain, love over hate, freedom over control? And what if every single person can choose to create the most loving life possible if we can just decide at all levels of our being that we deserve it? These are the questions I have spent over three decades pondering. My quest for freedom and peace became an internal journey. I now rest assured knowing I *do* deserve love, healing, and freedom and I am living it. I believe we all deserve that same gift.

We have always been able to heal and live free. It requires that we embrace and accept ourselves exactly where we are. Instead we choose to endure pain, denying our self-worth, all on a quest for love and acceptance while never giving it to ourselves. It is our desire to control the outcome that often causes our pain, coupled with our fear that we are doing something wrong. We don't want to fail or be seen as bad. To awaken, consider that we do not need to control others, nor be controlled. We need to see that we are enough, completely worthy of love and acceptance. Our wholeness comes from within. However, before we can experience this freedom we must begin to doubt all of our truths. We must reveal to ourselves the unconscious beliefs that are ruling our lives.

My perceived "soul" purpose was a substantial part of my unconscious belief system back then. My belief system obviously needed some work if I was willing to fully sacrifice myself to attempt to heal the abuser. Ultimately, to achieve healing I began to reevaluate my belief system as a whole. Why did I believe what I believed? What was right? What was wrong? What felt right to *me*? It was time to question all that I "knew," and doubt is not something that came easily. However, once I began looking at my situation and **doubting** its appropriateness, I began to exponentially fast track my life to greater awareness and living Awake. I began asking myself, *Why?* If you believe that something is or is not acceptable, simply ask yourself *Why?* or *Why not?* You should be able to answer these seemingly simple questions, although it is not always an easy task. It is in answering the simple *Why?* that you begin to reveal, and then likely reformulate your belief system. Your belief system is what you use as a standard against which you measure every aspect of your life. When you ask yourself, *Is this right? Am I happy? Was that appropriate?* your belief system is the yard stick to help you determine the answers. For some, the most difficult part of evaluating and then reconstructing this belief system is that you must do so without looking outside of yourself. Initially, don't look to a book, an authority, a religious text, a teacher, or a parent. While these things can be good resources, it is not the time for them yet. This book or any other resource should not direct your thoughts; instead, it should simply help you with a process to discover the answers within yourself. You have always had the necessary power and authority to build an abundant life of love and acceptance. YOU are the creator of many things, including your own belief system.

You likely have already had plenty of influences on your belief system, some beneficial, some detrimental. You may already be living based on someone else's belief system. Entertaining the idea of following a belief system that you yourself have designed may feel counter-intuitive or even scary. You may feel as though doing something against your previous belief system, even if it feels right to you, will make you a bad person. While that certainly makes sense, remember that following any given path without question does not make you good, it simply makes you a good follower. You must follow a path that you define. Living something because you believe you have to, and then judging yourself as "good" for doing it, is a deception.

Unlike the prescribed belief system you may currently be following, the one that you define will give you peace when you operate within it.

While things outside of yourself are not good starting points, once you embrace specific thoughts of your own, you can, and in fact should, always go outside of yourself for more information, but never lose sight of what **you** believe. You must balance being open to new information without shifting to a belief system that is not in alignment with your own values. Always assess and decide based on what feels right to you. Don't hide from who you really are—live it.

How can we claim to be free when we feel we must hide our thoughts and views for fear that we will lose something or someone outside of ourselves? If we don't discover who we truly are and then stand for our thoughts and beliefs, haven't we already had a major loss? Haven't we lost ourselves by denying our own truth? We must find our truth and not hide from it. It is easy to find self-esteem and self-confidence when you have both the inner and outer peace of operating in alignment with your beliefs.

Living free is about defining who you are by honestly evaluating your own experiences and inner knowing. It is your everyday life moments that teach you what you don't want; use that information to begin to create a life around what you *do* want. Living transparently, revealing the fullness of who you are and what you believe, and making choices with acts of love as the premise, takes courage. I invite you into the courageous life of living free.

For now, imagine any possible belief is a valid one and potentially the very one you may want in your life, even if until today you may have perceived it was unthinkable. Then, as you determine that a certain belief is not truly in alignment with your core, make a mental note of that, and use some of the tools I will outline for you to shift to beliefs more in alignment with who you really are—even if others have told you it would be unacceptable. Even if people you view as an authority have told you it is unacceptable. Who is your authority?

Often we use avoidance of our truths because we have been programmed to never question authority; whoever we perceive authority to be. This single premise is designed to keep us under the power of another. It is effectively stealing the life force from our souls. We can stop it at any time—in our personal world first; then together on a grander scale.

Our beliefs are a byproduct of our experiences. Our experiences are only what we take away from them. Whether they are good or bad experiences, they will provide us with the building blocks that we have for our entire worldview. The letters DOG are meaningless. It is only through our experiences that we attribute meaning to them. A person in rural China who has never seen any words in English, will not find any meaning in the symbols DOG. We have learned that the symbols DOG refer to a four legged mammal that may present itself in a variety of sizes and colors. However, Timmy from *Lassie* and the victim of a brutal attack by such a creature, will react very differently to the symbols DOG. That phenomenon stems from our experiences. The beliefs that we hold throughout our life with every fiber of our being, even if there is not a smidgen of truth in them, have power over us. These beliefs were and are our foundation, and we create our lives accordingly. We believe them and often choose to never let them go, until we do. Start now. Begin to question your thoughts about everything, whether it be your idea of a healthy relationship, success, money, loyalty, God, or the characteristics you attribute to a DOG. So, what do you do with this belief system once it is defined? How do you use it to determine if you are asleep? I believe the tool to use is to ask yourself if you are at peace in all the key areas of your life:

- ❖ **Spiritually**
- ❖ **Financially**
- ❖ **Emotionally**
- ❖ **Physically**
- ❖ **Mentally**

Each of these things take on whatever meaning you attribute to them. The goal is for you to really assess what your beliefs are in each area of your life. Often we are awake, or at least more awake, in one or more categories than others. However, we must examine our beliefs in all categories. Once fully Awake, the delineations we have created are no longer necessary. There will be no use for the idea of the spiritual self, or the emotional self, we will simply be "ourselves."

Redefining your belief system is not simple, and neither is self examination. Try not to look at it as an insurmountable task, instead just look at it as beginning to really get to know yourself, the self you likely abandoned many years ago. Reexamine your belief system as it pertains to every aspect of your life. In doing this for each belief ask yourself:

Why do I believe that?

- Is this my inner self speaking relative to a principle or value *I* established and hold or am I simply following the path that others have laid for me?
- Do I associate some negative consequence with changing this belief?

Decide that you have the ability within yourself to align your beliefs with your own values and principles. Intricately assessing your own beliefs will put you well on your way to achieving self-awareness, the largest part of your path to freedom.

The same way DOG has only the meaning we have given it based on what we have learned from our past experiences, all our beliefs have been established this way, through our experiences. Our beliefs are a result of our perception of the lessons learned in those experiences. Think of your memories, your defining moments as a child. The stories themselves are only minimally important, although understandably you may feel differently. What is of paramount importance is what you decided about life because of that story. Each of our stories often takes up only a moment, an instant. Those moments have nothing more than the meaning we give them. Our life is not so much about the details of the moments we can recall, as it is about the beliefs that they helped us form. When we begin to discover the lasting impact of our stories, we can begin to dissolve the resulting false beliefs we carry that can mold our lives into a living hell. Instead we must find those beliefs that can and will create heavenly bliss. We cannot change the content of our stories, only the decisions we make about life because of them. Our goal now is to become aware and through that, find our freedom. It is up to us.

Many people identify with their story so much that the bad things that happened to them define them. *I am a rape victim, I am a victim of abuse, I am ill*. I encourage you instead to not label yourself as the bad things that happened to you, as then you see yourself as that event, or more clearly as that victim. You are not a victim in this moment unless you believe you are. As long as you continue to see yourself as victim, that is what you will remain.

You may have been raped, abused or have a medical disease or diagnosis; decide you are not those things. Those are things that happened to you but they do not need to define you. If they are how you define yourself, how can you release them? Letting go of something that you define yourself by may feel like losing yourself, when in fact, perhaps releasing it is precisely what you should consider doing to find who you are. You are not those negative experiences. *I am...* is a very powerful statement. Follow those words with only loving words. *I am fat*, will cause you to live all the behaviors as if it is so…whether that means starving yourself as one might do if anorexic, or over-feeding yourself until your reality matches the "truth" you tell yourself; satisfying your belief: I am fat.

I will tell you pieces of my story to help you see that I have stood where many of you are standing, and to help you see how it shaped my beliefs and kept me in my own way for a good part of my life. Yet, I want to re-emphasize that our story, what happened to us in the past is not really all that relevant. What *is* relevant is what we decided in those moments and how those decisions are affecting us now. It is only in overcoming the negative power of the beliefs we created as a result of our stories, that we can allow our stories to hold blessings rather than pain. In your triumph of healing, you can share the wholeness obtained **because** of your story. It is in your peaceful wholeness that you can help others heal. I hope this message about our stories is penetrating your thought process for consideration. I also hope you realize it isn't about minimizing what happened to us, it is about finding our joy in life now, regardless of what happened to us.

We have a tendency to be our own "minimizers." We may think that someone's story is worse than our own. Or we may think that someone doesn't have the right to feel pain because we have lived through "worse." However, it is important to realize that it is all subjective. If it is real to us, then it is real. If we are still holding on to the past, it acts as a rubber-band pulling us endlessly backward. Even if we are attempting to move forward, that pull makes our forward movement exhausting. We need to cut that rubber-band holding us to our past, so we can catapult into the present and create a joyful future.

Me and My Shadow   Diana Rose Iannarone

Creation of Our Beliefs

In an attempt to ensure that your path toward awakening is more direct than my own, and hopefully less painful, I will walk you through each of the key areas of assessment in my life to illustrate my own path from sleep to wakefulness. In doing so, I hope to give you some insight as to what you might discover should you choose to evaluate your own life. Before I walk you through those critical components, allow me first to lay a foundation, so that you can fit your own experiences into the blanks and see the truth of the impact of your beliefs as you examine your own life. Once the foundation of how our beliefs are created is laid, I will reveal to you significant details of the abuse I endured so that you might look deeply at just how far our misperceptions, our determination to stay asleep to our reality, can go.

My intention is not to compare your story to mine. This is not an issue of "better or worse." Instead, in my revealing my truth, sharing my vulnerabilities, disclosing some of what I allowed myself to endure, I hope to remind you that no matter where you are on your path, healing and freedom are possible. More than possible, they are an absolute given. All you need do is awaken from deceptions and see the entirety of your reality. From that space, you will embrace the full power that has always existed within you and unequivocally know, you are free to Stand Up and create the reality you long for. It has always been just within your reach. You can Live Free.

What is the essence that creates our beliefs?

When I think of my distant past I acknowledge that competitive swimming was a huge part of it. I swam all the time and all my coaches would say what I lacked in talent, I had in **stamina and endurance**. I would give whatever it took to be seen as a winner. However, I wasn't concerned with being seen as a winner by just anyone, I wanted to be a winner in my father's eyes. If he was proud of me, I perceived that he loved me. So I thrust myself fully into whatever it took to make my dad proud. When I was young, I focused my energy on being a good swimmer. When I was an adult, I focused all my energy on my career, pushing for my dad's validation. Today, I know he loves me even if I do nothing, but even if that was not the case, I no longer need his validation to feel whole. I finally realize the love and acceptance that creates our wholeness is about who we *are,* not what we *do,* and we should never become something we are not to achieve love and acceptance. That kind of conditional love is not real. It is only our love and acceptance of ourselves we should be seeking, any outside love should be granted simply for who we are.

Now I recognize that it wasn't just my dad I wanted to please; ultimately, it was anyone I perceived as an authority, or that mattered to me at some meaningful level, even my brother. He was five years older than me and therefore I saw him as an authority figure. One day when I was about 8 years old, he asked me to help him build a radio. Wow, was I excited! My big brother wants *me* to help *him*.

My instructions were simple. "Diana, hold these two pieces while I solder them and don't let go." And so I did. I held those two pieces and did not let go. I didn't let go even when the solder was burning two holes in my knee. I

36

recall saying to my brother, "The solder is dripping." As he looked down to see the solder landing on my knee, he said, "Let go! What the hell is wrong with you?"

This memory of mine stayed with me as a testimony to beliefs I had as a child and carried to many future years. It exemplifies my beliefs for most of my life perfectly. Beliefs I didn't consciously know I had until many years later. Keep in mind this is the story as I remember it. Also keep in mind, how I remember it, is the only truth that matters. Regardless of what may or may not have actually occurred, this is *my* truth.

My behavior in that experience with my brother represents a belief I had about the power of authority that was established well before that moment. I believed that I must listen to authority, even if doing so caused me harm. I don't know for certain what exactly caused this particular belief, but that too is unimportant. What is important, is that we wake up to the truth about the power we give our authority and who our authority really is.

I purposely chose a story of pain unintentionally being inflicted on me. My brother didn't hold the solder gun to my leg and watch as holes were burning through my knee. Even those with the best of intentions may give us fuel for the fire of our false beliefs. All that matters is we realize we make decisions in every given moment of our life and some of those decisions are crippling us! Didn't I have the power to let go to stop the pain of the dripping solder? I didn't let go. It was that fact that begged the question, "What the hell is wrong with you?" I was then, and remained for many years to follow, incapable of not following what I perceived was an order. To me men were the strongest authority. I gave men my power. Who have you labeled "authority" and given your power to? Who or what are you allowing to abuse, manipulate, or control you in your home, work, family, school, church, or any or all-important areas of your life?

Those scars from that childhood experience still exist on my knee; no longer do they exist in my heart.

While I never experienced abuse from either of my parents directly, there was a fair dose of fear that if daddy was unhappy something terrible would happen. I don't recall any actual physical pain or anything I can classify as "terrible" being inflicted on me by my father, although the constant threat of *"Wait until your father gets home..."* often left a palpable fear of the unknown. I knew that mom always wanted daddy happy. She never wanted him to be mad, and I perceived that it was the responsibility of us children to ensure his happiness. I trusted that was reason enough to stay in line. I had good, responsible parents. It is clear to me, especially now, how much they loved me. As a child, this love was shown more through devotion to my sporting events and strict supervision rather than hugs and kisses, but it was and is a deep love just the same.

As a child it was unacceptable to express my emotions. The thought of expressing my emotions carried with it too much risk that someone might get mad. I perceived it was not safe to stand up to my parents. It was safer to be silent, to hide who I truly was, my feelings, and my truths. My parents were my first authority as your parents likely were yours.

If you cry, "I'll give you something to cry about." If you laugh too much, "Better stop laughing or you will end up crying," if you were angry, it was not safe to speak. You get the idea. I grew up in era where children should be seen and not heard. It is just the way it was. So I chose to quiet my voice in favor of love and acceptance from those around me.

Again, I can carry the "poor me's" all my life of how I didn't feel free to speak or I can release it. Authority ruled regardless of what the reality was from where I sat. So what? How long should I allow those experiences to rule my life? Until I release those experiences and the associated false beliefs they formed, life will keep putting me in situations where I can't be heard by "authority" in one facet of my life or another. What occurred back then simply doesn't matter now and if you still think it does, you are trapped in a misery of your own creation. Let it go. Decide instead what those experiences taught you about life. Learn what beliefs you are carrying as a result of your experiences and what sabotaging impact they might be having on the life you are currently living. In doing so, you can begin to create a life that serves your soul truth.

As a child, sometimes the fear of the consequences is bigger than whatever the consequence might be. As a child the fear was enough. We all make decisions based on what we perceive. Perception is reality. After significant self examination, I have identified some misperceptions I have had most of my life because of my childhood experiences:

- ❖ It is not okay to speak of my emotions.
- ❖ Women are weak.
- ❖ Men are authority figures.
- ❖ It is my job to be sure the man is happy, and, therefore, if the man is unhappy it is my fault.
- ❖ It is up to me to keep the peace.
- ❖ I must do as authority says, no matter what the personal consequences.
- ❖ I must endure intolerable pain if necessary to please authority.
- ❖ If I stand up and speak my emotions, something terrible will happen.
- ❖ I do not deserve compassion, only blame.
- ❖ If someone or something hurts me it is my own fault.
- ❖ If someone or something hurts me there is something wrong with me.

This is just a short list of the many damaging beliefs I had, you can see how some of these played out in the solder instance. These are some of my earliest beliefs, ones that I was unconsciously allowing to destroy my life. You have them too although they are bound to be different. As I disclose to you portions of my life you will see how each of my beliefs perfectly reflect the decisions I made to stay in a life of abuse; the beliefs I decided to adopt as a result of various childhood experiences, regardless of whether these beliefs were actually true. My beliefs would create years of circumstances that aligned with them. That is because our lives will be congruent with our beliefs about it, which is what makes examining and adjusting your beliefs crucial.

What if it is true that your outer world will continually give you situations where you are unconsciously confirming the beliefs you have? In grasping that thought, might you be moved to delve deep and find your unconscious beliefs? In an effort to determine them you might first simply evaluate your self-talk and many will be revealed to you. Listen to your own *I am...* statements. You can start by writing down beliefs you perceive you have or you can begin by writing down memories. Simply write down the memories you recall and ask yourself what you might have decided about life given you had this experience. If you look at the single story I shared with you about my brother, you can likely see the congruence in how I experienced that moment and my beliefs. Unfortunately, the congruence is with my destructive *false* beliefs, which are **incongruent** to the beliefs in my core, my *soul* beliefs...only I had chosen not to examine the true nature of my life. I ignored the inner voice trying to alert me, I was too busy trying to please others to evaluate the meaning of my inner prompting.

Digging through your memories will help you to find the meaning buried within them. If you do not recall childhood memories, you can still uncover your beliefs by becoming more aware and observant in the key areas of your life. As you become more aware, you will begin to see patterns or themes in either what you remember or what you are currently experiencing, or both. You will see patterns of self-sabotage. Finding your patterns and learning your "truths" will ultimately lead you down your path to freedom.

Again, it is easy to find evidence confirming an already held belief, since you see the world through the lens of that belief. When you have a belief, even if it is false, your outer experience will evidence for you that your belief is true. That experience helps you to keep holding onto that belief. The fact is though, because alignment between your thoughts and outer reality is absolutely inevitable, changing your belief will also change your outer experiences. Relative to your beliefs, alignment or congruency is absolutely a given in life. Your soul has been trying to awaken you to look at your beliefs, so that you might remember you are worthy of love and acceptance. This realization will allow you to again experience that feeling of wholeness you desire. Your beliefs and your resulting actions and inactions are creating your life. If you are unhappy with the conditions of your life, changing your mind, your beliefs, will begin to change the conditions of your life. I want to emphasize that your life is a reflection of your beliefs, many of which were adopted by you as a small child. That child, armed with those beliefs is running your life. Your soul or inner knowing is prompting you to Wake Up and Stand Up, so that the child in you no longer has to carry you. Instead you can protect them, and they can live free and play.

Assess the decisions you have made. You may have decided all men are cruel, all women are manipulative, it's your responsibility to carry others, people can't be trusted, or any number of other debilitating beliefs. I know the experiences that brought you to those beliefs were actual experiences. However, the beliefs that you decided in those moments are severely distorted and detrimental to your joy. So as you progress on this journey with me, please, consider that those childhood experiences were real and **only** your beliefs have created a reality that confirms those beliefs for you throughout your adult life. Your beliefs are determining the quality of your life. You can change the quality of your life, start now. Begin to allow a little doubt to be applied to your beliefs, and begin to enter your new life. What if the decisions you made about life and lived with *thinking* they were *your* core beliefs throughout your life simply are false? What if?

To exemplify this reality, many of us were taught that it is our duty to find a spouse and make a family. This has been instilled in us since we were very young. As women, while asleep, we often feel that if we don't have a man society thinks there is something wrong with us. Without a man, we perceive we are failing in the eyes of society, or worse, failing in the eyes of our parents and family. Perhaps men have a similar feeling. We don't understand that we can be whole and happy with ourselves rather than journey to find happiness outside of ourselves. We don't understand that once we experience our wholeness, all the rest falls into place. We can't see that we are complete, even if we are "alone."

The depths of our wounds may lead us to think that someone "completes us" and that belief drives us to fill the black hole with whoever signs up armed with a fairytale love. Often in our desperation, we never even assess who they really are and if we even really like them. They tell us the fairy tale we always dreamed was possible, and we believe them. We think we are so lucky that we found the man or woman who wants that fairy tale too. It is our confusion, our delusion, our refusal to honor our prompting, that allows for the real truth to be hidden and causes so much of our pain. We sign up, unconsciously thinking we can make it work. After all, this may become all we have dreamed of. It may finally be our turn. Perhaps we truly *have* found love. It does exist, but we will never know love if we remain blinded to the truth before us, seeing only the parts we wish to see in our partner.

Some people sleep through life, or should I say, never in fact come to life by Waking Up. They chose to be asleep when they were very young as it was safer. When they became adults, they never let go of their childhood fear, sadness and anger. In this space they are stuck in their childlike state.

Tragedy has a way of awakening us. Today I hope to inspire you to live awake in all areas of your life. I challenge you to awaken on your terms, instead of waiting for the harshness of the reality you have created to force waking upon you, as it did me. Who likes the sound of a blaring alarm? Wouldn't it be more enjoyable to wake to the gentle touches of reality than the sense of urgency that comes from crisis? It's up to you. You can decide right now.

Face it, we all have been denied in one way or another. No matter how noble their intentions, no parent, spouse, partner, boss, or sibling could ever give you everything you needed, because there is no way possible for anyone else to actually know precisely what you need. Those people who cross our boundaries to harm us, to take advantage of us, to violate us with their words, their hands, their bodies, their penetrating use of fear, their weapons, their power, can today be behind us, if we are willing to Wake Up, Stand Up and Live Free. We must reignite our hidden power.

I have given you a snippet of some of my false beliefs that were established in frozen moments in time, as a reflection of my childhood events. It stands to reason that as you begin to see the choices I made in my adult life you may be able to imagine some of what occurred in my childhood to cause me to make such harmful choices later in life. I had repressed memories about some childhood experiences that didn't come to my conscious recall until my thirties. Given that, the evidence of their truth is more than anything represented by the quality, or better stated, the lack of quality, of my adult life. It is from this awareness that I state, it doesn't really matter what happened in childhood relative to truth, it matters what we chose to believe.

I will tell you that big trauma, like sexual and physical abuse, and potentially little trauma, like your parents placing on your shoulders the responsibility of keeping the boat from rocking etc, have a similar impact relative to how we maintain those patterns throughout our life. However, the more significantly we perceive the negative experience we had as children, the more abuses that are likely to be present in our adult lives. Remember our perception of the level of significance of those childhood experiences is all that really matters; even more than what may have actually occurred. Can't you think of scenarios where two or more people had an identical experience and all parties recalled completely different renditions of the occurrence? What they perceived is what will stay with them, often in spite of information to the contrary.

Let me point out that when you are a child, the degree of suffering is measured by what you know, and therefore is very hard to measure. If your brother, father, or cousin molested you when you were very young, then would you have any reason to actually think you were being molested? I mean, until you are old enough to have an understanding of what is appropriate or inappropriate behavior, you don't have a word to label these experiences. It may be you recognized that some of these experiences didn't feel right, but you also would likely trust and love this family member so, therefore, you trust that your feelings are wrong. I want to reemphasize this point. At some point you decided:

The feeling I have that this is wrong
must in fact be what is wrong. My feelings are wrong,
not the act of what is happening to me or being told to me.

We decide that is the only reality that makes sense. We must be wrong. This leverage point is utilized by the master manipulator. They immediately see our willingness to deny our own truth in favor of theirs. We have been conditioned to be a victim and not trust ourselves. We have been conditioned to believe the abusers' words over our own assessment of truth because we assign them the label of authority, and assign ourselves the label of something less; something less knowing, less deserving, less worthy. It is in our childhood these decisions were made.

**The feeling I have that this is wrong
must in fact be what is wrong. My feelings are wrong,
not the act of what is happening to me or being told to me.**

It is easier to believe that our feelings are wrong than to believe that the people who are supposed to love us, care for us, and protect us, would instead violate us, abuse us, and diminish us. So at a very early age we decide, that feeling inside, that voice inside saying this isn't right, should be ignored, minimized, stifled, for what seems like a safer belief to adopt; this must be normal and our feelings are wrong.

And so our life of denying what feels like our truth begins and continues, until we make the decision to stop it.

We disconnect from the truth inside ourselves. It is in these decisive moments that we give up control of our belief system.

Soul Purpose

In examining our belief systems, we may often find one overarching belief that guides us. That is our "soul purpose." I felt that my soul purpose in life was to heal the heart of the seemingly broken man; the abuser. I devotedly worked to help them heal while ignoring or excusing away the abuse that they inflicted on me. I felt their pain while ignoring my own.

Stamina and endurance, two of my strongest qualities I would boast, came in very handy in this purpose. Make a mental note; our greatest strength can also be our greatest weakness. These two, **stamina and endurance**, nearly killed me; literally. I refused to walk away from the abuse. I could take it.

My guess is you too have a perceived driving soul purpose or belief that may in fact be killing you. Can you recognize it? Maybe it is to get validation that you are good enough from your dad; or loved by your mom; or recognized positively on a more public level; or more privately by your spouse or your

need to realize I'm not judging them as a person, but whether they are good/bad for me

45

don't want to be judgemental

children; or maybe you are seeking the love and acceptance of God, or you simply never want to be perceived as mean. Find what is driving you. You need to; it can save your life.

Consider now that if it is causing you pain, this belief has nothing to do with your soul, or the truth of the core within you. If only I had known.

My perspective that my soul purpose was to heal the abuser ruled my life. I used therapy to learn not how I could escape the abuse, but how I could help the abuser. I used every word and applied that knowledge toward others, all the while enduring the pain at their hand. So now I ask you, what is the lesson? Is the lesson that I needed to stop trying to heal them, the abusers?

Yes, and no. Instead what I needed to do was redirect who I saw as the abuser. Yes, it is true, the people I was choosing to be in relationships with were abusers, but who could surpass *me* as the abuser? I allowed the intolerable abuse. I allowed the blame. I took responsibility for their cruel behavior. I endured the suffering and worse; I invited it in. Once I was an adult, the quality of my life was always up to me. While many of us eventually seek help in leaving the external abuse, we often neglect to face the role we have played in the abuse, which allows the pattern to continue. By simply allowing the abuse and control you are a self-abuser, too afraid or asleep to stand up fully for yourself.

Since you likely see yourself as a caring, compassionate person, who is devoted to those around you, you may feel uncomfortable considering yourself as an abuser in any form. However, who is it that has allowed such harm in your life? Who has left you unprotected? It may be that you feel you do stand up to people who harm you. In some situations, you may stand up, but are you willing to completely walk away? Are you willing to fully disassociate from those who cause you pain? If not, then you are not fully Standing Up. Your neglect of yourself is a form of abuse. You may Stand Up for others, but aren't you worth protecting? What precisely is happening to you and your life while you are being so valiantly noble? I bet you have endured more pain and more sacrifice than you would have ever inflicted on anyone, other than yourself. Remember the depth of what you are willing to tolerate reflects just how asleep you are.

Let me break it to you gently. Your abuse does not happen by accident. You ask for it and it arrives, just like mine did. If you can't see this truth it may be that you prefer to remain asleep and cry victim. Not to say that you aren't a victim when you are abused, instead I am suggesting that you signed up for that role by continuing to walk forward enduring immeasurable pain. It seems evident that at some level we perceive we are getting something out of it, however obscure it may be. In our assessment this must be examined. Perhaps it fills a void for you to feel needed, or to feel like the hero, or the strong one, or you are choosing to believe in the promised dream and that is what you hope to get out of it. Often we simply do not want to harm another, never noticing that we are being harmed. We want to be nice. We never want to be accused of being mean. Yet, is it mean to protect yourself? Is it mean to consider *your* pain?   (just wanted to be loved.

Whatever you are getting out of the abuse is not serving you and you can stop it at anytime. I didn't say it would be easy. I am saying I am clear that it is possible, although at this moment it may not seem so. I understand that it is almost impossible to consider that getting away from the abuser is an option. We hold so dear to the possibility they may change.

The distortion of our view and how much we want to save them, how much we want to see them reach their potential, reach what they claim they long to become, is a seemingly never ending force to be reckoned with. We endlessly want to believe they want to be better and do better, no matter how much evidence we see to the contrary. In the desperate moments when they seem to beg for compassion, where they drop to their knees and plead for forgiveness in their seemingly child-like innocence, we believe them. In these moments, I stayed, because I truly wanted to be a part of their healing and I *knew* I had the **stamina** and **endurance** to stand with them.

What are you allowing your stamina and endurance to trap you in with a sense that the circumstances will change?

For me, it was that I could heal and change the abuser. I was recently reminded of the intensity with which I felt that belief when I found a book that I had once given to an abuser in my life.

In the inside cover it read:

This book helped me understand your heart so much better. It is also confirmed for me that your false self can be minimized by God and you need to know- You have what it takes.

I love you,

Diana

Do you know what I remember about the night I gifted that book with this message? I was in a little cabin near my home. I was working through an exercise that was about healing. I found a lovely little place with a hot tub and asked him to meet me there that night. I planned to spend the day working toward healing and discovery.

Rather than spend the day on **my** healing, which is what the experience was supposed to be about, I read a book about how to better understand the soul of a man. So when he came to the cabin that night I had all sorts of highlights and messages all designed to help him know I understood him, that I just knew he could heal and I wanted to help **him**. He took the book and wrote this inside the cover:

God give me an open heart for your word and guidance through this book to be all that you want me to be. Amen

I saw the remorse and the hope of change in his eyes, and so I stayed. Again.

He never read the book.

Accepting that you have allowed the abuse is an important part of waking up. Equally important is acknowledging what level of abuse will prompt you to Stand Up. For instance, it may seem comparatively easy to experience a physically violent act and respond by Standing Up and leaving the relationship, or it may not. Consider also that some of the deception and manipulation may not be quite so tangible. Perhaps your abuser does not threaten violence upon you, but does upon himself. Perhaps you are subtly made to fear your abuser by reminders of their physical strength, social standing, or of your own economic dependence. To Wake Up to the entirety of your reality enables you to Stand Up in a more effective and empowered way. This also translates to any aspect of your life where you are being controlled, not merely romantic relationships, as it was most significantly for me.

I ultimately stood up to abuser after abuser. Valiant fights nearly always ending in my favor through courtroom battles, legal documents, and an endless barrage of evidential claims, always after suffering physical, financial, emotional and mental warfare and subsequent pain. But the bigger question is why should there be *any* of these experiences, never mind a plethora of them? Because I stood up, but I hadn't woken up, therefore I continued the pattern over and over with a string of willing participants. If you find you Stand Up only after you endured more than should be tolerable, know that you are asleep. With awareness comes wisdom. With wisdom comes responsibility. Our awareness of this pattern and the shapes the abuse takes are key.

If you are out of the unhealthy relationship, friendship, job, church or whatever was controlling and diminishing you, congratulations. Now, to ensure that you do not repeat the pattern you need to learn what you were doing there in the first place. You need to Wake Up fully. You see standing up and getting out of the relationship is good, however the pattern remains intact. The key is you have to Wake Up, then Stand Up, in that sequence, to truly break the pattern and change your life forever.

<u>Discovering the Truth</u>

Most of my abuse was in intimate relationships, although from where I am now I can see that it crept into my life in other areas as well. After all, ultimately abuse is about violation of self, and if we are good at it, it carries over to all areas of our life. The names, dates, and specific instances of my abuse are not important. They are all the same story with different antagonists and a new script. My romantic relationships were merely a series of nameless, faceless abusers. Not to say the occasional "good man" didn't sneak in, but the relationship was often short. He didn't need me; he was not a part of my comfort zone. Abusers are everywhere. Mine are not all that different from yours. In the end, the story is the same, if we want to live, we have to get out. If we want to experience true joy and love, we have to never get in again.

Our choice to have abuse in our lives is often a life-long pattern of destruction. We allow this under the guise of trying to save, or at a minimum,

51

spare the feelings of another. We have the belief that when we do this well, we will have that glorious experience of deep love and acceptance. It is so important to us to not be mean, to not feel that we have abandoned someone or let them down. We long to be nurturers. We are "nice" boys and girls. Now we must realize our problem is not them, it is us. It took me over a decade to begin to recognize that I was in fact the problem, and then almost two more to Wake Up, remove the abuse from my life, and begin Living Free. However, it didn't have to take that long. I could have woken up at any time, if only I was willing to look **inward**.

It's time to let go of their piece and have the courage to look at ourselves. I repeat myself, it is time to have the courage to say it is not *them*; it *is* us. We can choose to recognize the manipulation for what it really is. It has always been up to us to create a joyful life. We are love, and love starts with us. We must first and foremost love ourselves, and any unloving experience we allow to happen to ourselves is a destruction of any perceived soul purpose we may have. Continuing to put our sacred energy into saving the person or persons who are destroying us is not a worthwhile endeavor.

We must embrace who *we* truly are, the whole of us. The pieces of our lives cannot come together as one, until we do. We must embrace the truth that we are the creator of our world. We must acknowledge the fullness of our power of love and acceptance and through that knowledge we will be empowered to create real change, not only in our lives, but in the world as a whole. We will be in a better position to offer kindness and love to others once we learn to show it to ourselves. Certain responsibilities come with this title of creator. We must no longer leave room in our world for hate, control, or words that diminish our spirit. There must be no room for *us* to diminish ourselves either. To allow yourself to examine the deceptions in your life, takes great courage. First, you need the courage to look so that it may be revealed, and then to act in your best interest armed with what you now know. It is at this time you can begin to Stand Up.

When abuse or neglect of the self is how we choose to live our life, it will bleed through in all facets of our life to one degree or another. I have discovered that I was not only willing to abuse myself in my personal relationships, but in my work as well. We tend to operate under the assumption that our needs are unimportant or at least less important than the needs of others. Deciding that YOU are a priority in your own life is an integral part of attaining your freedom. Don't allow anyone to dishonor you, not even you. When you think about honor, you must think about all the players in your life. Even authority should not be permitted to dishonor you. Not your spouse, boss, parents, siblings or even your children.

In any abusive or unhappy situation we readily decide that there is no way out. This is a delusion we choose to embrace to keep us in our suffering. We have known our suffering for so long that we find comfort there. No matter how much you may feel that there is no way out, consider if only for a moment, that this is a deception. Once you open your mind and heart to that possibility, you might be surprised by the pathways that appear. There is a way out of any abusive situation, no matter the source of the abuse, even self-abuse. As an adult, you can Live Free.

Begin to assess your life and determine where there may be abuse. It is then that you can start making small stands that will lead you to awaken. Then you can Stand Up in your full power, never allowing yourself to be diminished again. You must consider all areas that you are allowing a violation of self. Be extensive in your search.

Often we find abuse in our professional lives.

I started my career in financial services working 60-90 hours a week, responding to the perceived demands of what became a high paying job. I started at the bottom of the company and my determination to receive that seemingly elusive validation enabled me to quickly rise to the top. It was in this role where I first learned the concept of living in alignment with my values. I not only heard it, I taught it, and became nationally known within my company for my ability to train others in this concept. My training helped people assess the beliefs at their core, and acknowledge that their perception was in fact, their reality. While assisting people in building their self-esteem and self-confidence through changing their perceptions, they were often empowered to create the life they wanted. I, however, was dead asleep in the largest parts of my own life.

It is important to note, that my high self-confidence was always intact. It was my self-esteem that was nearly invisible. The deep sense of who I was and my right to just "be." I thought my value was *only* in my "doings," my measure of accomplishment based on what I could do. I didn't realize what little regard I had for my right to feel, and have those feelings honored. I was in denial of the misalignment in my life. Teachers teach what they most need to learn.

For many of those years that I would work excessively neglecting myself and my life, I didn't see any of it as abuse. I saw my hard work and dedication as a well rewarded effort for the greater good. This belief was really no different than the belief that kept me in abusive relationships. Here again, my **stamina and endurance** prevailed. I distorted reality, denied the truth with this martyrdom belief that I was serving some uniquely profound service for the greater good of others. I never looked at the personal consequences on myself or my life with my daughter. In an odd way you might say I thought I was doing God's work, another form of that sort of "soul" purpose. My career felt like part of my spiritual journey, because I was leading others to success and helping them discover their path, their greatness inside. Alas, I saw the financial and emotional rewards, but never stopped to assess what it was doing to my physical, emotional or mental self; my life as a whole. I never looked at the impact on me. To avoid my words possibly being misconstrued, know that I believe that devotion, hard work, and certainly serving others are key consideration to serving one's true "soul" purpose. However if we are abusive to ourselves to get there, we will never truly arrive. Loving and honoring ourselves on the journey are required components to reach the destination of serving our highest purpose and Living Free.

Abuse comes in many shapes and sizes. It can be dramatically obtuse or discreetly calculating. All forms of abuse are more readily visible when you decide to observe the truths about your life. Most of us are allowing abuse in one form or another. Often the cruelest of these abusers is us, in how we treat ourselves or what we allow into our lives. I ask that you stand back and take a broad view to investigate where there may be *incongruence* between what is for your highest, greatest good, and the true circumstances of your life. Reexamine *every* aspect of your existence. My guess is you will find somewhere you are asleep, somewhere that deception has control.

Once Awake, *incongruence* will be immediately recognizable. You will acknowledge your lack of peace…and know. Taking action to resolve that condition becomes natural. You will unquestionably understand you are worth it.

Author, Don Miguel Ruiz suggests that we will only accept from other people the level of abuse we are willing to give ourselves. That single thought resonated deeply through me many years ago and I now realize why. I was my worst abuser for allowing such horrific treatment of myself by others. Our threshold of pain is based purely on what we are willing to accept in our treatment of ourselves. It is only once that threshold is exceeded, we are willing to attempt to stand. What I have learned is as you release all the abusers in your world, and you can, you may realize the one abuser that might linger longest is you.

It may surprise you to learn that once you Wake Up to the whole picture of your life, Stand Up and then make the challenging decision to have patience in your healing, you will easily move to gratitude and love and have the joyful experience of Living Free. However, you cannot jump to this destination; you have to journey there.

Acknowledging that we have allowed ourselves to adhere to a belief system other than our own is an important step. The more you are aware of your own thoughts, feelings and beliefs, the less those outside of you can manipulate you into believing anything that violates those thoughts, feelings and beliefs.

It is our fear of something bad happening, our fear of shame and the resulting need to control that causes that tight rope, that restrictive environment where we carefully focus on each step for fear of falling. That focus, and our lack of self-awareness, causes us to build the prison that contains us. We deny our freedom to feel, which numbs us. It is in honoring our freedom to feel and acknowledging those feelings that we gain awareness, not only of ourselves, but of others. Awareness enables us to experience freedom from manipulation. This is not to say you cannot be influenced. This is to say that you will only be influenced by those who you allow to influence you. This has always been true, but now you will be aware of what you are allowing. If the influence is not in alignment with your goals, or your values, you can choose to ignore the influence.

What if the very thing you are trying to avoid comes to fruition because of your desire to control? We tend to attract those things that we focus on, and what could possibly require more focus than attempting to control those things that are out of our hands? The more you try to control people and situations, the more out of control they become. Sometimes the tipping of the applecart brings great awareness and strength. Sometimes letting things fall leads to a new understanding. Remember the jigsaw puzzle? Any attempt to hold another's "piece" for them is an attempt to control.

How many other instances are there that we attempt to control? We strive to control because we fear the potential outcomes. There are two potential outcomes that we tend to fear, but they are really one in the same. The first is an outcome resulting in the loss of a tangible object we are attached to (money, possessions, a person, or even a lifestyle). The second is an outcome resulting in our own shame. Guilt triggers us; we worry something bad will happen, so we act to avoid shame. This one may be slightly harder to grasp than the loss of a tangible object. It is often seen when we attempt to control a person or situation. To provide an illustration, perhaps we are attempting to "change" our significant other. This person is abusive, but we know that we can help. As stated earlier, it is our soul purpose. But perhaps there is something other than our kind heart keeping us in the relationship, perhaps there is fear. We must change him or her to avoid the shame of failure, the shame of being unable to fix them. The shame of another failed relationship. When we fear loss of something tangible, the fear feels different, but it is still rooted in shame. The shame of how we will be perceived without the people or possessions that define us. In each of these instances, this fear tends to manifest itself in the form of worry. "I am worried about my marriage" or "I am worried about the economy." These "worries" are merely fear in disguise.

It is by releasing control that we release the fear, and thus the worry associated with it. The only thing we can control is ourselves, and while we cannot allow others to manipulate and abuse us, we must allow life to happen. Life is going to happen either way, but the joy in life is found by relinquishing control.

We saw this shame once before, as a child, when we were taught to ignore our own perception of right and wrong. When we are violated as children we experience this shame and as we have discussed, it shapes our beliefs. It is our fault. We caused this. We so readily own this sense of humiliation. We are bad and we mustn't speak this to anyone. If we share our experiences with anyone, something terrible will happen. Isn't that what we were told? Aren't we told that if we speak this experience or feeling to anyone, something terrible will happen? And we believe authority. As a child it is our only conceivable option. We know we need that authority for our survival. We don't want to lose them physically and we fear their rejection or abandonment. We adapt our behaviors to become someone they will love. Many of us have a difficult time letting go of those feelings of guilt and the resulting fear of further shame. We remain asleep, imprisoned.

Holding your own piece and only your own piece is key to waking up. Stop trying to control those around you. As we progress together on this journey, you will see how as we each hold our own "piece" our collective power will create the world we all desire—one filled with peace and love. In this space we will have the strength to help those that truly need our help.

Now I know some of you may be thinking that if I knew the details of your situation it would explain to me how *you* are the exception to this idea of freedom or peace. You may believe that if I only knew your situation, I would understand what an impossible task holding only your own piece is for you. Maybe you are helping an aging parent or a sick spouse, and in those instances you may be doing what is necessary. Remember, there is a difference between assisting and attempting to control. I am not saying you should never carry someone's piece in circumstances that might warrant it. I am saying, be aware. Look for intention. Look for what is real. Evaluate the truth about the life of this person, and observe what they are willing to do to help themselves. You cannot help others if in the process you are sacrificing and destroying yourself. Are you paying attention to you? Are you paying attention to your health, your well being? And if you are not, before long resentment will step in as you exhaust yourself from giving when you have nothing left to give, and then anger and then destruction of the love that led to the support. Soon there will be negative physical outcomes for you. If the support you offer to those around you stems from guilt and not from love then the resentment will appear faster. Offering assistance out of guilt is another form of control to avoid shame, the shame of being a "bad daughter," "bad wife," "bad son," or "bad employee." The fear of shame is released when we are aware of, and at peace with, ourselves. Self-esteem is the antidote of shame. To reclaim our self-esteem we must begin to honor ourselves and our feelings.

If you have children who depend on you, I recognize that we need to hold our children's piece until they are capable enough to hold their own, but we must do so out of love, and not out of guilt or fear. We must also remember that they can likely hold their own piece long before we allow them to. By holding their piece for too long, we may actually be hindering them by reducing their ability and confidence to hold their own piece. Most commonly, more damage than good is done when we attempt to hold the piece of others. In addition to this practice's tendency to diminish our own strength and ability to love and grow, it also sends a clear and loud message to the very person that we are trying to help. Our act of holding their own piece, of taking over their responsibilities tells them, "I don't think you can hold your own piece therefore I will hold it for you!" This does not encourage the independence and stability that each person should strive to achieve of their own volition, but perhaps more important, it is this very trait that the abuser will take advantage of. They will sit back and coast through life with the knowledge that you will not allow their "piece" to fall.

In short, we may be holding someone's piece because we have our own desire to control them or the situation we are in. We may be allowing ourselves to feel guilt, or we may be manipulated into holding someone's piece. If we were self-aware to our own standards and boundaries, and willing to look at the whole of us, we would not be deceived and we would instead only help when it was good for another **and** not harming us.

An image that might be useful as you take a look at the truth about your circumstances, is to see your loved one kneeling in water screaming, "Help me, help me, I am drowning!" As you throw rope after rope to the screaming person and reach out in futile attempts hoping they will grab one or two of the life-saving devices you throw, how are *you* feeling?? Your heart races, as you frantically search for a longer rope, a better tool, another way to save them, but if you take a breath and step back you will notice that it is often only a puddle that they are kneeling in, and the one thing that they must do to keep from drowning is the one thing that you cannot do for them. They must Stand Up and they will be safe. While you may be able to give them a hand if appropriate, they must choose to stand of their own accord.

All you can do is observe, support, encourage and let them decide. That is all.

Perhaps our job is simply to encourage those who are **capable** but **unwilling** to help themselves, to begin to believe in themselves, not by acting on their behalf, but instead telling them we trust their ability. A simple, "I know you can figure out what is best for you" or "I believe in your ability to make the best decision for yourself." Even assisting in this manner is only acceptable to the point that you are not harmfully sacrificing yourself. The moment that the burden of another begins to cause you pain, you must evaluate if you should stop carrying it. There are times, like an ailing spouse or child that you will carry it to the end, out of love, not guilt or shame. In instances where you cannot carry it any longer you can tell the person that you are helping, "I'm sorry, but this load is too heavy for me to bear." One who truly loves you will accept that, and will bear more of the weight on their own, or if possible, they will seek help elsewhere. They will not want to cause you undue pain and suffering. See the truth of what our relationships are telling us. Open your eyes to the truth of your life.

Carrying someone's piece who can carry their own is destructive to all parties and our willingness to do so, ignoring the burden it may inflict on us, makes us ideal candidates for manipulators to find a home with us.

At this moment we must acknowledge it is time to take care of and love ourselves, to heal our mind, body, and spirit. Unlike the abuser that victimizes another, we can rest assured that our love of ourselves will not cause pain to another. True self-love is seen in a healthy balance of self-esteem and self-confidence, which we will discuss in penetrating detail as this is key to Living Free.

As I have said before, one of the keys in this game of life is awareness.

As you begin to recognize your belief system, becoming more self-aware, you may begin to accept that you are your own worst abuser, you may begin to see that guilt and shame and a need for control are key factors in your life. So what do you do with all of this information? How do you actually begin to let go of these roadblocks? As you walk through the process of establishing *your* belief system and acknowledging *your* emotions, inevitably you will become aware of your truth and begin to trust your inner knowing.

There is value in allowing ourselves to feel the pain, sadness, and anger of all those childhood losses. All the terrible things that happened to us, the ways we were minimized and led to believe we were small and meaningless. The feelings of helplessness that were created for us in some of our stories can stay with us always, until we take our power back. I don't think we should "suck it up" as we have so often been told. We should feel it, and then let it go. Carrying that burden is allowing poison to live inside of us. I believe buried emotions do not die, instead they harbor in our bodies creating illness and physical pain. If you are sick or suffering, I believe there is likely a negative belief driving your existence. Release your negative experiences and associated emotions and begin to heal and Live Free.

Some people never speak their truth. Until they speak their truth, even if it is only out loud to themselves, those terrible experiences fester and accumulate inside. Until they set those thoughts and feelings free, it may be like a movie that won't stop playing causing them to relive, re-experience, and continuously feel the pain of that event or events. The thoughts and feelings that we hold on to about our experiences must be released in order for us to be healed. While merely acknowledging those memories was enough to gain insights into our belief system, we must release the emotion associated with those experiences in order to move forward with our new belief system.

You will see that I am a strong advocate of journaling as a healing tool and believe there is enormous compelling evidence of its benefits. However, you must find the release that works for you. Above all else healing is what you are after. Please seek how you can best begin to feel rather than avoid your emotions. For many people songs, books, or movies can speak to their pain. I found that if I was open to hearing or finding something that would help me heal, it showed up. I find most often God speaks to me in songs; so I listen. And, if it doesn't feel right to address these potentially buried emotions at this moment in time, don't. At the deepest levels you really do know what is right for you. If you will listen to and trust that knowing you will find your way. Just begin to raise your awareness of who you truly are.

If the person who harmed you, or you perceived may have harmed you, is still in your life and you are okay with that, okay. If the person who harmed you is not in your life, either because they have died, or because a choice was made that they not be in your life, okay. Your healing, in most cases, does not require you to actually confront this person or persons with the things that happened many years ago. What matters is that **you** confront these things. Confronting these things is really a private matter. In confronting our experiences and the associated feelings through journaling or speaking through the experience, you move toward freeing yourself from the emotions and the lingering impact of those experiences. Regardless of the ultimate truth, if you believe these experiences happened, your life is a reflection of that belief. You must begin to heal from that place. Treat the experience as if it is real, as it is real to you.

<u>Laws We Live By</u>

As I type about buried emotions or releasing things we are still carrying, I am reminded of an old Zen story. It is about two monks who come upon a river where they are met with a distressed woman. The woman explains that she is afraid of the current and ruining her clothes and asks for help to get to the other side of the river. The senior monk decides to carry her on his shoulders across the river. He gently places the woman down on the other side of the river and continues to walk. The junior monk feels that they have done something dreadful, they have touched a woman and they have violated their "law." He is offended and tells the senior monk the error of his ways to which the senior monk calmly replies, "I left the woman a long time ago at the bank, however, you seem to be carrying her still."

Why is he still carrying her?

In his heart, do you think this monk really feels he has done something immoral? Or is it possible that the beliefs that have been ingrained in him, the beliefs that create the laws he is convinced he must live by to be perceived as "good," is precisely what is leading him to feel "bad" about his actions? If he relinquished the concept of laws as he knew them, as they were ingrained in him, and defined them instead by his own inner moral system, by love, would this monk still struggle?

What if the intention or premise behind our actions is the key rather than the law? How does it feel to use the concept of actions for the greater good, as the tool in which to assess our contribution to the world? By this I simply mean, are our actions out of love? Are they for our good and harmful to others, or are they helpful to others?

It is operating within the confines of rules out of alignment with our true beliefs that is destroying our joy and hindering our ability to be free. We feel bound by something defined as a rule or law, even if only in our own mind, and we become riddled with guilt and plagued by shame if we violate that "law." Self induction of pain due to laws that were created by someone outside of ourselves is an overwhelming negative pattern that, in my view, needs to be broken.

For this monk, I would recommend he journal. "I feel guilty because…"

Through journaling, this monk could release the guilt as he discovers and understands that the action of helping the woman was from a place of love, to serve and not take. Be free. Don't let the laws that violate your goodness be the laws that damn your soul and leave you feeling guilty and ashamed. When living by the law has you feeling bad about who you are, then the law is probably flawed, not you. What laws that have been instilled in you are you using as a weapon against you or others? Who or what are you carrying out of some distorted obligatory law that has been imbedded in you?

Imagine a life where you trust yourself to decide which laws to live by. Imagine the freedom that comes from that choice. It is available to you now. Every action has a natural consequence. If you live in alignment with your own beliefs, the beliefs founded and aligned with who you really are, those consequences will generally be acceptable to you.

If rules are the only thing guiding your actions or inactions, then you are not actually choosing to think for yourself and make wise decisions for any highest, greatest good. You are simply compliant. Instead the rule is the authority, or you feel that those that enforce the rule are the authority, and for those reasons you feel you have no choice. But you do. To illustrate this point let me share a story from a client of mine.

He was taking his son to the hospital in the middle of the night. He came upon a red light and he stopped. The light seemed to take an inordinate amount of time to turn green and he was nervous because he wanted his son to get to the hospital.

To those of you that haven't been rule following people because fear was not instilled in you at an early age, there is an easy solution, go through the light. It was late. There were no other cars in sight. It was perfectly safe. Why didn't he go through the light? He didn't go through because breaking the rule simply seemed impossible to do. He was like I had been. This is the rule, therefore I must follow it, regardless of how nonsensical it may be to follow it. Regardless of the fact that if I follow the rule it might harm someone I love. People like us are perfect candidates to be manipulated because people will use the rules as leverage against us.

Consider the purpose of the rule that states we must stop at a red light.

We likely could agree that the *spirit* of the law is safety. To the *letter* of the law, one must stay at the light until it turns green.

If my client had stopped, waited to be sure it was safe and then went through the red light, would he be in violation of the law? Yes, the black and white legal law. The question becomes, is it the law that it is imperative to live by, or is it the moral law that should be given stronger credence? It certainly seems valid that the most important considerations were safety on the road and safety for the child in need of care. Not violating the law and, therefore, choosing to sit idly at the red light could cause harm to someone he loves.

Today, without question, it is clear to him and me that going through the light is an acceptable decision. By not violating the black and white law there could be greater negative consequences. In life we need to learn to weigh our decisions based on what **we** think is right, using our moral compass, rather than the black and white letter of the law or what has been instilled in us as "law" by some authority other than ourselves. The outside authority may very well not have our best interest at heart.

I am aware that people who have impure moral standards and ethics will use this exact freedom to choose to harm. But remember, those who will harm will not be thwarted by mere law. Everyone is doing what they have conjured up is right based on whatever sense of logic and reason they wish to apply. People can always find justification for their actions, as their actions had some good reason to them. In the end everything is about who we really are at the deep core of our existence. Our values, our principles, drive us.

This particular point of choosing our own beliefs, our own laws to live by, is of such grave importance in the creation of our life. It is also important to consider that if we allow ourselves to use our moral judgment based on highest good, the lines of our laws will keep moving and swaying based on the vast multitude of circumstances that present themselves to us. If you grasp onto the newfound law you find now, with the same rigidity you may have applied to the other previous laws you followed, you are denying yourself freedom yet again. Freedom is about the "in the moment" choices we can make, moment by moment. It is our denial of this power to choose, that keeps us in a holding pattern year after year, relationship after relationship, job after job. We must and can break free.

Look at what laws or beliefs you have that are running your life. Be sure they are the ones you would choose, if you embraced the fact that you in fact have a choice. I believe the structure of looking at them in the key areas of your life such as spiritual, financial, emotional, physical, and mental self is a good approach. Perhaps you want to choose your own process, which of course you are always free to do.

To understand that you can and should live by your own laws is an important step to freedom. We must evaluate the beliefs we have and the resulting laws we create. If I had learned this single point years earlier, then I would have experienced peace rather than manipulation and pain for so many years.

I can say with passion and certainty that I give little credence to laws outside of those that I have defined. I am clear now that my moral compass is my lawmaker and, generally speaking, black and white interpretation of the law does not allow for that. When you choose to abide by your law verses the black and white law, you have a risk of negative consequences. I would rather be arrested or ticketed for going through that light, perceiving it is the morally right thing to do, as opposed to living with the death of someone I love trying to follow the letter of the law.

While to many the idea of disregarding the law in such instances would seem obvious, when we are asleep this decidedly accurate conclusion is almost impossible to muster. While in my asleep state I would have been immobilized at that light. I would have been sitting at that light, desperately wanting it to turn green. I would want to go through it, but my penetrating fear would not allow it. Only if it truly became life or death, might I break that rule; survival might move me, especially if it was someone else's survival. While taking that chance, choosing to violate the black and white law, I would have been terrified.

I recognized my internal conflict relative to rules many years earlier, when I realized my discomfort as I watched people break the rules I felt so bound by at work. In business sometimes I felt cheated as others skirted the rules and got ahead. I had a simultaneous feeling that the rules were not right and was maddened that I had to live by them. Of course I had to live by them because of my dreadful fear of consequences from authority. This was not about survival; it was about being a good, rule-following girl. Did I really have to live by those rules? I was in constant inner conflict and would remain there for many years to come.

When I voiced my frustration with the rules to various associates, it was suggested to me that rules are largely made for people that didn't have the common sense to do the right thing otherwise. For people that had the common sense to do the right thing, it was suggested that the rules could destroy them if they allowed it.

To validate this thinking a mentor of mine presented to me that our own morals should be our compass and our only rule. He asked me a series of questions that led me to confirm my possible capacity to break a rule if it was truly life or death. He also led me to discover a deeper startling truth; I was incapable of convincingly lying to someone I perceived was an authority figure no matter what the circumstances, even if the circumstances were potentially life or death. My fear of authority was too great.

In summary, he spoke of the Holocaust when the law was that the Jews were to be arrested and ultimately killed. He knew my integrity and stated that he was sure I would be hiding Jews in the attic, to which I vehemently agreed. I would be terrified, but would likely still break that rule. But then something strangely uncomfortable happened. When he asked me how I would reply if someone had knocked on my door and asked if I had seen any Jews, I felt paralyzed. I told him that with everything in me I would want to say that I hadn't seen any Jews, but I truly and completely did not know if I could say those words with any level of conviction. I was incapable of effectively lying to authority. This reality is often true of those of us who are asleep. We offer full disclosure and we do not lie. This proves very useful to our manipulators. Our distorted sense of character and integrity are so important to us and they know they can use this as leverage for harm against us. They will threaten to ruin the image of ourselves that we have worked so hard to maintain, or perhaps they will *actually* try to destroy us with their words or claims to others.

We believe that to have integrity, to have character, we mustn't lie.

I had such a black and white view of lying that I never allowed for my own morality to powerfully supersede this thinking. I never factored in who I would be lying to or why. We do not have to be good, honest servants to those that wish to march us or others into harm's way. Back then I would have said, "No. I have not seen any Jews," however with the quiver in my voice and the lack of conviction in my words, we likely all would have been escorted to our deaths because my *lie* would be so evident the search would ensue.

What I didn't understand until I woke up, years after this discussion, was that the difference between what you outwardly speak and inwardly believe makes your actions congruent. I could outwardly say "No. I have not seen any Jews," and then say inwardly *...because if I told you I did, you would kill them.* This congruency of words and actions aligns with my integrity and, in my view, is for the highest, greatest good. Since being awake this has been one of the places I experienced the greatest liberation and it has granted me freedom from evildoers.

Our character matters deeply to us. We always want to operate with integrity, be in good standing, be honest, pay our bills, have good credit, be charitable and helpful...and we allow these virtues to be leveraged against us to dance to a beat of someone else's drum. This drummer may wish to beat us with their drumsticks, yet, in this dance, they lead and we blindly follow.

The "set-up" is that if we don't pay these things or take these actions, there will be impending danger to our credibility or some negative consequence to someone. A family member may be forced into a nursing home or there will be a bankruptcy. They will lose a home, a car, or there will be legal trouble, or a bad debt will be created that will destroy our flawless credit structure. Perhaps our manipulator will die from our lack of care, or they will commit suicide. All tools used as leverage that keeps us dancing to the beat of others needs or illusion of need, at the exclusion of our own care. We always want our character in check. We want to feel that we are "good," potentially to our complete and total destruction. We only know a definition of good as it was instilled in us, we must look closer to see what **our** true definition is.

In my instance I was so devoted to my ingrained belief that the man had to be happy, my belief that if something went wrong it was my fault, that in essence I gave every man the same "trump card." This "card" would ignite my guilt or shame. It could be used time and time again to manipulate my money, my behavior, and my love.

My Trump Card: Something bad will happen to me or someone I love if I don't do something to stop it. As a result, I will experience feelings of shame if I do nothing.

I saw it as my job to protect them, like a parent might. I would stop at nothing to see that I did protect them. I believed if I didn't save them, if I didn't keep them happy, then something bad would happen. Their suicide was a huge threat that worked for many years. They would die if I didn't act.

They wanted me to feel responsible for what happened to them and I allowed them to manipulate me with that fear.

I can remember one such time when a man was with me on a business trip, and he didn't want me to attend my business meeting. After making every attempt he could think of to detain me, he threatened to kill himself if I went, a threat he had made before.

I was, as usual, beside myself. What a quandary. I felt if I didn't go to my meeting I would be in trouble with authority, my boss. If I did go to the meeting I was terrified something bad would happen to this man, the man I believed I must please, who I also viewed as an "authority." I pled with him, as usual trying to **control** the situation. Terrified of the **shame** I would feel if I allowed him to die, if I let something bad happen. This internal conflict was a constant presence for the bulk of my life. In this instance, I attended my meeting with a great sense of urgency to return immediately.

As you might imagine I was very **worried** at my meeting. I was distracted, filled with anxiety. What was he doing? Was he going to harm himself? I hurried back to the room and found him standing on the ledge outside the window on the 10th floor of the hotel. He was crying and screaming that he had no reason to live, with his all too familiar claim that I was cheating on him and he knew it.

I now see how this was simply him raising the stakes, because at the time, the lower stakes game was no longer securing a reaction from me. The ploys he had always used that would put me in turmoil and have me tripping on myself trying to save him, had more recently been met with a more casual and unemotional, "I hope you don't do that." He had to raise the stakes in order to get me jumping again. I was beginning to wake up, and he was not happy. When you are not playing by the terms that have been set, things will escalate. There may be a quiet interlude before the next move, but that next move will happen, and it will clearly define a higher stakes game. Even though I realize that now, at that time, I was both terrified at what felt like an imminent tragedy and humiliated that this was occurring at a high level executive meeting in a high class hotel.

Even though this incident should have jolted me awake, especially since I had already begun to open my eyes, it did not. Instead it had me feeling more sympathy and compassion for this man who professed that he longed to be a Godly man. I was left with a feeling of sadness as I watched him carry so many demons.

I don't know how much time elapsed, it felt like an eternity. He reluctantly came inside as I lured him in off the ledge, constantly professing my love. He started drinking straight from the open wine bottle. I helplessly watched as the wine poured down his face. Of course, I had no idea how much alcohol he had already consumed, but it appeared to be plenty.

Still speaking in despair, he raced into the bathroom and came out with a disposable razor and began attempting to slice his wrist. Of course, it is nearly impossible, if not *actually* impossible to slit your wrist with a disposable razor, yet it felt terrifying just the same. Through repeatedly gouging himself he actually managed to draw a little blood.

Today, now that the fullness of the picture has been revealed to me, I see only his desperate plea to control me. Taking a disposable razor that couldn't possibly slice his wrist and screaming he wants to die now seems pathetic to me, maybe even humorous. At the time, I saw no humor at all. I couldn't see him then as a desperate soul kneeling in a puddle. I saw him in the deepest ocean screaming, "Help me or I will drown!" I grabbed his hand hoping to stop him from slicing his wrist.

In response to my touch, he immediately picked me up and literally threw me on the bed. He then put his arms around me from behind and began to strangle me. He was spewing hate and telling me how he was going to have my father killed, how my whole family was going to die and it will all be my fault; these threats were new. In the past he had spoken of the unspeakable ways he had harmed others. He had spoken with such remorse, such pain about the person he had been before his redemption, before he found me, before he found God. These threats were different, never had he threatened to harm those I loved. This was nothing more than his latest attempt to raise the stakes. I couldn't breathe. I was thrashing my legs and trying to kick him so I could escape. I finally got free and ran out into the hall, I was completely disoriented. It was as if I was acting in a dream, a nightmare. That's what those moments feel like, it is like you feel the experience but it isn't until you are awake that you realize how terrified you were, or perhaps you should have been. He followed me out the door. He ran a bit down the hall and, since I was sober, I was able to run back and get in the room ahead of him to deadbolt the door. He managed to break the bolt off the door by kicking it.

To this day I can't imagine how no one called security. To this day I don't know who I worked with that may have seen this event unfolding. To this day, I find it amazing that I chose to still stay with this man for several years after that.

In the morning, not surprisingly from where I sit now, he claimed not to remember a thing. How convenient. A simple, "Well wow Diana, if that happened I am sorry." If? The shallow gouges on his wrists didn't seem to be evidence enough for him, neither was the broken door latch.

When any threatening escapade is over and we are exhausted, it is commonplace for an abuser to simply say they don't remember a thing. Alcohol and/or drugs may be their excuse, or perhaps they simply claim that they never said those hateful words. Maybe they will say they don't understand where the bruises came from—they didn't hit/grab/push you *that* hard. Excuses are their greatest art form.

And of course, there is no police report, no report to security, nothing; just another day in a life. After all, isn't it our job to protect them?

The Reason to Stand

Not all of the moments of control and manipulation are this violent, this "in your face." As hard as it may seem to miss this glaring red flag, I did. I saw only a poor broken soul, and I allowed the control to continue. I continued to ignore my soul's efforts to awaken me. As you read my words, what were you experiencing in my story? Did I seem insensitive to his needs? Did you feel fear for my circumstance, or maybe did you feel a deep sense of compassion for him? Poor guy, he is in so much pain and desperately needs help. That just may be because you simply do not know what you don't know. As you learn more about my reality, you may begin to see things in your reality in ways that you have never been willing or able to before. It is my intention to awaken you to some truths you just may be unaware of. The obvious consideration is if I can miss something this big and not see a red flag, imagine the small day-to-day manipulations that I may have ignored, that perhaps most of us ignore.

We have taught people how far we will go, and whether with ill intent or just capitalizing on the benefits presented, we are marionettes responding to every pull of that string. We allowed these strings to be placed on us slowly, as we gave up our control to them. To be free you must remove each and every one of those marionette strings that cause you to act in a way that is harmful to you. This also means you should not *place* a string on another. Any effort to control another will have harmful results. Regardless of the degree of harm, I ask you to ask yourself, *why do you deserve harm at all?*

I realize that some people are kneeling in the puddle seriously believing they will drown. I also now realize many people know they are kneeling in that puddle and are absolutely clear they won't drown. Either way, we need to look inside of ourselves to decide what is the right and appropriate action, rather than just hearing the chants that are being spewed at us and believing they are demands we must respond to…or else. Guilt, shame, or fear of either should not be manipulating us to act.

I want you to hear, perhaps for the first time truly hear, that you do not deserve abuse in your life at any level, for any reason. I also want you to hear that you may need to define abuse differently. I say this because I often hear people tell me they are not abused, while they proceed to tell me how they are ignored, shut out, not listened to, and abandoned. The name I would like you to give that is *neglect*.

With neglect there are no visible scars, but neglect can cause some of the deepest wounds. Neglect is significantly painful and we are left with nothing tangible to memorialize our suffering. If you were a puppy, would you rather be left in a dark room without love or interaction endlessly, or would you prefer that periodically someone came in and offered affection, spoke kindly to you, even if sometimes they were cruel? Most people would take pain over neglect…at least it evidences we exist. Abuse is anything that diminishes your light, your life. Expand your definition and know that it is only acceptable that you be surrounded with love. Verbal abuse, physical abuse, sexual abuse, emotional abuse and neglect, to name a few, are all forms of abuse. You can end abuse in your life completely. No matter how difficult it may seem, you can.

74

When we allow abuse or manipulation in our life, the reality is we don't allow ourselves to fully see, accept and feel that evil side, the danger or pain we are in. We instead prefer to excuse it away with some vast assortment of false beliefs we have established. If the truth be known we would realize that at some level we don't regard ourselves enough. I think if someone told me years ago that I didn't care enough about myself I would have objected. Standing here now, I know it was true. In order to assess the reality of your situation put a child in your stead. If my child was choosing for herself any number of the relationships or situations I was living in, I would have done all I could to get her out. If we truly regarded ourselves as we do others, we would not tolerate abuse inflicted on us that we would find intolerable for another. If we feel that our child or someone we love should be out of that relationship or situation, why can't we see that we should be out?

In the case where physical, mental, or emotional abuse is being inflicted on us, we often believe these individuals want to be better, or don't mean to treat us this way. We believe that because they often tell us so. We believe it because *we* want to be better, so it is easy to believe that *they* want to be better as well. Again I ask, besides manipulating you, what are they actively pursuing on their own to aide in their own healing or resolution of their claimed circumstances? Are we pushing them to act, or are they acting on their own? If we are working on their healing more than they are, we need to consider this may be nothing more than a manipulation.

Our distorted beliefs make us what I call **a target**. A target for whom and what circumstance is driven by just how asleep we are. In my case, I was dead asleep. I was in complete denial of my full capacities and, therefore, the realities of my life.

I will discuss the concept of target in intricate detail as we progress, for now just know that abuse is allowed or permitted whenever one party fears that they cannot let go of the abuser or the situation for any various number of reasons. Guilt, shame, security, perceived love, appearances—these can all be factors. Whatever the reason, it is simply an illusion. It is an illusion that anyone or anything has dominion over us. We only perceive we are trapped. To live free, we must realize that we are our own authority, we create our own security, and we can make any decision we choose for our highest, greatest good. Only then, are we truly able to help others experience that same freedom.

My emphasis is on abuse of the intimate kind as that is what I endured the longest. However, from where I stand now, I help people resolve all abuse because I am aware now that it is all played the same way. We decide that we have to act or behave as someone demands or even merely implies, and that we have little or no choice but to continue this pattern. We often believe we can't say "no" fearing that will be considered mean, or worse, fear we will be abandoned. This thought freezes us, leaves us unable to function for our own good. Ultimately, we allow this feeling of helplessness, this feeling that we are powerless in our life, to drain us completely of our energy. Our repeated neglect of ourselves acts as a positive feedback loop until eventually we ignore our own needs to the point of illness, or even death. Extensive abuse leads us to be so numb to our existence, we feel dead, even if we might still have some small breath of life left.

In many instances, it is our own assumptions that lead us down this path. The other party might not be trying to manipulate us, we may simply impose our own sacrifice based on our distorted beliefs; we wish to ease their discomfort, we feel it is our duty. Once awake, it is through our own awareness that we can see whether or not we are being manipulated with intent to do harm, or we are merely succumbing to the needs of others to our own detriment. Awake we see the truth. When we no longer hide from the fullness of ourselves, the fullness of others is no longer hidden from us. Regardless of the intent of others, *we* have the power to change the situation. It is our awareness that will set us free. It is important that we do not blindly assume their innocence. Perhaps we have simply missed their shadow.

This decision that we are trapped in our current situation is false. Deciding that you are not trapped, will help lead you to the freedom you deserve. Remember, *you* can choose to be aware. Imagine that *you* have a sword, and *you* choose when to use it. It is not being mean to protect yourself from ill intent, it is mandatory.

76

In nearly all of the abusive intimate relationships I experienced, I was the financial provider for the household and held a reasonably high ranking position, for much of that time with a Fortune 100 company. You may be surprised to learn that *targets* have high self-confidence and I had plenty to go around. It is our hidden sense that we are not worthy of love that creates our suffering. One way our lack of self-worth, our low self-esteem shows up, is how we allow ourselves to be accused of being something we are not, and choose to needlessly and desperately defend ourselves. A typical representation of this occurrence would be that when I would leave for work dressed in appropriate business attire, I would be accused of setting out to attract the men in my male dominated company. Today, I would find amusement in these accusations and the accuser would be quickly dismissed from my world. However, back then I so desperately sought love and acceptance from this type of man, a man that I now understand operated from the shadow, that I was compelled to insist they see the innocence I knew was mine. I wanted them to see me through *my* eyes, but they could only see me through *their* eyes which were clouded by who they are. Through our own denial of our capacity for evil or the shadow side we are unable to see their darkness, just as they are unable to see our light. My pleas of innocence, my vehement cries of love and loyalty, fell on the ears of men who could not know innocence. They were unable to grasp the concept of loyalty due to their own lack of experience with the term. The more I defended myself, the more they saw their own shadow reflecting back off of me.

If you ask my daughter what I stand for, she will tell you integrity. It is known to be my strongest value. To me integrity is walking in alignment. This means that my words and actions line up with my values and beliefs. Having said that, look at my life? Was my life *really* driven by integrity? I was allowing the men I chose to have in my life to violate everything I am and everything I valued. I was always out of alignment; always. I just couldn't see. Just as the men in my life were incongruent, inflicting great harm and having a misalignment between words and actions, I was as well. I presented myself as a strong and confident woman, and I was in many aspects of my life. My coworkers, most of whom looked at me with earned respect, would have been flabbergasted by the sight of me often sobbing on my knees, begging for forgiveness, insisting on my innocence for crimes I didn't commit. Are **you** truly living in alignment with your greatest value?

You will see that the moment in which I finally Woke Up occurred simultaneously with the moment when I could finally embrace all that I knew and chose to ignore. When I Woke Up, I could see what my soul was trying to awaken me to all along. I *was* worthy of love and acceptance, and to arrive, I needed to offer that love and acceptance to **all parts of me**. Awakening occurred when I could fully see what was in the shadows, the parts I disassociated from, the parts I compartmentalized away rather than examine. It was my refusal to embrace all of me that kept me from living free. I had simply refused to fully see me. That denial of the whole of us, all parts, is what keeps us asleep. I was invisible to myself. Instead, I saw only what I could do and be for others.

These disconnects between words, action, principles, and values that I refer to as incongruence or misalignments are the key to discovering the truth about the circumstances of our reality. I look for it in myself, and I look for it in others. What we allow to happen to us, creates that inner prompting when we are being mistreated or even when we sense we are about to be. Our soul wishes to warn us of the impending pain or the pain we may in fact be enduring. We also get that prompting when we experience incongruence between what is said and what is happening. Having conditioned ourselves for so many years to believe that people's words are the truth over their actions, we ignore this incongruence, the red flag before us. If we are not in alignment, and we ignore it long enough, there will be a huge negative impact on our life, our relationships, and maybe even our health. Another way to look at an obvious reflection of incongruence might be if I say I want to live a long and happy life, but I smoke two packs of cigarettes a day. I may not be in alignment, not just on the soul level but on the physical level as well. I am saying one thing, and doing something in direct conflict with it. I am incongruent. There are degrees of this too; perhaps if I smoke one cigarette a day it is a misalignment, but one that will likely be less consequential. There are more subtle incongruencies as well, for example stating, "I deserve to be happy," while we allow ourselves to be manipulated or controlled at any level.

I was living out of alignment because I was allowing the needs of others to violate my own principles. I would sacrifice myself to come through for them. Again, I needed to control because I was afraid of the outcome. They would tell me what they might lose if I failed them—their home, property, children, good standing, or most significantly, their life. I didn't want to let anyone down, especially the man in my life. My fear would lead me to act.

If I was in alignment with myself, I would have let them take care of their own issues. I would not fear abandonment or failure because I would have known that no one makes me whole. No one holds my life line except me. I would have known living in alignment with my inner soul, my true values and principles, will always be the right path. Taking care of their issues was violating my own principles. In my assessment you will see that in an effort to save the men in my life I was often diminishing my own financial security which I regarded highly. I would not have treated my finances with the same disregard in an effort to care for myself. My finances were disregarded in an effort to achieve love and acceptance from another. I was out of alignment because I claimed to value integrity and treating others with respect and dignity while allowing significant emotional, financial, and physical harm to be cast upon me. I didn't apply that principle to myself. I too needed to be treated with respect and dignity. I was not free.

As I said, I gave every man in my life a trump card. One they could use that always worked. I needed to Wake Up and Stand Up against the delusion I was living. I needed to see the fear that they were using to make me act was a fear I told them I had. We, "targets," tend to disclose what matters to us most. I needed to realize their acts were with harmful intent. I needed to release the idea that their consequences for their actions or inactions were somehow my responsibility. They knew what card to play and I allowed it to have power over me.

Obviously this card is going to be different for all of us and have a huge variance in degree and power. The key is to understand what the trump card is that has power over *you*. To help you recognize it, know that it is likely grounded in guilt or shame. For me there were always threats of harm that kept me jumping. There had been times, for example, that my abuser had

> Used guilt to keep me stuck - looking sad, crying, threats of ending the marrige

pointed a gun at me or themselves as a threat, and those flashes of warning were unconsciously with me, reminding me of the risks of my inaction. The more common threats were, "If you go to that meeting I am going to get drunk and drive my motorcycle into a tree." "If you don't pay my back taxes, they will take everything I own, and perhaps what you own." "If you fight back, I will yell for your daughter so she can see how violent you are." I couldn't see it at the time, but the effectiveness of this trump card was found in my own feelings of guilt and my adamant desire to avoid shame.

All of us have had different experiences, but the key here is to assess whether or not someone has a trump card they are using on you. It may be a small manipulation or a big one. Be clear, there should be no card that has power over you; none. It may be, "You owe it to me to take care of me" or "After all I did for you…" And it may just be the implication of these manipulations even if they are unspoken.

Fear is the emotion a manipulator hopes to trigger. These manipulations do not need to work. We do not have to allow it. In finding our wholeness, we will discover how to stop our suffering.

I don't know what your trump card is. However, I do know if you feel manipulated or abused, the weapon with the driving force is guilt, or fear of a perceived shameful consequence. Those are the tools with the power to control you. You want to avoid the guilt and the shame that is a byproduct of your "failure" to act. However, when you allow yourself to be manipulated, to operate out of alignment with your own belief system, do you feel at peace? Do you really avoid the feeling of shame that you were striving to avoid to begin with? It is time to embrace the idea that you are your own authority, you can create your own security, and you can live in alignment with your values. You can live free. You do not need marionette strings; no one should have the power to control you.

If you have abuse in your life then you, like me, let that marionette string pull tight. The manipulation, the excuses, the deceit, the trump cards—these are all ways that we have allowed others to control our every move. We will continue to live this way until we Wake Up!

The Disguise

How do these destructive relationships happen? Sometimes when you meet a person, there is some powerful attraction that you can't quite explain. Even if you don't feel an immediate attraction, their persistence often triggers a feeling of being deeply loved. You begin to feel like the most important person in the world, or at least in their world. You begin to believe you will be the person who will finally love them the way they have longed to be loved. The person they have longed for but could never find. Then, they tell you about their broken lives…broken until you came along of course. They often play the victim and express to you how they want to be a better person, they need you. You feel badly for their circumstances and want to rescue them. You give all you have to save them while never looking to see that you are being manipulated…played. You never even consider that for the other person it is more of a chess game then a loving encounter. You believe you are on the threshold of the most unimaginable love. This may be nothing more than a delusion.

While asleep, we see their actions as a reflection of their suffering instead of an effort to manipulate us. It is sometimes difficult to distinguish between suffering and manipulation. In our wholeness, Awake, we will more clearly know. It is as if a part of your being that was shut down can now see.

The hardest part for me was to consider that someone could actually be intentionally trying to harm me, that malice was the core of these repeated relationships, not love. Again, I was blind to the concept of evil. Those individuals who claimed to love me were *actually trying* to harm me by controlling me. We were playing a calculated chess game that I never even realized we were playing. Game after game, I lost. Their prize was simple; control over me.

Once I was awake, I could recognize their acts as evil. However even as I was on the road to awakening, I was slowly accumulating more awareness that perhaps what I was experiencing, was not what I was worthy of. As I changed my view of what I saw, the dynamics of the relationships radically changed. It was not until I was Awake, that I was clearly aware of the game. As I saw things differently, I acted differently. Over time, the marionette strings were cut, one by one. Once they were all cut, I was finally the driving force in my life.

In order to awaken, I began to observe the behaviors and words of others. I was trying to no longer allow others to scare me into action. In doing so I began to respond less to the manipulations. I would remind myself that they were in charge of their life. It was difficult and necessary to release their piece of the puzzle. They could walk out the door with their keys, saying they were going to drive into a tree, and I would not follow. This is not to say I became uncaring, had someone truly been in emotional anguish asking for help, rest assured I would be there. I was recognizing there was a difference. Those who were seeking help, because their own piece of the jigsaw puzzle had become too heavy and they needed help in that moment, would not routinely threaten harm to attain help. They would **actively and consistently** change their own behavior until they could once again hold their own piece. Those seeking to manipulate, profess their desire to change, but only have fleeting moments, if any at all, of actually attempting to better themselves. If

82

you are helping someone who is truly in need, you will likely also feel the wonderful power of true gratitude. Gratitude isn't why you do it; but those who are sincere in their need tend to be genuinely grateful for your help. Those seeking only to manipulate are likely to forsake gratitude for a sense of entitlement. As you become more of an observer than a controller, it allows you to back away from the situation and obtain a clearer, more accurate view.

I had taught my abusers how to control me and they knew precisely how I would respond. When I didn't respond as they expected, they were confused. They would try again, and escalate their tactics. If I watched him leave without engaging in a fight, he would quickly come back in the house claiming to have forgotten something and then claim that *now* he is really going to do whatever it was he was threatening to do. Keep in mind the abuser, the master manipulator, may actually leave, but they have no intention of driving into that tree, or jumping off that ledge, or pulling that trigger; they have no intention of harming themselves, only others. Even if they do harm themselves, **it is not our responsibility to save them**. Their intention is keep us *fearing* that they will harm themselves or us. The goal is control, and if the old tactics don't work anymore, they will likely decide they just have to escalate the plan so they can get you jumping again.

Remember, it is in our desire to control the outcome that they find their power. Let go of that control. Do not be afraid of the shame, or the guilt. Do not worry. You can only behave in a manner that is in alignment with your own belief system. The rest is up to them…

In spite of all the threats of self harm, none of my abusers are dead. Even when I stopped jumping to save them, they didn't die.

I shifted from the active controller of their outcome to the passive observer of their actions. This transition was not an easy one. My abusers went to great lengths to keep me engaged. They wanted to elicit the same guilt, the same shame. Your abuser may do the same. It has been my experience that they might come home with a bloody lip or a black eye and say something bad happened, like an accident or a fight. Perhaps they will tell you they are stuck somewhere and you have to come pick them up because they can't drive home. They may even go as far as to do harm to themselves (scratch their own face or have a friend punch them), so you will *know*, they got hurt and it was your fault, it was because of you. They know your guilt will make you act, and they are not above conspiring with others to help orchestrate their control over you. All this to ensure that next time you will jump again and maybe this time, jump even higher.

They do this so that you will run to their rescue confirming what matters most to them, you are under their control. Their calculating mind was only trying to figure out what they had to say or do to get you to jump. They won't easily give up. Their motivation is simple: they have to win.

Remember that image of your "loved" one kneeling in a puddle screaming that they are drowning? Again, see yourself jumping all around that puddle trying to save them...they have their face buried in their hands; you see their body shaking with sobs. You feel for their pain, but for the master manipulator, the shaking is not their pain, it is their laughter. The tears are not their fear, it is their joy at watching you dance and knowing that they are the choreographer.

When you are asleep, when you disown part of yourself, you are prey. In the wild a predator has to observe and study the pattern of their prey. They study so they know how to best capture their target. We make their job even easier by *telling them* everything in the depths of our soul. We write their script for them. But remember, the prey can observe as well.

There are other ploys to get you and keep you hooked.

They might tell you some noble act they did, like an undercover sting operation, without mentioning it was to avoid going to jail for drug use and dealing. Perhaps they will mention that in their last relationship their spouse was charged with domestic abuse, without telling you how they threatened and instigated that person until they reached breaking point. Decide to no longer take anything at face value. Perhaps they wanted to be wounded so they would have evidence that they were being abused in an effort to get sole custody of their children. Don't tell yourself that no one would do that, *everyone* has the capacity for evil and those who live from their shadow are much more adept at accessing that capacity. Those who operate from their shadow may have friends in authority, and they may remind you of this fact. They thrive off of your fear.

What can we label these people who act in such harmful and brutal ways and feed off of their ability to control another? I have found most often, one word seems to fit: ***Sociopath***. I had the constant pattern of choosing to be in relationships with men that I now deem as sociopaths. Despite their prevalence, most people have never heard the word "sociopath" in any real terms. I am stunned at what little warning of their existence is out there for us. When I use the word sociopath, I don't mean to do so as if making a medical diagnosis. I am not a doctor. Also, as far as I know, no one I have ever encountered has received this diagnosis from a professional. Although I'm sure if they did, they would not advertise that fact. What I do know is that when I say sociopath, I am referring to someone that has no conscience and therefore no genuine remorse for their acts of cruelty and deception, and I have met more than my fair share of people who fit that description. I have found that once I had an understanding of the mechanism enough to put a label on these individuals, I was on my way to remain free from them. Call them what you will. The label we give to these abusers and manipulators is unimportant. Call them teddy bears if you would like, as long as you willing to remove them from your life.

Sociopaths are known to be charming, often likable people, who can manipulate without remorse, given they have no conscience. It is all a game to them, a chess game, a manipulation of pieces they use as pawns. Any sense of compassion or love is an illusion. They blame others, live by no rules, and are incessant liars. Often we can't see through any of this until we are in knee deep, and sometimes not even then. If you have a sociopath in your life, know this chess game is not an easy one to walk away from. The only thing more difficult and dangerous is continuing to play.

Sociopaths are certainly charismatic, although even in your asleep state you may catch the occasional glimmer of a red flag. However, their charm causes you to immediately dismiss the warning. The sociopath will lure you in with stories of their past pain and their longing for love. They often allude to relationships with celebrities and influential people of the community in the hope of gaining trust by association. This name dropping is accompanied by photographs or other "evidence" to give some credence to their tales. These tales boast an ounce of truth, for every pound of lies. They will recognize your weaknesses and prey upon them. They will drop to their knees in reverence at the sight of a holy relic. They will weep during a feigned flood of emotion induced by a powerful sermon or a powerful hymn. They will speak of their love for their family as muted tears stream down their cheeks. They are the sensitive and spiritual partner you have been longing for. They leave you enamored with their promises of a life of happiness, love, family, support, or wealth. Through your sleepy eyes, you see only the poor broken soul as they recount how people have taken advantage of them in the past.

The people who sociopaths seek out do not see the fullness of their own beauty or power. They are often self-critical always wanting to be better, more attractive, or more successful. They want to be perfect and strive every moment for that perfection. They don't trust their inner wisdom with a man because they desperately want to be loved and valued for their goodness by them. They think they have to earn the right to be loved, so they work harder to be better, to do better. Put another way, they are **targets.**

We are those targets. As individuals, we targets are often proud of our ability to provide for ourselves so sufficiently, that we unwittingly shine that success as a badge of honor—it is that shiny badge that attracts the sociopath to us. They see us in all our success and self-sufficiency and they approach us, but they see something else; something important, they see that we don't see our greatness.

When you walk in a room, what do you perceive people see? Do you believe they see your greatness? Do you really see yourself as captivating at a deep level? It is likely that you are most often very "put together," you are dressed to the nines, you exude confidence, you are over prepared for whatever you might have to present or do...but what do you feel on the inside? The part that defines who you *are* rather than what you *do*? We must embrace ourselves for who we are, not objectify ourselves as our appearance, or skill, or any compartmentalized aspect of ourselves, as abusive individuals do to us. To be free we must embrace the fullness of who we are; all parts of ourselves. As hard as it may be to believe and accept, these type of abusive individuals see us as objects, pawns in a game to win, and nothing more. Despite any presentation to the contrary, they do not see us as breathing, loving, feeling humans. They see no one as such.

Targets are definable. They are individuals with high self-confidence and low self-esteem.

You see as women, both good and bad men see our beauty, our success, our independence and both types of men approach us to discover more of who we are. I suspect this is the same in the inverse, meaning if a man doesn't truly see his greatness and a woman approaches. The good man is drawn to us, yet upon closer examination he realizes something quickly—we don't see our own greatness and beauty. Once the good man recognizes that, he generally turns and walks away because he sees that deep insecurity at the core of who we are. He knows that our insecurity will lead us to dishonor ourselves for love. An honorable man would know we weren't ready for them. It is not his job to rescue us, it is ours. That very characteristic that makes that good man walk away is what makes that bad man hook on. He knows he can charm us, he knows he can hook us, and he knows we will do anything for love. He sees us and says "Ah…she can't see her beauty, her greatness…she's mine." This is not to say that we won't occasionally end up with decent men, for awhile, but the relationships rarely last. Either the men decide that our insecurity is unappealing, or we decide that their security is boring. There is nothing for us to fix, no one to save.

We have to decide, the person that needs saving is us, and we are our rescuer.

Given we cannot see our greatness; we spend all our energy trying to help them see theirs. Even when they present themselves as great, there is often this subtle presentation that they really need our love, our support, to feel the fullness of their greatness. Somehow they convince us that they need our help to reach their full potential…and we sign up for the task. In doing so we violate every honorable code about how we should be treated.

They pick up on our signal, and the entrapment begins. We are magnets drawing them in. Often they pursue us relentlessly. Initially, we feel their desire to know where we are or their frequent "check-ins" are loving gestures, they miss us. They may show up where we are unexpectedly. We think; what a surprise! In some ways we feel hunted, yet somehow we find a way to let their efforts makes us feel valued, important. Over time what felt like devotion becomes suffocating control. The progression is subtle, until we find ourselves in over our head. After the charming and romantic "honeymoon period" we continue to prove we want them in our life by tolerating the intolerable treatment we receive from them every day. We love them through their "healing," while we ourselves are being destroyed.

We allow ourselves to believe the message that we are bad or disloyal or a failure in some way if we don't make it work. We apply this principle even if our abuser is not found in an intimate relationship, but a job, a community, a family, anywhere there is a manipulator getting us to move at their will. We hand them our marionette strings and then lose sight of the fact that they are in control.

We allowed those strings to be placed on us, and if they remain there long enough, the strings become ropes, and the ropes become chains. We had the option to release them at any time, but our ability to do so gets more difficult as their hold on us gets stronger and tighter. Once we allow the ropes to become chains, we need to use power and force. We will need to use our sword. In order to use our sword, we may have to first reclaim it. As you will see, we likely dropped it long ago. As women or nurturers, we often prefer not to use a sword. We always have had the power to keep ourselves safe and be gentle...by releasing the abuser at the first sign, breaking the string before it becomes a chain. Once it is a chain, it is not so simple.

Manipulators have to hurry. Their goal is to get you in too deep to easily escape before you can see the truth. Suddenly you may be living together, married, engaged, having children, merging your finances, and you find yourself asking, did I agree to this? Urgency, speed to advance the relationship is a red flag. The rules that we place upon ourselves that were created outside of ourselves become the wonderful tools that the sociopath or abuser will use against us. These men will leverage your fears and shame, your sense of duty. Somehow they convince us that if we are not willing to move quickly we must not love them…and so to prove we love them we begin to jump.

Over time, their goal is to make us have the sense that now our whole survival depends on them. So they may encourage you to quit your job and trust them, or buy a bigger house and they will take care of it…or move to another area where they can make more money to provide, meanwhile you are now far away from any support system you may have.

In reality, if you could just speak sociopath it means, "I want to remove from you all sources of independence you might have. I want to eliminate everything that can take care of you from your life, so that suddenly, you feel as though all you have as your source of survival is me. I want to separate you from your friends, your money, your family, your job and anything that might be deemed a provider of your security. I want you alone, completely and totally to myself."

One of my abusers used to say, "I want us to be in our own little cocoon of love. I want the kind of love that when people think of me, they automatically think of you. I long for people to not be able to think of one of us without the other, almost as if we are one." I believed this to be a statement of undying love …but now of course I can hear it as the truth—isolation. Having lost all sense of community and independence, you now feel exactly what they hoped you would feel: helpless.

Consciously or unconsciously, these abusers see who we are and know that we will let them in. They test us on a small scale and we pass with flying colors. They test to see if we will feel for their sad situation or bend our plans or ideas because of them. They see us because we choose to be a target. They test to see if we are vulnerable to them, and act once they are certain we are. If you look at your life, the part of it that is behind you, you can likely see that you have had a pattern of allowing others to control you at some levels. Those that have not had that pattern can still be susceptible. Often we become susceptible to engaging with a sociopath after we have a traumatic experience such as a death, divorce, job loss; anything that shakes our stability and makes us vulnerable, makes us a more likely target for a sociopath or someone who wishes to control us. These individuals troll for vulnerable people. It is like they can smell us; we are bait.

The soft and charismatic beginning often shifts to what we see as passion, although it is really just anger and control. We believe that their jealousy is understandable; they have been hurt in the past. We will gladly remove any remnant of a past relationship such as a photo or keepsake at their request or more likely, their demand or insistent pleas. We are surprised by how few friends they have or how they are alienated from their family. They tell us it is because of their past. Their past mistakes perhaps—everyone loves a good redemption story. Perhaps they lost everything through no fault of their own. They spin a tale of victimization, something we can relate to. They tell us they had wealth, had success, but it was taken from them. In contrast, they may be quite successful when they enter our lives. These people will claim to have earned their success like many who have gone before them, but in truth, these people have littered their paths to success with the destruction of others.

I speak of these men in my past as if there were never good times, but there were. Perhaps recognizing the abuse would have been easier if there were not glorious breaks from it. The moments of joy sustained me, as I hoped and longed for the next one. I have spoken of the fairy tale beginning to these relationships. They were full of grand romantic gestures, soul-bearing conversations, and laughter. This charade would often be repeated if the abuser suspected I may be pulling away. However, the illusion of romance was not only for my benefit, it was so that everyone we encountered, friends, strangers, relatives, would think I had found Prince Charming. They saw the dinners, the flowers, the limos, the vacations. What they couldn't see was what went on behind closed doors.

We stay in these relationships tolerating the intolerable because of the moments where they show us love, that is just as powerful as their hate. We do not see their hate as malice, but as wounds they long to heal. To gain that love feels so good. We keep hoping that we can heal them enough so that someday the love will be our life, the hate will melt away, and our fairy tale will come true.

Those moments that capture our heart and bring us into the delusion of their love so deep, a tenderness so seemingly real, that we stay hoping for another morsel, another moment that gives us the illusion we are loved. Those are the moments that set the hook ever deeper.

To me, the abuse I experienced was nothing more than a demonstration of his pain. Asleep, I was unaware that what I was experiencing was in fact abuse. I saw nothing wrong with occasionally sharing with a family member an interaction that illustrated this pain. I would tell them of his tormented soul, and I expected compassion for his suffering. I was confused when these stories were met with the occasional suggestion I should leave him. I didn't understand their perspective. Obviously, I never listened. It wasn't until I could see for myself that I was being abused, that I was willing to walk away.

I see why others struggle to understand why we stay. Why would someone choose to be in an abusive relationship? To those of us who stay, it is not a conscious choice, it is an outcome. Everything happens so quickly! In some of these dangerous relationships the victim, like I was, is completely unconscious of the reality that they should fear for their life. If they became conscious of this fear and felt they could not escape, they would be terrified. Neglecting to experience this fear helps to keep us asleep.

How safe these abusers must feel knowing they can harm us in any way possible, while also knowing we are devotedly concerned with their safety. We do all we can to help them avoid consequences or harm. And even when they inflict harm upon us, we will never call the police, or if we do, we may also bail them out. They know we will never give the full details of the gravity of what they have done to others or to us. We will minimize the harm they have repeatedly caused. In fact our most compelling lie, aside from the one we tell ourselves, would be the one told in the interest of protecting the abuser whose spell we are deeply under.

Once Awake, all of the distortions in our views vanish, seemingly like magic.

Within days of waking, I was for the first time introduced to the concept of the sociopath. All this time I was living in their world, asleep to the fact that they existed. I didn't know what I did not know, and that proved very dangerous. If you are unfamiliar with the term sociopath, let me share that one in 25 people or roughly 4% of the population is sociopathic according to Martha Stout, Ph.D., author of *The Sociopath Next Door.*

Remember in all areas of your life there is potential for an encounter with a sociopath. Throughout this book I speak more about men being sociopathic. I want to state that I only do so for two reasons:

1. It is statistically true that it is more prevalent that men are the abuser/sociopath.
2. Being a woman, it is the experience I encountered.

Be clear though, men have and do fall victim to sociopathic or abusive women. Sociopaths harm, regardless of gender. They are indiscriminate in their search. They seek only qualified targets. Remember too that these predators are not just prowling the streets for romance; they are simply looking for games that look fun to play. Fun for the sociopath is premised on the belief they can win. Winning is about control. So although I refer to the abuser as *him,* since for me that was the case, I hope to reach all people enduring abuse at all levels of life by any abuser. Given their prevalence, it is almost inevitable that all of us have crossed paths with a sociopath or abuser of some kind, so it might be wise to see and know the signs of their presence.

The amount of harm the abuser or sociopath in your life is capable of inflicting is unique to them. My history has given me more than my fair share of experience with these individuals, and I have seen no two precisely alike. It may be possible that they can heal if they want to. However, if you find yourself with a person who fits the parameters I have described, I suggest removing yourself from the situation until you have solid evidence of that healing.

Once you are awake, your awareness allows you to see that which you denied before. They sense your wholeness, your acceptance of your greatness, and they fear your ability to recognize them. Awake, you can see now that they are living from the shadow. You alone cannot cause them to live from the light, any more than they can cause you to live from the shadow. You will finally realize you cannot shine your light on them in a manner that will bring them out from their shadow. Instead you will realize that you are covered in their darkness and will move toward freedom.

They want easy targets. Choose not to be one. Observe the red flags. Be aware.

Let your eyes be wide open to who might be the sociopath in your life. As I said, it may not be your intimate partner, it may be a sibling, a parent, or a boss ...and you are tormenting yourself trying to get them to love, respect, honor or care about you or the circumstances of your life. You want desperately to elicit their compassion. You need to realize they are incapable of true compassion, although they can "act" compassionately if it will serve them. In fact, sociopaths are wonderful actors. They can feign the most complex of emotions if it serves them. Love, compassion, remorse are emotions they can portray, they can play the part, but you will not find these emotions in the blackened heart of a shadow dweller.

Once you awaken and know the truth, you can and will be free. It is about learning, no, *remembering,* to trust yourself to act from a place of wisdom and stay safe. When we Wake Up, seemingly inexplicably, the sociopath seems to know we can see them as the manipulators they are and then their interest often moves to avoiding us. Not at first perhaps, but over time. And once we are truly Awake, the sociopath no longer seeks to engage us in a relationship. We fail their test. Like magic, sociopaths hide from us. They prefer easy prey.

I commit to you that once you wake up the information you need to help you get to safety will appear, because when you wake up, in essence, your energetic makeup changes and you invite in those who can help you. This reality is very powerful. The fact that I was introduced to the concept of sociopath days after waking was no coincidence, and the messages I needed kept arriving.

If you feel diminished, exhausted, confused, numb, depressed or helpless, you just may be under the control of a sociopath or a master manipulator of some sort. To escape that life you need boundaries and awareness. You can be free from the hell you are in. It is not easy, but it is well worth it.

The three questions I most often ask my clients when I suspect they are dealing with a sociopath are:

1. Does he offer compassion, genuine true compassion when he hurts your feelings or harms you?
2. Are you free to express your emotions, even if it means expressing anger or crying?
3. When is the last time you stood up to authority?

The answers to these questions paint a picture. One you will clearly see with your awareness of this phenomenon.

Who is Your Protector?

One of the challenges you may face is when you finally realize you need help and begin to reach out, some of the places you reach to may be littered with sociopaths. Private or public sector positions of power—lawyers, police officers, priests, ministers, military, especially high ranking positions within those institutions are likely breeding grounds for sociopathic individuals. They charm their way into an arena and then manipulate the environment to their benefit. If you are asleep, I commit to you that in the moment you walk in the room, these predators know you can't see them and know they can manipulate and take advantage of you. They know that under the guise of assisting you, they can drag your suffering on and on, potentially endlessly to serve their own desires. I know this to be true because I have experienced it, not just in my intimate relationships, but also with some of those I turned to for help before waking. Once awake, I turned the tables and so can you. The key is to do what will keep you safe and get out.

These individuals, wherever they are in your life, are orchestrating strategies should you try to exit before there is even any indication in your mind that you would leave. The strategies are being put in place long before they need them; they just don't call them into action until the time is right. While you were building a relationship based on love, commitment, or business goals, they were strategizing how to keep you from ever being free. If they don't have a strategy, they will quickly devise one the moment they think you might leave. They will stop at nothing to control you.

In one such instance I ended the relationship and finally got my abuser to leave my house. Hours later he called, stating that he had nowhere to stay and asked if he could come to my home for just this one night. He promised, just one night. Today, I would be able to reasonably predict that this next action would take place, but in that moment I was still asleep. Instead, I believed him. He asked for just one day to make arrangements for where to stay. I had mercy on him, as he knew I would. We have this sense of guilt and duty that says we can't abandon this person and, in my case, I felt financially responsible for these men who seemingly could not take care of themselves. I didn't want to be mean.

In these moments while asleep we say to ourselves, *"What kind of person would abandon someone they once loved in their time of need?"* We don't know we are playing a dangerous game, we just think we are doing the loyal and devoted right thing...until we wake up.

Thinking I was making a stand, I actually asked him to sign a piece of paper promising he would leave in the morning. I don't remember if he signed. What I do remember is that he spent the night in the guest room and when my daughter left for school I was straightening up her room. I was placing things in her closet and was kneeling on the floor. He came to the doorway, he began to tell me that he wanted sex and he knew that I wanted it too. I told him that was the last thing I wanted, and he told me he could see it in my eyes, I wanted him. Moments later, he was on top of me, holding my hands to the floor as he tried to rape me. I felt that I was truly going to be raped by him, so I bit him to get free.

96

Once I bit him I clearly remember him screaming at me that I had overreacted to his *playing* and then kicking me in the ribs. What is important for you to hear is when he told me that I was wrong, when he told me that I overreacted, I believed him. He was right, I overreacted…because he wouldn't really rape me, would he?

I realized I had harmed him. I decided that was bad. The man is supposed to be happy and now he was not. I started to cry. "I am so sorry. I thought you really were going to harm me…"

Do you believe it? I apologized.

I always intended to honor people, of this I was certain. People were able to manipulate me by telling me that they weren't honored. I knew that I had tried to honor them, but I was still willing to take the blame. I would apologize, no matter what. I apologized for honoring my right to not be raped over his right to not be bit. All along I was neglecting to honor someone very important in my life—me. I had to awaken to the knowledge that I was my protector and there were more resources than I could imagine available, if I would just embrace all parts of me.

If I was awake I would have understood that my actions were me swinging my sword of truth, that he harmed me, and my acts were about protecting to avoid MY harm. I wouldn't have apologized. I would have stood in my convictions, while dialing 911. If I was awake, I would not have found myself in that position in the first place.

Know that the abuser may call in other positions of power as part of a fantastic strategy that they hope will leave you looking abusive, crazy or both. They want to destroy you, your credibility, and your character. They want to be seen as the victim of your crazy accusations. They want another story to tell their next victim. They will hide in the darkness while trying to put your behavior or antics in the limelight, even if those behaviors were all devised by them. They never want *their* "image" of grandeur tainted or worse, destroyed.

In my experience, every move is strategic. Reflecting this truth, one man suggested that we begin going to the shooting range and get our concealed weapons licenses. The relationship was shaky and this was something we could "do together" he claimed. This hobby was later used as evidence that I was armed and dangerous. Conversations were taped without my knowledge or consent and edited. They were played out of context to make any point he wanted about my sanity, credibility, etc. The sociopath will use any tactic that serves their purpose. They have absolutely no loyalty to you, in spite of their claims and they have an unwavering need for you to prove your loyalty. My favorite line of one of my abusers was the saying, "I would take a bullet for you." What a thought.

I couldn't see I was an object, a thing that they wished to control. I was the central piece in their game of chess. *They* knew my power that I refused to see. They leveraged my strength for their own benefit, knowing I did not understand and embrace my power and how it might serve me. When I Woke Up I learned I was the Queen, with more power and freedom than I had ever known. As the Queen we are indeed the most powerful piece in the game. In the past I simply awaited my capture by the King, but once awakened the game had changed. I finally realized the belief that I was powerless was a deception.

Recall that years ago I was asked if I would ever do to another what was being done to me. My answer was an adamant no, yet it did not awaken me. Perhaps it is time we look at the inversion of "do onto others as you would have them do onto you."—What a great assessment tool I neglected to use for all those years. This is why seeking the truth about your values and beliefs is so critical. You need to have a clear understanding of your standards and embrace all your abilities to assure that they are never violated.

It was through first looking at each area individually that my awareness catapulted and led me to far greater understanding. As I said, once you evaluate all areas, you no longer need delineation, because you will know a deeper sense of wholeness. It is this reality that made integrating my own personal assessment into my story difficult. In our growth and healing process there are so many things happening simultaneously and yet, I needed to extract the assessment pieces from the whole to reasonably illustrate their meaning for you. I chose to delineate these categories to present them in a format that might offer some considerations for your own healing. Once you are on the other side of this assessment with me, you will see how the integration of these thoughts must occur for true wholeness and completion to come to fruition. From these disjointed pieces of awareness, we are able to finally embrace our full selves.

As I take you on my journey to freedom I need to be clear that my path to waking up may not be the only path. I only intend to help you know there is one, and to encourage you to seek the wisdom inside of yourself to find your path. You must look at all the pieces separately before you can see the whole restored image of you. As you do, you may realize that we are one in mind, body, and spirit. Walk with me as I share my assessment in each of the five areas. As you observe my shift in awareness and share in the lessons that I learned along my journey, I believe you too will find the path that can set you free from *any* chains that bind you.

Spiritually (Spirit)

"Spiritually" refers to your belief

regarding your connection to something

larger than yourself and what role

you feel it plays in your life.

As I have expressed, to begin to wake up I believe you need to deeply assess your beliefs in all the key areas I have mentioned. In my life, I started with spirituality. I seemed to be willing to make this assessment as a child, and have continued through adulthood, whereas assessment in the other areas came much later in life.

I was always baffled by the idea that God was an exclusive God and not an inclusive God. I didn't understand all the rules. I didn't understand how God could give us free will and then damn us for using it. I loved God. I went to church, I prayed, I was curious about the meaning of life. I thought I was going to find the secret to all life and help people be free; even as a small child I believed that.

Who knew what I would choose to endure to accomplish that vision; that purpose.

At some level I believed in an inclusive God, one that accepted us all with our similarities as well as our differences. I considered that there did not need to be one single religion or belief that was right or wrong, but I was too afraid to acknowledge this belief. I believed that the intention was Love, but I focused that love outside of myself. I gave love and acceptance of others, believing it would lead to all healing.

I was taught that to enter heaven I had to love everyone and I heard that to mean, no matter what they did to me. I accepted that I was supposed to sacrifice myself for the good of others. In the many years that I focused on Spirituality, I was embracing it as it was being doled out to me. I felt guilty all the time. It just seemed so hard to live up to the rigidity of all the rules that were required to follow to be seen as *good*. Most importantly, I had to obey my parents and honor and respect all authority no matter what. If I didn't, something bad would happen. Fear and threats of hell were prevalent and felt terrifyingly real.

So often we decide early on to deny what feels like our truth, in favor of what is being taught to us by "authority." We often continue this pattern throughout our life, yet at anytime we can choose to realize we are our own authority and trust the wisdom inside of ourselves.

My greatest breakthrough in my early Spiritual growth was achieved when I read *Conversations with God: Book One* by Neale Donald Walsch. I remember the liberation I felt as I read each word. It was as if the words were speaking to the core of my soul. They spoke to the beliefs I had held, but kept hidden for fear of speaking or embracing them. These were all parts of my truths that I had rejected for fear of not being loved and accepted.

In essence, I denied my beliefs in favor of love and acceptance. The funny thing is that when we deny our beliefs, we lose love and acceptance of ourselves.

As I read Neale's book, I started feeling that maybe I could move slightly off the tightrope I felt I had to walk, the narrow path that needed to be followed to be seen as *good*. As I read words that confirmed my beliefs from someone outside of myself, someone who at the time I viewed as more of an authority than myself, I began to consider that there may be broader truths than the ones I had been taught.

The acceptance of the possibility of a broader truth, the willingness to apply doubt to what I had been taught was true, allowed me to feel that I now had permission to read anything that might educate me to the possible explanation of God. I was on a quest and a mission for understanding. From that moment to today, I have read a wide range of content covering vast and varied schools of thought from quantum physics to Buddhism, Christianity, Judaism and metaphysics. I place no limits on what I read. I have since adopted beliefs that are my own and not tied to any religion. I started to believe that my Spiritual beliefs could be my own, that I could decide what was right or wrong for me to believe. This was the beginning of my liberation. I would still have a long arduous journey before I would be fully free.

I was focused on how I could use the wisdom that life was about love to heal others, while ignoring the dramatic healing *I* needed. While asleep, I didn't acknowledge all the harm I was allowing to be bestowed on me. In spite of all my reading and learning, I continued to sleep through the important messages because I had an outward focus instead of an inward focus. Today I would call this an external locus of control. This means that I was still vastly driven by things outside of myself; beliefs, people, things that do not come from my own internal self. Having an external locus of control allows us to believe we are the victim of our circumstance, as opposed to their absolute creator.

Victim of circumstance, just how far reaching is this? What if we may have knowingly entered into our environment, from the moment of conception, so that we might have certain experiences? Of course we are not conscious of these choices in our present form, but what if we are a participant in creation of every facet of our life? These are the kinds of questions I encourage you to allow and consider. What if every moment is of our choosing?

For now, regardless of what power we may have over our circumstance, I am going to say that as children, we have little to no authority over what happens to us. As children we are not big enough or strong enough to overpower those larger humans who may be harming us. When we were first born, we naturally thought we were one with our mother. As we grew and developed over time, we learned that we were separate from her. There are many facets to this understanding. One key facet is learning to say 'yes' to some things and 'no' to others. When our natural 'no' and 'yes' isn't acceptable to the people around us, we experience limitations, because our goal is to not lose the love and acceptance we know innately even before we are born. What if when we feel love and acceptance being pulled away we change our behavior to make love and acceptance from others appear to return? In our formative years we are so responsive to the environment and people around us that we trust what they teach us, we trust that it is true. We do not look at ourselves to see our truth or what harm might be coming to us; instead, we look outside ourselves and ask, *Who do we need to be to be loved and accepted in our current environment?* We lose ourselves in favor of combined limitations and become the Limited Self. "Adapted Self" may be a more appropriate name. We may choose to remain there all our life.

The "adapted self" attempts to keep us safe, it gives us the illusion of love and acceptance. This adapted self is who we learn to be, not who we are.

In essence, as children we were filled with love, and then we sought acceptance. When we feel some aspect of ourselves is not accepted, the negative force of rejection by those we view as our authority, our caretakers, diminishes us and redefines what we think love is. From our heart of love, we begin to learn fear. What we fear most is losing love and acceptance. We need love and acceptance to feel safe. We become whatever we perceive will allow us to be given love and acceptance and/or will keep us safe.

I believe that we are born knowing only love, because we are aware of our connectedness to God. Then we are taught to fear. It is this fear, mainly fear of being rejected or harmed that teaches us to adapt our behaviors. These adaptations may not feel right to us, but we follow the path that we believe leads us to love and acceptance.

> **The feeling I have that this is wrong**
> **must in fact be what is wrong. My feelings are wrong,**
> **not the act of what is happening to me or being told to me.**

That fear of not being loved and accepted forces us to shift from our whole-selves to our adapted-selves. Our adapted self is the person we perceive we need to become, and eventually do become, so that we might feel loved and accepted as a child. The adapted self hides who we really are. The adapted self is our wounded self. That adapted self we became to feel loved, accepted, and therefore safe as a child, can be released once we are an adult. We can release our adapted self any time we decide. Through finding your beliefs you will learn who your adapted self is, and begin to rediscover your true self buried underneath.

In order to free ourselves from our false or limiting beliefs that created our adapted self, we first must identify those beliefs and wake up to the true reality. Once awake, we must stand up for who we are and our beliefs, even if they seem unacceptable to the world at large and, perhaps, by whomever we view as an authority. This is easier to do as we begin to trust ourselves. This courage is contagious.

There was a time in my life while in a very abusive relationship that I went back to foundational religious beliefs that were ingrained in me as a child. I knew my beliefs were not accepted by those whose love I craved, so I changed. Until we are awake, fear will push us back into that adapted self if we let it. As we trust ourselves, our self-esteem grows and we no longer need the acceptance of others. Trust in the Universe as a whole, and in ourselves as a part of that Universe, is the antidote to fear, just as self-esteem is the antidote to shame. When we no longer trust ourselves, others may approve of us, but does it matter if we don't approve of ourselves? Silencing our beliefs and reciting the script that has been handed to us is just one more way we can live in misalignment. It is a stressful existence and can have significant consequences, even on our health.

You see it was largely my spiritual beliefs that led me to put others before myself. I made myself invisible because I believed the world was about others' joy and love, not my own.

In all my deep adventures and journeys on my Spiritual path to learn about love and God, I had missed the point. God meant for me to love myself, the whole of myself, all parts of me. I can trust in my own ability to see those who wish to harm me. I can release those that wish to harm me without harboring hatred. I can send love to them and prayers for their healing; I just didn't have to stay in a relationship with them! It was okay to send anyone who didn't treat me well out of my life, and never look back at them.

As I said, what if people are brought into your life in a grand Universal effort to help you wake up? Of course their role is not something they are conscious of. Those individuals who are cruel to us are just being who they are on their own unconscious quest for wholeness. They are on their own path learning their own lessons, or perhaps not learning any lessons, but on their own path just the same. However, I have learned to have gratitude for those who have harmed me. If I was truly listening, if I would have let any one of those moments awaken me, I could have Woken Up a long time ago and stopped abuse in my life, as I have now. They served their purpose as the mirror in my life reflecting back at me the image of my own wounds, the wounds that I would need to heal to attain freedom.

Going through my life without an understanding of boundaries and having a distorted belief of the "love one another principle" created much of the harm I experienced in my life. The simple truth is I believed other people mattered more than I did. I also believed that I could never violate or disobey authority, and I gave too many people the authoritative role.

I didn't understand boundaries. I didn't understand my body was my body. I didn't understand my spirit was my spirit, I didn't understand my emotions were my emotions. Clearly, I didn't understand it was not only my right; it was my responsibility to Stand Up to protect myself. If I would not or could not protect myself as an adult, no one would.

All my life I was teaching people how I deserved to be treated by what I was allowing in my life. I taught them what I would tolerate, and I ask you to consider that you too are teaching others what you will tolerate and accept.

Embrace this thought:

> You matter and it is your responsibility to ensure that your life is filled with love, honor and respect. It is the path to freedom.

- ❖ **Always honor yourself.**
- ❖ **Honor others as long as honoring others doesn't cause you to dishonor yourself.**
- ❖ **If someone is asking you to dishonor yourself for them, that is not okay. Say no.**

Those of us who are *targets* chose to live the opposite of this Mantra.

- ❖ **We dishonored ourselves.**
- ❖ **We honored others, even if it dishonored us.**
- ❖ **We didn't say NO.**

Saying "no" is a powerful right that we have always had. So many of us decide that saying "no" is mean, or denying someone else of their rights. Instead we need to embrace our power of NO. We must speak it often until it feels natural. I often encourage people to simply practice saying "no". It is about learning to be comfortable with no. It is about knowing NO is not only your right, it is your responsibility. Being firm is not the same as being mean!

It is not selfish or mean to take care of yourself in honorable ways, although sometimes people may lead you to believe that it is. The consideration is, are you intentionally harming another or are you merely protecting yourself? Are you considering only your needs, and not the impact taking care of your needs will have on another?

The men in my life would tell me I was bad when I would offer kindness to anyone but them. I used to tell the men in my life, "You make me feel like I have to choose between who God longs for me to be, and who you long for me to be," and yet, I didn't see the truth that could awaken me in those words. I simply couldn't see that therein lies the conflict; a conflict that can literally make us sick. They would take all my noble intentions and make them into something dirty or sinister...taking it to places I would never even think of going. They would repeatedly crush my spirit.

To be deemed as *good* we are often taught to remove all our boundaries when it comes to what we allow others to do to us. The turn the other cheek concept perhaps has been distorted into a belief that we should keep enduring. Maybe instead it means we should turn our cheek to walk away. I do not believe that the intended message is to allow more pain to be continually inflicted upon us.

If you are to love your neighbor as yourself, then perhaps you need to first love yourself, your whole self exactly as you are. If you love yourself, you must learn to only allow loving treatment of you, as you would only bestow loving treatment on others.

We must become conscious of our thoughts and beliefs to create the life we truly want. Whatever convictions we have in our beliefs, manifest themselves in our life. We decide what our beliefs are. Therefore *we* have the power to manifest all components of our life in all areas of our life.

The way to release negative energy in our lives is to express those feelings which need to be expressed and let them go. If we continue to dwell on the negative experiences of the past we are giving them life in our present. Holding onto our story acts like a rubber band around our waist holding us back, pulling us back even as we try to advance forward. It keeps us from being free. We are meant to move past the lies and false beliefs that were instilled in us as children and recognize that we are the creators of our life. The quality of our life is a direct testimony to our thoughts and beliefs about it. I believe that any hatred, gossip, judgment of others, or jealousy, keeps us in a living hell, and faith, trust, and love can create for us a heaven on earth.

I also realize that there are circumstances that seem completely out of our control—death, accidents, illness, but it is our response to these tragedies that decides what happens next. We have far more power in our life then we may be willing to acknowledge. Do not underestimate the power of positive energy, or prayer, if you are more comfortable with that term. If we are truly accountable for all aspects of our life and our life is a mess, or not where we want it to be, perhaps it may be time for *us* to change.

After assessing myself spiritually, I know that I honor all the pathways to the loving source of God. I honor if you choose not to believe in God. We each get to choose which path brings us peace and comfort and aligns with our own beliefs and values; hopefully from our heart not from our fear.

We cannot heal without accepting who we are, exactly where we are.

As I awakened in all areas of my life I began to see the larger picture. I began to see our quest for wholeness on both an individual scale and a larger scale of the world. I began to see that I was always connected in mind, body, and spirit personally, yet it was my lack of understanding of that connectedness that in part caused me so much pain.

I wasn't listening to the external red flags or promptings, nor was I listening to the internal ones. As I learned to connect all these dots, I found my wholeness as an individual and am now embracing our wholeness on the grander scale of the Universe. I believe God, if you will, gives us exactly what we are asking for. The trouble is some of us never stop to look at what it is that we are asking for!

What if we are all one, bound together at an energetic level? What if embracing this interconnectedness is what can lead not only to our own healing, but planetary healing as well? From this place of connectedness we will have love where before there was hate, we will have compassion where before there was rejection. We will not compartmentalize. We will accept the different parts of ourselves, without harshly judging those who are different than us. What if as we learn to accept and embrace all the parts of us as individuals, even those parts right now we think we would rather reject or deny, we will experience the joy of that wholeness and begin to lead others to wholeness on a larger scale?

Until we embrace the truths of who we truly are as individuals, we seek acceptance outside of ourselves. This quest for the love and acceptance of others often fails because we must first love and accept the truth of who we are, before we can expect to receive love and acceptance from others.

Once we accept and trust ourselves right where we are, we will be building our confidence and self-esteem in that trust and acceptance. We will know that eliminating abuse from our lives is necessary if we want to be truly happy and free. We must not focus on changing those outside of ourselves. We must only focus on changing ourselves. Our suffering has always been our choice. The more we embrace our deservingness, our divinity, the stronger the presence of love.

I believe that God is love, the most powerful force that exists. I believe in our wholeness we experience the full expression of God and all the majestic powers. When we know peace, we know God.

As a coach, I encourage people to find their *happy place*. The reason this is critical, is it will clearly illustrate the power of your thoughts on your physiology. Before I share this with you, note how you feel right now physically. Your body, your mind, your heart; tension, breathing, the presence of your whole body. Now, ask yourself to think of the happiest time of your life—a precise moment when you felt utter joy. For many, this is not as simple as it would seem. Regardless, give it time, you have one; we all have at least one moment of joy. If you truly cannot access one then make one up. Something you wish to experience. Now close your eyes, breathe deep. Let all your thoughts go and go there, to your *happy place*. Use as many of your senses as possible. Be in that moment. Allow yourself to stay there for a moment, or many moments. Don't create a photograph in your mind, experience it multidimensionally. As you go to release that image, then imagine it like a photograph. See yourself placing that photograph in your heart. It can always be with you. After having that experience, comparatively, how do you feel right now physically? Your body, your mind, your heart; tension, breathing, the presence of your whole body?

That joyful feeling is a decision. Isn't that oneness with God part of what we are searching for? You don't have to go anywhere to find it; it is within you. It always has been.

Perhaps more than the potential exclusiveness of religion, we need acceptance of the power and love of God regardless of the path you choose. Years ago someone gave me an image of this concept that really resonated with me. If God is the elephant, the huge and the powerful, and I only choose to see one leg, then I may only be seeing a part of the whole, but I am still seeing God. What if by our segregated and exclusive views, we are only enjoying part of the whole? If we stood back a little further, we could see we are all connected to the same source. What if we are actually connected *by* that same source…what if we are actually part of that "elephant"?

In part, the idea that one path is right and another is wrong, is often intended to keep the world divided, so that there is a place for "fear of" and "power over." Religion often promotes believing we are better than another or perhaps better stated; that someone is less than us. This promotes a continuation of the idea of separation, which weakens our ability to prevail as unified humanity. The tendency of religion to be divisive and based in fear just may be part of the issue.

Perhaps this concept of "fear of" and "power over" is instituted in a broad scale so that we never allow ourselves to live totally free? We walk a tight rope created for us, fearing that if we fall we will be rejected by the highest source of all, God. A God that is love accepts us with the knowledge of the truth of who we are, as we are. If we choose to accept ourselves with that same unconditional love, we will keep moving toward healing and wholeness; oneness with all that is. While asleep we deny the truth of who we are and limit our lives and all the potential we hold. We hide our true power.

Perhaps God, the Universe, or whatever name you give to the loving energy between us, is all things and the one thing that will forever have us all connected to each other, exactly as we are. To embrace that truth is the beginning of our healing on a grander scale.

Love, and the acceptance that we are all one and that love is why we are here, could go far to heal many wounds and create peace, even if it is just a peaceful life for us individually.

When you embrace the truth that you are free, you can be the eye in any storm. You can remain in your hammock no matter what appears to be storming around you. You can experience peace no matter what the outer circumstances seem to reflect. You can float down the river accepting the view, calm in the awareness that you have the freedom and power to change the course at will.

You do not need to embrace any of my beliefs. Instead, why not decide what yours are?

Decide what you believe, and begin to live free.

You need not impose your beliefs on others, just Stand Up for your right to have beliefs of your own, and live them.

Financially (Material)

"Financially" refers to your thoughts regarding money.

What your perceptions are relative to the role

and importance of money, and your beliefs

regarding how much you deserve or don't deserve.

Still at a relatively young age, I began to address some elements of my financial beliefs as a result of ending a relationship of significant length. Astonishingly the abuse in this relationship, although painful and diminishing, was on a much smaller scale of the abuse that was yet to come. So why did I remain in a largely unhappy situation for all those years? My **stamina** and **endurance** told me I had to make it work. Guilt and shame are we allow to be used against us, to make us violate our own ѕ·ce, our own inner knowing. Stamina and endurance prevailed.

At that phase of my life I still believed that I was not the ruler of my life. I felt that I had to abide by the laws created by someone outside of myself. I had to try to make it work; it was what was expected of me. Keep in mind my belief system. It was my job to make the man happy, to heal and protect him.

If only I had known then to:

- ❖ **Always honor yourself.**
- ❖ **Honor others as long as honoring others doesn't cause you to dishonor yourself.**
- ❖ **If someone is asking you to dishonor yourself for them, that is not okay. Say no.**

What do you know is wrong that you are still **enduring?** Who are you trying to protect or save believing that it is the path to love and acceptance?

Earlier I spoke of that voice, the inner prompting that tells us, *This isn't right.* That voice was always prodding me. I just didn't understand it was my soul talking to me. It was as if it was saying, *Will you listen, will you listen now? Can you hear me?* ***You*** *matter and deserve to be treated with honor and respect.*

Was I listening? No.

Leaving that relationship did send me head first into Financial, my next area to begin to awaken.

Sometimes our relationships are giving us the opportunity to see what we *don't* want. This allows us to be clearer about what we *do* want. As I have said before, we attract what we give energy to. This means if we focus on what we *don't* want in a relationship that is exactly what we'll get. Turn it around to focus on what you *do* want. Instead of saying, "I will never be with someone who is dependent on me financially again!" say, "In the future I will choose someone who is secure in themselves."

After that relationship, I didn't take time to assess myself. I didn't ask myself how I ended up in that relationship and how to create something different. The only thing I felt I needed to focus on was being a provider for my daughter. I knew and believed with every fiber of my being, that if I wasn't careful, something bad would happen. That belief more than any other, drew negative outcomes toward me. My fear was attracting to me exactly what I feared. Life has a way of rising or falling to our level of expectation because we are powerful creators, powerful attractors.

I recall when I finally told my parents that I was ending that relationship. My father warned me, "Diana, you will end up on welfare!" Of course, that was just his fear talking. He still didn't believe his little girl could take care of herself. My greatest fear was that he was right, that I couldn't do it on my own. I believed I was not enough. I believed it was not going to be okay. I longed for validation from my dad. I wanted him to believe in me. I began the next phase of my life with my fear and false beliefs guiding my path.

In that moment, when I heard my dad say "welfare," I made a decision. I would never be on welfare. My parents instilled in me that success was defined by money. There was little mention of love or its importance. If I was not financially able, I perceived I would be unimportant and unaccepted. That fear drove me. In addition, I was taught that the way to show someone you love them is to provide for them financially. If I was not a provider, I would be doomed to a life void of love.   *Wes?*

My father's words, my fear of being on welfare, these outside forces were ruling my life. I was still very much asleep. I was letting my fear create a trump card for every abuser that was going to enter my world. If there was financial risk, I would act.

If the men in my life were unhappy, I was willing to make drastic changes to appease them. I would change jobs, move across state lines, respond to whatever demands they put forth, under the illusion of creating their happiness, their security. They knew they could ask these things of me without risking their own financial security, because they knew I was so driven by fear that I would always continue to provide. I provided for myself and my daughter, but I also provided for the men who parasitized my finances. I allowed them to. They knew how I feared the shame of proving my father right. They knew just how hard I was willing to work to avoid that shame. They knew I was working hard to prove my "love" for them. I was exhausted.

I never looked back on this exchange with my father until my world crashed once again. Why would it crash? Because I still wasn't looking at myself relative to **all** the areas: Emotional, Physical, Financial, Spiritual, and Mental. I was never looking inward.

I wasn't assessing my priorities for the whole of my life. I was in survival mode, fear mode, living to avoid welfare. I was living to meet the needs of others, others who saw me as nothing more than a meal ticket, and someone who could resolve any of their alleged financial issues.

Almost immediately after this conversation with my father, I fell for what I believe to be my first sociopath. Of course at the time I had no knowledge whatsoever of sociopathy and would not learn for many years.

I have come to believe that sociopaths, or any other abusers or manipulators, find us because we send out a clear energetic message that suggests we want them in our life. That message is fear, caused by our lack of understanding of our worth and power.

This "sociopath" came in to my life not only because of my fear, but because I was being provided with an out. As part of a Universal plan, this man was brought to my life to wake me up. I was supposed to allow this relationship to enable me to see the error of my ways. The Universe granted me the opportunity to wake up; however, I remained engrossed in my slumber. I was a single mom and all that mattered was avoiding welfare. This meant that I was so consumed by my work and my fear, I neglected to acknowledge the abuse that was happening all around me.

So I worked and worked. I didn't pay attention to what was happening to me or to my life. I was a loving mother to my daughter whenever we had quality time together; however, my driving fear was that I could not fail at my job. If I failed at my job, I believed I failed as a provider; the role that I believed would bring me to love and acceptance. At no time did I evaluate what was important to me as a mother or as a woman. I was living to align with the belief system that had been dictated to me—money was the goal. My distorted view kept me focused on establishing myself as the provider, so I worked.

I was so busy working, I never examined the abuse. I excused away all of my abusers' false accusations of my affairs. I chose to believe their repetitive convictions that I was nothing and I would never survive without them. I ignored the holes they would punch in the walls and the fact that they would disregard my home, my property, and me. My own lack of regard for myself showed them that I was willing to let them minimize and belittle me.

Over time, the abuse at home would intensify and my career would keep getting bigger and more demanding. My business success was a reflection of my self-confidence, while my self-esteem was being further dismantled and destroyed. Self-confidence is what the world sees. It is the part of us that can "do." Often people who are successful in business have a high degree of self-confidence. Self-esteem is a little trickier. Self-esteem is what we believe about who we are on the inside, the unseen. I watched myself time and time again anger the man who was the authority in my mind. Given my belief system relative to men, I was a failure. I couldn't keep him happy.

My world would need to shatter before I could really see. I was focused on the financial, the external. I was so consumed by my fear of losing my financial security that I neglected to look at any of my internal realities. I was blind to the pain I was feeling inside.

I recall at one point, in the middle stages of my career, receiving advice from an assistant that worked for me whom I respected…she presented a question to me…"Why do you live like you are poor, when I know you are not?"

Believing that success was defined by finances and business, it was my focus to earn, but not to spend. I was ignoring myself, my needs and my desires, living as if impoverished, while working and living to earn. Her comment did not awaken me.

My parents were a good balance on educating me financially, dad being a banker and saver, and mom being a little more open about money. My father gave me my hardworking business ethic, my mother taught me to believe in my business capabilities and that I could do anything. She told me that no one can make money on *scared* money. She was trying to teach me to believe that my hard work would result in abundance of money, even if it was not immediately visible. Yet I always had a fear of not having enough.

I have mentioned that our memories create our beliefs. I want you to know that this is true relative to both negative and positive beliefs. In once such instance I recall being about 8 years old and on a cruise ship with my family. There was gambling on that ship and when the ship was at sea, even children could play slots. And so I did. I was amassing a rather large pile of dimes as my dad stood behind me and observed the pile. The pile was beginning to diminish and I kept dropping in the dimes. I remember feeling my father's presence behind me as I excitedly grabbed each dime from my pile and placed it back in the slot. My dad encouraged me to walk away, take the dimes I had won. I thought I was so lucky and could win more, so I continued to drop those dimes in, one by one, my dad encouraging me all the while to walk away. Ultimately the pile was gone, and with the most adorable brown eyes I could muster, I turned to my dad and asked for more dimes. My dad's response was "When the money is gone, the money is gone." That was a precise lesson that I have never forgotten. His wise lesson was distorted, due to my irrational fear.

That fear, and my fear of welfare, led to my hoarding of cash, perhaps to an extreme. It was my mom who always encouraged me to take business risks and have faith. Very early in my work life, I would leave good jobs for what seemed like cuts in pay because I could see what I could build it into, and it always worked. While I may have been a risk taker in some financial aspects, I lived by a set of rules. I feared that if those guidelines weren't followed to a T, the money would inevitably run out. Unbeknownst to me at the time, my success was more about my powerful quest for my lost self-esteem. My financial situation was the only thing that I felt proved that I had value as a person. I believed I was what I did for a living and what I could provide. My strongest *I am* was always followed by my executive title, my position of power. The one place I considered, I am *somebody*.

I always had paid myself first and in fact, as I mentioned, I lived as if I was impoverished for many of my early years, knowing I had to build a cushion. In my career I saw far too many people with poor discipline in this area, and as a result I was over the top at my devotion to savings and avoiding debt.

Unlike me, the men I chose to be with were very vested in finer things. They cared deeply about how they looked financially to the outer world; their "image." This resulted in bigger homes than I would have chosen, construction to expand those homes, lavish travel and so on—All on my dime. I thought I was on my path to love and acceptance rather than destruction. My relationships with these men caused me to spend, in an effort to give to those who claimed to have been robbed of so much. Do not underestimate the power of this spell. It ignites in us a need to fill their desires and restore their losses. We help them succeed in whatever endeavor they claim they would strive for, if only they could, so they might someday believe they are worthy once again. We so want to move them toward healing. In one such instance, after hearing his tales of woe—the failure of the once thriving business, through no fault of his own of course—I found myself placing a significant sum of money in an account in his name as business seed money. I wanted him to know I believed in him. Coupled with the loss of his business was the story of betrayal which led to his beloved Harley being "stolen" by those he put his faith in. He had titled certain assets in the names of others for "safe keeping," you know, until he could resolve all the misgivings the IRS had about his failure to pay various taxes. Distraught for his painful losses, I surprised him with a brand new $23,000 Harley Davidson Road King Custom. I was driven to these acts of "kindness," both the Harley and the business seed money, within three weeks of meeting him. I was rejoicing in my ability to help restore this poor and broken man. Surely he quickly knew he hit pay dirt. I can now see his sobs were not his pain, but instead his laughter at his power to manipulate me into satisfying his desires through the illusion of his being victimized by others. I now see that all was a ploy to maintain assets reflecting his flashy success while looking penniless to the entities that would want him to pay up. It was always about looking successful, but when possible, avoiding that paper trail.

I have said that my trump card was that something bad will happen if I didn't do something to stop it. Given that a key component of my belief system was that I must be the provider to prove my love, I responded to whatever the abuser wanted by providing financially. Even in the countless times I would insist on "no," somehow the master manipulators would shift this to a "yes."

This play of the trump card can be done through many techniques.

For me, guilt would cause me to take actions that I knew at some level were wrong, but I felt I had no choice. The power of that trump card would lead me to sign property into joint name to those that I now know wanted to claim what I owned as their own. I was asked to make the transfer to prove I trusted and loved them. Or the repeated times I would loan them money to show I believed in their ability to create a way to provide or co-sign loans, or buy property, or homes, or...you get the idea.

Know that during the "honeymoon" period these crafty individuals are excellent at setting the environment to create trust. They tend to keep their word and express the illusion of remorse if they fall short. They make it explicitly clear through their language, that your needs are the utmost priority. Where it matters most to *them* however, they work hard to build their credibility with you through their actions as well. They don't want to let you down, especially and above all else, in the areas where it is most important that they can manipulate you. For instance, early on they pay back monies you loaned them as promised, like clockwork and speak often of their devotion to this goal. You believe it is important to them that they don't disappoint you. Awake, you will know their promise was devious. They simply didn't want to lose the game. Their ability to fulfill their promises has nothing to do with true trust. Remember; they have to set the hook.

As time progresses, they claim a vast array of challenges making it difficult to meet their obligations or commitments as promised, to which we often offer compassion, given we perceive they just need a break. They have had such hard luck. When we do start to doubt their words, they rise to the occasion, over and over again. The trap is masterfully set, if you are asleep enough to trust the untrustworthy.

The important thing you need to know is that manipulation is about the trump card. It is simply about where the manipulator knows they can have power over you. Your trump card may not have anything to do with money, it may have to do with work, children, God, family or even pets....but you see in spite of how it may appear, each of those circumstances are not about the money or what they seem to be using as leverage, it is about the entrapment it creates. It is about control. The same is true of how your trump card is being used.

A true manipulator knows the more enmeshed your life is with theirs, the harder it will be for you to escape, so that is what they are after.

Their goal is simple, they want you fully vested in them. They want to keep you in the game and under their control, like nothing more than a chess piece. Know your opponent. True chess games may merely be about winning, yet in this game, for the most calculating players, it is about annihilation.

If you find yourself in one of these types of relationships, know that once you have tolerated the maximum you can tolerate, it is imperative that you realize exiting initiates a game at a much more deviant level. Prior to waking, the fighting was endless, exhausting, and difficult. It remains endless until you are awake enough to see that this game is strategic, not emotional. You must get out of your emotions and stop applying the same human thinking you have in *your* mind, to how *their* mind works.

This is true in business or other family dynamics as well. When you become nonchalant instead of reactive because you can stand in your power, and not your emotions, your sense of security throws them off and empowers you. It is all the same, a chess game.

121

It is important that you see that wherever there is abuse in your life, this chess game is something to consider. It should be no surprise to you that my assessment largely focuses on experiencing and ending intimate sociopathic relationships, yet know that departure from abuse is about having the courage to see the truth, and then to act on that truth. We must awaken, heal, and embrace our wholeness that has been ours all along.

Ending relationships often ends in battle. You may be battling over the children, dogs, art, cars, assets…but you must consider that they may not care about these *things*. They may just want to grab a hold of what you care about so they can win. They want you to feel as though you owe them. They want to play on your compassion. You feel that perhaps they deserve to see or have the dog, or maybe even the children. You want to have their rights honored…and so you compromise. Or perhaps you want to be free so badly that you are willing to walk away in ways that are harmful to you.

As you know more, you will consider what you may not have considered before, that you are not dealing with a genuinely emotional individual; instead you may be dealing with a master manipulator. Every single thing in their life is an object, an object that can be used as a tool to harm and control you. Once you understand that, embrace that, and feel your heart shift as a result, you are awake. Do not apply this concept to all divorces or all departures from church, work or any organization or person. The situation I describe is not always the reality. It is true, however, that you must be awake to the possibility. Observe who you are battling with and if your experience is nonsensical and harmful, you just may be in a vicious game of chess, instead of a true above board dissolution with benign beings.

When it is time to severe any joint financial life with someone, there is always the issue of "my stuff" and "your stuff." However, when you have been the provider for a sociopath, that division is not simple. I spoke of grand romantic gestures, lavish and expensive gifts that my manipulators would "spoil" me with to show the world how much they cared. I neglected to mention that those gifts were all purchased with my money. The abuser tended to believe that they were just as worthy of those gifts as I was. Shopping is always more fun on someone else's dime. The true sociopath has a sense of entitlement like none the world has ever seen. If you are the provider, then during the dissolution of the relationship they will claim that nearly every purchase made during the relationship was intended as a gift for them. It is true that many purchases were made as a result of their glistening eyes as they came upon the desires of their heart, so you now find yourself asking, *Does that mean they are gifts*? They may also request a few items of purely sentimental value—a gift from your child, a Bible, or a photo of a time you spent together. This is merely a strategic move to show you, your child, the court, your friends, that they are not interested in taking anything from you. They do this as they take all that they can carry. They will claim that they did in fact *earn* their right to these things. They will **falsely claim** they did home maintenance and repairs, cared for the children, or made extensive financial contributions etc. and therefore they should get all that you have, all that you had even before you knew them. They will play on your emotions, your charitable nature, and your sense of integrity. You may find yourself questioning, "Did I say he could have that?" "Perhaps I should give it to him, it's only right." Do not feel guilty—they do not genuinely need your charity. You have likely given them more than you will ever know and there is no need to give more.

On the other end of the spectrum, perhaps they *were* the provider. They will now see you as worthy of nothing. Perhaps you quit your job to raise the children, but that means nothing to the sociopath. They will strive to keep everything, even those things with no monetary value. Possibly even your children. They do this, not out of love of the children, but because they know exactly where to hit you to make it count. Their winning is not so much defined by acquiring wealth of assets, the children or pets, as much as their winning is defined in celebrating their power and ability to manipulate their way to your destruction, devastation, and harm. The longer they can take to drag your suffering out, vacillating between agreement and appearance of conscience, to confusion and reneging on any commitment, the happier they are.

And if we say, "Take it all!" they will find a new way to keep us hanging on. As you learn more of what you do not know, you should be more able to play a strategic game of chess. It is your job to protect yourself. If you feel that a chess game might put your life at risk, it may not be wise to play. You can seek help. The material goods are not worth your life. This is a judgment call only you can make. Awake you will know. Awake you will listen to that still small voice that before, you ignored. Its guidance will be very powerful.

Once awake you can and will play this game differently. Once awake, perhaps for the first time in your life, you will find yourself operating from the shadow. Suddenly you can lie and stand in your integrity like my Holocaust scenario, only now you will be free to end your own internment.

You might say "No I purchased those items for the home, not for you, they were not gifts"…*because if I opened the door that they could be yours you would take them, not because you want them, but because you want me to lose them.*

If you genuinely gave a gift and want them to have it, you can give it. Just realize that the person you are giving it to is not the person you thought you were buying it for, they are nothing more than a great manipulator. Step out of your delusion.

As I have stated, be clear that when a relationship is ending, their goal is to get back in the door if you have evicted them, or to get you back in if you have left. They need to win. If you do not find evidence of this attempt, either they are hoping that their absence will draw you near, or they have trolled and found the next victim. Rest assured, if they are trying to get back in, it is to harm you, although they will attempt to convince you it is to better love you, to talk things out, or they will convince you they are in need, knowing you will come to their rescue. They might say that they have lost something important, they fear the dog or child is sick, they got in a car accident or hurt themselves—anything to get back in so they can perform their next act of violence or set you up so they can win in court. Compassion is what they are trying to draw from you; your guilt being the tool. Remember that ALL humans have the capacity for evil, and if you are dealing with someone who is truly living from the shadows, you cannot underestimate the lengths that they will go to win.

A life of full disclosure and transparency is what we strive to live…but to be safe we must only offer our information to someone that would hold that information as sacred, not use it as a weapon to harm us. Once awake we can distinguish between those that would harm us, and those that would treat all of who we are, with sanctity. We can distinguish this difference because we now know, to look for incongruence between words and actions. We know to be aware of our inner prompting, our voice. We will know to trust their actions and not their words, and that we can finally trust ourselves. When you know, you are able to play chess; you will be on the offensive, and you will have a diminishing need for defense. They are not expecting you to be different than you always were, and that is to your advantage. You can no longer be predictable. Together through these pages we can help develop your skills.

The cost of being asleep can be quite devastating.

As I completed my assessment of myself financially, I realized that I have had many good disciplines. I know that I have vast knowledge on the subject. I have been both student and trainer. My entire career was based on my sophisticated grasp of finances. I have educated others and learned complex strategies regarding investments and estate planning. I taught Series 7 for more than two decades, which is the exam one needs to pass to become a stockbroker/financial planner. I even earned my Certified Financial Planner designation (CFP®), which is quite comprehensive. I had always devoted myself to advancement in the business world. Once I was a single mom my passion only escalated, motivating me to start at the very bottom of my company making only $26,000 and energetically working my way through the organization; ultimately making upper six digits at the high point of my career.

As I saw the extravagant lifestyle these men wanted to live, my fear went in overdrive, yet I listened to their promises instead of that nagging little voice in the back of my mind. I would *invest* in them enamored with their promise that it would be my turn to sit back and have them provide for me, "soon." Financing their dreams almost drove me to financial ruin. Although none of these men received anything from me upon departure, or at least very little, leaving them was very costly because of the manipulation and games. Legal battles, stock market crashes and need for my capital to protect myself with private eyes and security cameras, disputing conjured up statements presented as facts, and arguing over legal documents, was costly. At one point more than 70% of my relatively significant assets were gone. Not to mention the money that they had managed to skim from my accounts during the tenure of our relationships. All my saving had positioned me perfectly to have the assets to sell my financial soul for love. At some level I believed my money could buy me love. What do you believe about money?

I keep talking about alignment. I feared I would lose my security, which I perceived was solely my money, and this caused me to be disciplined and a saver. However, once I was knee deep in these repeated relationships, my finances were terribly abused. In one area of my life, financial, I acted based on fear. In another, emotional relationships, I engaged in behavior that was sure to bring about the very thing I feared. If fear is your driver, it will ultimately send you crashing…you can't be afraid to lose something and truly expect to hold onto it. Scarcity mentality will lead to scarcity.

I was awake financially relative to how to save, the importance of saving and all the detailed methodology and reasoning. However, because I was asleep emotionally, I repeatedly gave up my financial security in an effort to support someone else, who I thought would in turn, give me security and take care of me…some day. I confused their laughter as sobs, their lies as promises. What would make me think they could take care of me, if they wouldn't even take care of themselves?

So as you evaluate yourself in all areas, be sure you are really looking in-depth at those areas. Any room full of people who know me would say I know finances intricately, and I was awake to every area about the topic. My being asleep emotionally however, nullified my knowledge and almost destroyed me. How are you using money in your life? Or who are you staying with because you perceive you need them for your own economic survival? Wake up…freedom is always attainable; you are not trapped, even if you perceive you are.

Emotionally (Heart)

"Emotionally" refers to your feelings, your awareness of them,

your ability to feel and express them, and what may be acceptable

or unacceptable to you in this venue.

I continued to seek wisdom for the express reason of healing others while still not acknowledging the ways in which I was neglecting myself. I never set boundaries intended to keep myself safe. I was choosing to remain asleep, never taking the time to address my own emotions. Evidence that I was remaining asleep was found in the cruelty I allowed in my life. The conditions of your outer world are a direct reflection of your inner thoughts about yourself. Every negative thought and emotion allows for the creation of the same.

I was not trying to protect that imaginary little girl holding my hand. I wasn't paying attention to my emotional needs. I was working and trying to hold the piece of those that claimed to love and need me. In spite of all that occurred, I was still so focused outside of me. Did I even exist?

I felt invisible.

So often we ignore ourselves and our feelings for so long, that in our numbness, we are unaware that we are alive. We feel dead and deny ourselves even our breath.

I believe that sometimes part of our self allows pain to remind us we are alive, much like someone who cuts themselves. As I understand it, one reason people do that is so they can experience pain and know they are alive. They bleed, therefore they are real; they exist.

In that regard, I think it is important that we discuss the lack of emotion I felt when the abusers in my life attempted to rape me, strangle me, or otherwise endanger me. The reason I need for you to assess this, is that I need you to see how someone who is a target, someone asleep, sees their story versus how someone awake would see it. I want you to see it so maybe you can assess where you are on the spectrum of awake vs. asleep, and move to a more awake position if necessary.

Ask yourself, if you witnessed someone attempting to rape your child, or any child for that matter, or strangle them, point a gun at them, or set them up in some way that they would be harmed or in trouble, if *your* child was bullied in these terrible ways, where would your level of emotion be? My guess is even as you read those words you may be feeling the anger beginning to brew inside of you. You are likely adamant about your intolerance of such behavior and you would want to take action to stop it and prevent further harm.

This might be a good moment to ask that you actually imagine some of those events. Imagine any of the hardships you have allowed in your own life happening to someone you love. Notice how powerful the imagery can be. The images can elicit a physical and emotional sensation. Images are part of

128

our life every day, even though we may not notice. We have movies playing in our head. If I say, "What did you have for dinner?" or, "What are you going to wear?" don't you see an image? Imagining your experiences and then changing the image to one that is more favorable, more bearable, or more empowering, is very instrumental in healing.

As you see those images of something harmful happening to someone other than you, someone you love, might you more readily call the police? Might you worry less about the consequences to the abuser? I would like to think that is always true, but alas, many people are too afraid to protect their children too...and therefore, in their asleep state they will also ignore the magnitude of their children's pain. They are too afraid, too numb, or feel too helpless. That said, as a coach I know that most people are more willing to experience their own anger, pain, and sadness when they picture the victim as someone outside of themselves, especially someone they love.

Why can't we love ourselves as much as we love others, especially others that we often perceive as helpless? We need to see that we are acting helplessly, although we may not be in fact helpless. We have compassion for those who we perceive as unable to defend/care for themselves without our help, but we do not see that *we* are in fact helpless, if we do not choose to care for and defend *ourselves*!

Why are we not as appalled when these things happen to us? Shouldn't our anger and protective response mechanism jump into gear to save ourselves? Our decision to use our **stamina** and **endurance** to facilitate our continued pain is a testimony to our own lack of regard for ourselves. When you Wake Up, that will change and you will have a love for yourself that, sadly, you might have never known existed.

To demonstrate our own emotions about ourselves, in this moment close your eyes and say, "I love myself," twenty times slowly and note how you physically feel as you say those words.

Are you uncomfortable already? I hope not, though many people are at first.

Now I would like you to do the same exercise repeating "I love myself" twenty times, except first imagine yourself as the container of the perfect quantity of your favorite food. See that image then speak of love of self!

Was that easier? Many people giggle their way through that exercise in delight. What does that tell us about our feelings for ourselves? It is time for us to deeply and completely love ourselves. What if we all did?

What if we captured that childlike joy that we left behind so long ago? We must take that child whose hand we are holding and do such a wonderful job parenting her that she feels safe to be who she really is. As she begins to trust that you, the knowing grown up, will keep her safe, she can use her energy and strength to remind you to make time for the playful, joyful side of life. Personally, I can say that was the side of life I had never ventured into and today, I have finally touched that level of joy.

When you imagine that child holding your hand, how old is she or he?

That may be the age you are emotionally stuck at. Think of your false beliefs; were any of them established around that time?

Our lack of self-love moves us to numbness which enables us to remain in denial of the obvious truth of our suffering as we sleep. To demonstrate this let's revisit the moment of my near rape.

What was blatantly missing from what I told you about the attempted rape? What strikes you as I simply stated that someone tried to rape me? When someone is asleep, their abuse is just something they have accepted, so all the appropriate emotions in the experience are missing, shut down. Where is my fear, the details, my anxiety? Why am I so matter-of-fact, as I tell that story or any other story of abuse inflicted on me? Asleep, I recounted these events as if I was merely commenting on the weather, it simply *was*.

Today that rape story does feel just matter-of-fact because I am healed, having chosen to really feel the pain of that experience and release it. You see, once you are free from the buried emotions, through accepting and feeling your experiences, no or very little emotion will appear when you bring those experiences back up. That is a good indicator that you are finally free from them. So in part, my healing enables me to matter-of-factly tell the story, however, I chose to tell the story in the same manner that I recounted it while I was asleep for illustration purposes. When we are in constant trauma, as a survival technique, we choose to minimize our experience.

I once similarly told my daughter that after receiving a devastating letter, the man that I was in a relationship with tried to strangle me. When I told her this, I wanted her to see his pain, feel sorrow for *his* experience. How distraught he must be to do something so drastic. I did not speak of any fear. I was unaware I felt fear. In fact, while asleep I did not consciously *ever* fear what this man might do to me. I only feared that he would leave. I clearly remember my daughter responding, "What amazes me Mom, is that you can use his name and 'strangled me' in the same sentence and not realize there is a problem."

You see my daughter could see the value of **my** human life. I could only see the value of *his*.

When we are living in the abuse, we lose sight of it. Our friends or family may question physical signs if we have them, and we may excuse them away. We may even open up to someone in our lives about our abuse. The incident I told my daughter about remains in my memory, though it no longer haunts me. Shaking with a red face, the man who claimed to love me wrapped his hands around my neck. I could not breathe and I remember slapping him across the face to attempt to get free, a futile effort to release his grip. Eventually, he released me. I gasped as the precious cool air filled my lungs once more. That evening we had company, a cop no less, and this man told "the officer" and his wife that I slapped him across the face that day. I looked at him in dismay and bravely proclaimed, "Yes, to release your hands from around my neck." He responded, "That never happened." I imagined in my mind that he must have been so upset, that he couldn't remember what he did. That poor man.

Logically, what my daughter said would seem eye opening, a jolt of reality to help me see. Yet to me, she just didn't understand his suffering like I did. He

131

was hurt. He didn't mean to hurt me, he loved me. The emotions I should have felt, the hurt associated with the man I loved strangling me, were merely reflected back at me as if he was feeling the pain. I recognized his "pain" instead of my own.

We disassociate from our pain, we choose to feel numb. If you were in a war you could hardly feel and acknowledge all the tragic experiences that are occurring minute by minute, and still function vigilantly as you need to for survival. So our bodies and minds find a way of coping with reality until we are ready to move away from that reality. Unlike true war, in our personal world *we* dictate when we can move away from that reality. What is absent from these stories is the truth about my fear. What is absent from these stories is the truth about my vulnerability. What is present in these stories is my ability to ignore my fear and vulnerability. I was not ready to acknowledge how painful these experiences were, or at least should have been.

Let's assess this on a broader scale.

When you live in abuse it is not an isolated instance. It is not a rare event; it is instead a chosen way of life. Abuse has many different forms but often it is a certain pattern of actions.

In these types of relationships your partner often has a reasonably consistent routine of violent acts. Even if you are not the direct target, they may put their fist through walls or intentionally, deliberately, and almost flamboyantly destroy property by throwing things, breaking things, threatening to do harm, tearing photos or any number of destructive acts. When you live in an environment wrought with this behavior you become numb to it. The action is evident, you see it happen, but being asleep you likely never looked at what that violence was actually doing to you internally, or what messages you were absorbing from that violence. In a different manner, these things can show up in business, churches, and political arenas as well. Less gravely, in the business world these fears may show up as threats to your job, or to your level of pay or ability to move up the ladder. In churches the fear might be about falling out of grace with God.

132

No matter what the message, it is fear that can leave you believing you are rejected, not good enough or unaccepted, unless you do or change something. It is always about instilling fear, so that another may have control over you.

When someone smashes their fist through the wall, they are sending a message, one of fear. Internally, whether you are conscious of it or not, you are asking yourself, *If he can do that to a wall, what could he do to me?* Unconsciously we decide we need to walk on egg shells to keep ourselves safe, while never being conscious of our fear. Our life of vigilance begins. We deny our fear *so* deeply, that we truly believe we are not afraid. We are not even conscious of the truth that rests beneath the surface. We are afraid to look. We are choosing to stay asleep because it is too overwhelming to wake up.

As an awake outsider, if you were watching someone bashing their fists through a wall, or intentionally destroying property, what might your thoughts or feelings be?

This man is scary. He can hurt me. Each time he hits that wall it is a reminder he can harm me. He is telling me, *I dominate you. I am more powerful than you. You are not safe. I don't respect you. I don't respect your property. I will hurt you. I am hurting you.* Someone who is awake, someone who is aware and trusts themselves, would see this behavior and choose to remove themselves from this person.

Recall for a moment those times you broke down and cried. What happened? You were made to feel even smaller. You were likely ridiculed and dominated further. These abusive individuals like to take advantage of people they know they can dominate. By us choosing to allow ourselves to feel smaller and less significant; in their sick way they feel larger and more significant. This has them feeling they are winning. When they are in control they are winning, you are losing, and that is all that matters.

The process of awakening sees an evolution of our fear. While completely asleep, we do not realize that we should be afraid for our lives or our safety. We fear only that we will let them down, that they will leave, that the relationship will fail. We fear the shame associated with these outcomes. As

133

we observe their threatening behaviors we become subconsciously aware of the danger that we are in. Subconsciously, we enter survival mode. Our survival instincts ensure that we will also conceal our fear from our abuser. We do this because we know that if they see our fear, our hurt, they will take advantage or harm us. They will kick us while we are down, so to speak. We also hide our fear from ourselves. We believe that if our fear were to fully surface, we might actually experience the reality of our situation. We are not yet ready to acknowledge that we are in danger. We are only in danger if we are afraid, so we mustn't be afraid. As we begin to wake up, we become aware of our fear. The reality of our situation starts to sink in. We begin to accept that we are in danger. When we Wake Up, we are terrified at first. We fully acknowledge the danger, we must act and from our awake place we *can* act.

Prior to waking, even if you do share your story with someone, you will not share that you are afraid. Perhaps, we are truly *not* afraid of our abuser. Remember, while we are asleep we are incapable of acknowledging that every human has the capacity for evil. We don't believe that this person we love could *really* hurt us. We have neglected to see their shadow. Even if we realize this person could harm another, we are certain they couldn't harm us. They love us. We are special to them. We are safe, no matter how big and strong they may appear. Their dominance, in a very weird way, makes us feel like we are safe. They would protect us, after all they always said they would. Once we are awakened, and as a result, can see their shadow, we acknowledge the fear, and we see the danger we are in. Upon seeing that we are in danger, we begin to accept the fact that we must act. This is why we often do not allow ourselves to see the fullness of our fear until we are awake, as until we are Awake, we are unable to fully act.

When you do finally begin to feel this fear, others around you may think that you are paranoid or irrational. Perhaps you are, but do not begin to doubt your feelings of fear simply because others can't see it. Some of these manipulators really *are* worthy of that much fear.

Reiterating, the words that we use while asleep do not illicit fear because our violent experience is just another day in our life; a life we have learned to

134

accept. I had learned to accept this rage from my string of intimate partners; I excused away their behavior. Regardless of the relationship, I always carried the belief that if they were mad, it was my fault and I had to fix it. It was my responsibility to see that they were happy; this was both in business and my personal world. In business I had less tolerance for abuse, but even a small amount of abuse is unacceptable.

The night my abuser tried to rape me, I did evict him for good. However I continued to invite in much worse. The Universe is constantly providing us with wake up calls. When we ignore them, the message tends to get stronger. This was certainly the case for me.

If I had been awake, he wouldn't have been back in the house to rape me. I wouldn't have let him in. I would have seen the danger. If I had been awake, there would have been a call to the police as soon as conceivably possible. If I had been awake, I would have pressed charges. If I had been awake, I would have realized his capacity for evil, and been appropriately terrified. If I had been awake, I would have gone to the hospital to have my ribs checked after he kicked me. I would have left a paper trail of his assault.

I couldn't see that I didn't deserve to be treated in this way. All I could see is I could do better, be better, work harder and if someone harmed me or was angry, it was my fault.

As you recall, I bit him. When I realized I had harmed him, I felt guilt, remorse. The man is supposed to be happy and now he was not, because I hurt him. Recall, I start to cry. "I am so sorry; I thought you really were going to harm me..." If I was awake I would have understood that my actions were me swinging my sword of truth, that he harmed me, and my acts were about protecting me. If I had loved myself I would have understood he deserved the natural consequences for his actions. I would have known it was not my job to protect him. It was my job to protect me. I wouldn't have apologized. I would have stood in my convictions.

You see, I stood up to him ultimately by biting him and evicting him, but look how far the abuse had to go before I would really act in my own defense! Sometimes even while asleep we have limits to the abuse we are willing to endure. My tipping point was rape. Rape was over the line. If only I had known to swing my sword, if only I was whole, things would have been so different; largely because I wouldn't have been in the predicament in the first place.

Since we are unwilling to acknowledge their capacity for evil, we assume that any pain they inflict on us must merely be in response to our behavior. If we had acted differently, we wouldn't have been hit/raped/screamed at/diminished. This is why we often do not report these acts. There are no hospital records, no police reports. We accept that it was our failures that brought about this situation. Our **endurance** will prevail. We have the **stamina**.

All the men in my story knew that I believed it was my job to protect the man, no matter what they did to me. They witnessed it enough to know. They pushed the envelope in small ways and saw I did not run to my own rescue, nor did I wish to cause them harm, so they violated me. You set your boundaries, however poorly, and your abuser knows exactly where that boundary lies. You choose how much abuse you are willing to take. People are accountable for their own actions and the natural consequences that occur as a result are just that, natural. If he hits you, he may go to jail. That is okay. We must acknowledge that his consequences are an acceptable outcome. Instead, we stop these consequences by excusing away their behavior and taking ownership of the blame. This helps no one.

Intimidation and fear are the abuser's tactics. They want you to believe you have no choice, that you are stuck. They want you to believe you are trapped. You are not!

In these relationships we so often feel trapped. To walk you through this experience, imagine yourself as if you live in a box. You are therefore surrounded by four walls.

Imagine the wall to your right is the Murder/Suicide Wall and it is the first wall we each hit when we are in turmoil. At some level we believe if we kill that person who we perceive is harming us, our life will get better. Most of us however have enough logic and reason to realize that killing another person

136

would yield us dramatically more trouble, and our conscience won't allow it. Of course it is evidential that some people unfortunately do not have that logic or reason. Either way, if we can't kill them, then we often move to considering suicide.

Suicide is generally choosing to kill ourselves, to stop the pain that we believe someone or something outside of us is inflicting. Therefore at many levels it is an admission that we are victims, irreparably so, which we are not; unless we choose to be.

Sometimes suicide is pushed upon us, especially if your abuser can somehow benefit from your death. I remember a conversation that began with my abuser finally beginning to show me the thing I long for more than anything: Compassion. He arrived home and he poured me a glass of wine, and sat down with me so that we could talk. This was very surprising to me as it is not his nature. Throughout this conversation he continued to fill the wine glass when I was not paying attention. I realize now his intention was to have me drink too much, he wanted to cloud my judgment. Perhaps he even drugged me that evening; I doubt it would have been the first time. This was all a part of his plan. After drawing me in with compassion and kindness he then told me that he has been receiving calls from people concerned about me almost daily. He claimed they were concerned about my behavior and feared I was "losing it". As he spoke I was not grasping his words because they simply did not make sense to me. I was unaware of anything in my behavior that would have set off an alarm from those who love me. Then, after I began to finally feel what seemed like genuine concern, he shifted from concern to vile hatred. He began badgering me, belittling me, telling me how worthless I was. He did this for what seemed like more than an hour, I was crying and confused. I was hurting. I was in agony and then he said seemingly totally out of left field, "Why don't you just blow your brains out, no one will miss you." I was stunned. "What?" I said. "Of course people will miss me, what are you talking about?"

His words deeply penetrated my being. It was as if these were the words I had heard all my life, in all my relationships, and they had mounted into this one moment representing all that pain I denied. The pain was unbearable. I kept waiting for his kindness. I wanted to feel kindness, I wanted to feel love; I was tired of the hate. I was breaking, I felt broken. He then nonchalantly told me to go get one of the guns and shoot myself, "after all no one will miss you," he insisted. He told me I was nothing but a burden to the world.

In that moment, I was hyperventilating. I was in total anguish. I told him in absolute desperation, "Fine, I will go get the gun. Is that what you want? Is that what you want? You want me to kill myself?" As I was going in the other room, I thought to myself, *He will stop now. He will realize the magnitude of what he is saying. He will stop me. He will come to my rescue saying, 'Oh My God what am I doing I love you.' He will say that. Won't he?*

I got the gun, I was crying, I was still yelling, "Is this what you want?" Then I stood before him, gun at my side, tears in my eyes, "Is this what you want?" I was not yelling. I was barely speaking. I quietly pled, "Is this what you want?" I was just standing there. Inside I was praying for him to break down. Praying that his awareness of his cruelty would kick in; praying he would hold me and say how sorry he was. He said nothing. He did nothing. He did not even look up. He turned the television on, the only intimacy he knew. He turned to me and said, "You will never be satisfied." He did nothing. *Wouldn't he want to stop me? Wouldn't he want to stop me if he thought I was really going to kill myself?*

Defeated and in despair I turned and walked away. I went into my bedroom; I sat down in my chair. I was sullen. I cried. I placed the loaded gun on the table. I grabbed my journal and began to write. I chose to write, but I can easily see how others would choose a different path to release their pain.

In my journal I said nothing about what he had just done. Nothing. Not one word. Instead I wrote:

"I remember how I was there for him, he was filled with rage and hate and I kept reaching out and building him up—when he [allegedly] tried to kill himself twice—I stayed with him insisting on my love."

As I wrote in my journal, he walked in the room and I thought, *Maybe now he will say something. He will speak to me in great sorrow for his acts; he will feel remorse and tell me he is so sorry*. I looked up at him as he entered the room; with a glimmer of hope. He just looked at me. He glanced at the gun on the table next to me and just walked out of the room.

Then in my journal I acknowledged my sadness about what had just transpired. I drew a sad face. One of the most devastating moments of my life, and I was so numb to my emotions, that the only response I could muster is a sad face sketched upon the page of my journal.

Then as a testament, one that only I would recognize, I drew a gun in my journal. I actually outlined the weapon that I could have used to take my life, I laid it on the page of the journal and traced it…then I wrote about how I thought I messed up my hormone medication. I thought I doubled up my pills and that was what had me feeling so low. I dismissed my despondency. I admitted only that I was upset he hadn't apologized, and that no one who harmed me ever had. However, I was clear that this devastating experience was somehow my fault. I must have done something wrong for this to happen.

I chose to draw the clear outline of that gun on my page perhaps because I could not bear to see the words. I believe too that the image was a reminder to me without uttering a word in that journal, so that someday, when I was ready, I could remember the dreadful experience of that day.

So why didn't I write the truth? Partially, it is the same reason that always came up. I didn't write the truth because it was my job to protect the man. I truly remember in that moment, saying to myself that I had to be careful what I wrote in case someone should find my journal. I feared that he would be in trouble if someone found my journal and read my words. **Fear *for* him I could always feel. It was fear *of* him I was numb to.** Only my fear of shame was ever present. I may have also feared reliving this moment if I ever chose to re-read my journal. I couldn't handle the reality. I couldn't write what I was unwilling to accept and face.

Sometimes when I read about people committing suicide, I am saddened by how society seems to accept as fact, that if there is no obvious evidence that they were killed, then it must not have been a murder. Well, I have firsthand experience, if someone can benefit from your death, they can go to great lengths to lead you there. They play with your self-esteem until there is very little left. Their words push us to the edge of our existence. When we are whole, their words of harm roll right past us. We would likely never even be subject to them as these individuals would never be in our life.

Many people choose not to kill themselves because of the fear that they will go to hell. This is precisely my point. Something outside of you has created laws that control you and yet, you decide you are trapped into a no-win situation. If I kill myself, I go to hell. If I live, I must abide by all these rules that make me feel bad about myself. If this is so, then aren't I already in hell?

I don't fear hell. I believe hell is nothing more than a place of our own creation. I lived in hell. I wasn't afraid dying would take me to hell. If anything, I thought it might free me from it.

I do believe however that suicide is a decision that indicates you are choosing not to grow in this life any longer, and this only sets you up for the same lessons again in another lifetime. You will see that in my healing process, suicide was a constant thought. It was only out of consideration of the often irreparable damage for those who are left behind, those who treated me lovingly, that I forged through life. I knew those that loved me would forever feel guilt, wondering what they could have done differently to save me. Having said that, survivors of such a tragedy need to know what I am saying here repeatedly, *it is seldom about you.* It is about the power we gave to the perceived negative circumstances in our life, about our believing we were powerless to continue through whatever pain we were living. How much power we give to the harm and pain bestowed on us from another is our decision. As I displayed earlier, certainly those who inflict such harm and cruelty, those that push us to disregard and harm ourselves, are not guiltless in our demise, however, in the end, all of our actions are about ourselves. Ultimately, we are still the decision maker of what path "out" we take. The sooner we embrace that reality, the freer we become.

Hopefully, we all ultimately move away from that idea of murder or suicide as a solution, and we move to the wall at our feet. Geographic Cure. At the

Geographic Cure wall, we believe changing our location or surroundings will bring us joy. If I leave the job, or leave the spouse, or leave the state I live in, then I will be happy. I am just not happy in this particular surrounding. This, too, is not true. Wherever you go, there you are. This does not nullify the fact that leaving any abusive environment is a healthy and correct choice. The problem is that if you don't look inside of yourself to see why you keep choosing those environments, the pattern will continue. So "growing" away might work, but running will not. If we do not heal and learn the lessons that created the life we are moving away from, we will recreate the same awful surroundings again.

Many people feel that they cannot leave their job or their spouse or their circumstance. That too is an illusion, generally built by fear. I can't leave my spouse because I don't have the money or because of my kids. This illusion is a testament to your lack of faith. If you really believe in a God or some Universal force bigger than yourself, then perhaps you need to believe it will provide, somehow, some inexplicable way, and those things will resolve themselves. Having lived through what I lived through, I would rather live in a box on the street, penniless, then live again in my self-created hell. If only I had known what a sociopath was, I may have allowed for the possibility that their cruelty was just that. I would have acknowledged that it simply was true. This person did not acknowledge the capacity that I thought was in every human—a conscience and the resulting guilt, remorse and compassion; the capacity for good. If I would have embraced my own capacities, all of them, I would have been able to see all capacities in them. Those capacities they acknowledged, as well as those capacities they did not.

My message is that there is rarely, if ever, a time when you truly have no choice. You only perceive you don't have a choice because, perhaps, you don't like the choices you have. You must be willing to expand your thoughts beyond what you know, into what you don't know. Perhaps the truth is that you don't want to trust yourself to take full responsibility for your material and emotional needs. Unfortunately, your ultimate joy won't come to you until you can. Even if you don't believe in a God or a power greater than you, you have choices. If you choose not to act, you just have chosen to be a victim. That too is simply a choice. That decision is serving you in some way or you would make a different one. That is not to say it will be easy, it may be the hardest thing you have ever done. Look within to discover the truth. Deciding you are stuck is a sad choice and one that requires little to no courage. You are clutching your fear, but you must let go of that fear to fully experience freedom. Feeling and releasing the fear allows you to finally experience all the good that has been waiting for you to arrive.

All those thoughts that say we have no choice are simply ways for us to remain trapped in our lives. We choose to remain under the perception that people or circumstances have power over us in our life. No one really has power over you; it is all your illusion.

Often we are too afraid to seek information, to see if that little prompting we have that something isn't right is in fact true. We are afraid to discover what we don't know, yet often it could save us from our pain. Often the controllers or abusers in our lives let us know that our snooping into their world is unacceptable and so we don't. We feel guilty about violating their trust, while they regard nothing of ours as sacred. They treat us as if there are no boundaries where we are concerned. We feel we cannot touch their property that is dubbed off limits, even if we just decided that on our own. If we were so harshly accused when we were innocent, imagine the consequence if we *did* actually do something to violate their trust. So we stay on our tightrope.

We must trust ourselves, we are adults now. We have been given the wisdom we need, we do have choices. Don't deceive yourself any longer into believing you do not.

So now that we realize Murder/Suicide won't work, and then Geographic by itself won't work, we move to the wall on our left. The Get Sick, Go Crazy Wall. At this wall we are in the height of believing we have no choice. We fear we cannot escape or grow past our present circumstances. I believe this is when our health issues show up. High cholesterol, high blood pressure, TMJ (Temporomandibular joint), these are all signs something is wrong at a deeper level, and generally here we medicate, either through prescriptions or the self-medication of drugs or alcohol. Not surprisingly, at the deepest level of my suffering my total cholesterol was 350 (Desired range often estimated between 134-240). We begin our process of hiding the pain that we feel rather than facing it; feeling it. We choose to be numb so that we can remain asleep. Our bodies absorb the stress/fear/pain that we are afraid to experience and then release.

At one phase I was stuck at the get sick go crazy wall and embroiled in fear and battles. I was trying to get safe, and I feared losing what I had left. In my situation, given that none of these highly manipulative men were the father of my daughter, there was no real opportunity for any of them to get my daughter away from me, although they attempted to do so through claims of my violent, crazy and drunkard behavior. They did so by calling 911 claiming I was flailing a gun, or trying to get me on tape claiming something about drinking or harming or simply being crazy. Embracing our truth, can release us from the impact of these efforts. We know the truth and therefore have no reason to fear or explain.

If we do not choose to change, we will allow the stress and the pain of our current unhappiness to eat away at us. We will slowly deteriorate. In not choosing change, we may be choosing death. We must be willing to acknowledge our emotions. We must be brave and face them head on. Only then can we begin to change our lives. The wall above our head is the Change wall. We must decide to change to be free from getting sick or going crazy.

My message is to Wake Up, Stand Up, Live Free. This is about the broader scope of your entire life; all abuses are signs you are out of alignment with yourself. Become aware of the many messages and red flags that are given to you every day from so many sources, if you would just pay attention. Those inner promptings are guiding you; all you need do is listen to them. Trust yourself in all areas of your life. You are your own authority. Become aware of the bigger picture and the many avenues that may be available to wake you up. You find much of this awareness through labeling and experiencing your emotions. Make yourself visible to you.

We must acknowledge our guilt, our fear, our desire to appear invulnerable. Emotionally, we may appear to be happy, to "have it all together." Freedom comes in the realization of the insanity of our situation. We must not only allow ourselves to label, but to *feel* each of our emotions. These emotions may have been turned off long ago, but they are vital to our path to freedom.

From where I am now, I can clearly see reading the book *The Gift of Fear* was a powerful part of my process of waking up. To show you the depth of my denial of my fears and emotions, in the chapter *Intimate Enemies,* Gavin DeBecker has a list of what he calls "pre-incident indicators of violence." It is a list of 30 warning signs "associated with spousal violence and murder."

While asleep and again seeking information to better understand the man in my life I had read this list. I went down the list and I wrote the initials of my then intimate abuser's first name next to every one of those traits I ever saw him exhibit during the relationship.

There were only two I did not put initials by:

> "The woman has an intuitive sense she is at risk."

> "His wife/partner fears he will injure or kill her. She has discussed with others or has made plans to be carried out in the event of her death."

My denial of his capacity for evil was so deep, that I denoted this as something that did not apply in my situation.

Then I went down the list again and developed my own rating system for those I signified as having experienced and asked myself whether this characteristic was still fully present, improved or seemingly gone.

Discovering that more than one third of the characteristics were improved, I actually discussed with my abuser that this improvement gave me hope. I was pleased, I felt I had shown him the light. I was helping him be a better man. I was healing him. You heard me right. I discussed this with my abuser with a sort of "attaboy" mentality. Now, it seems preposterous!

I was reading the list as if I was reading the ingredients of a recipe to make a poisonous cake, and I was celebrating that I could make this cake with less ingredients, instead of seeing that every one of those ingredients are toxic and dangerous, and I needed to move away from any part of this recipe. This is the power of denial.

When you are asleep, you remain asleep because you can only handle seeing your dangerous life as normal. This is why waking up is hard to do. Waking *is* hard to do, because it takes courage. Facing the reality of the state of your life can feel overwhelming.

You may wonder what began to open my eyes to my own fear. I was on a telephone meeting with a business coach. She and I had met a handful of times, but we had rarely discussed my personal life.

She told me in passing that she thought I was afraid of the man I lived with.

I thought that was absurd. She asked me if I realized that I whisper, stop talking or change the subject whenever he enters the room.

I hadn't been consciously aware of that reality until she brought it to my attention. God has sent you nothing but angels, there are people surrounding you to unconsciously or consciously guide you to wake up. Standing where I am now I truly see the perfect orchestration reflecting that when I was ready to look within; all the teachers appeared. All knowledge begins to lead you to awakening. Openly seek it.

Now recognizing that I was quieting my voice in his presence, I had to consider the possibility that I was afraid. You cannot be in fear and be free simultaneously.

Even my own acknowledgement of fear was facilitated due to my false belief. My business coach, my authority, told me I was afraid. In reality, I should have been aware of my own emotions, but I needed an authority to give me that awareness. Our emotions are our guide. Honor them; evaluate the circumstances that are driving them. Even "negative" emotions can teach us something. For example, guilt is not bad; guilt is the barometer we use to decide what is right for us. If we do something wrong, guilt is one of the things that distinguishes us from those without conscience. While guilt can be a good indicator that we are operating out of alignment with our values, we must be wary of those who use guilt as a weapon to be hurled at us in attempts to manipulate our behavior. Guilt is simply a prompter for us to look and assess, it should not be used as artillery externally forced upon us.

Anger and sadness or any perceived "negative" emotion, are both good and powerful. Those emotions are awareness. They let us know what we feel and give us the opportunity to assess and change ourselves or our circumstance. The key is to maintain healthy patterns of assessing and releasing, and not repressing or ignoring our emotions allowing undo pain on us. It is through acknowledging our emotions, and knowing that although they seem projected outward, we must look within to discover their true meaning.

It is through labeling, honoring, and feeling our emotions, that we allow ourselves to re-enter that space we abandoned so long ago; our heart. That space where God resides.

Physically (Body)

"Physically" refers to your body, the role you feel

it plays in your life, and your thoughts and actions

in regard to its care and feeding.

Personally, my examination of my physical self did not fully begin until after I was awake and stood up. Once we complete this assessment I will take you on my path from awakening to standing and healing at the deepest level. Connecting the dots on the value learned from each of these areas of assessment will likely ready you to see where you are on the path as we continue. For me, it was not until I had removed myself from the abuse that had preoccupied me for so many years, that I was able to really examine how I cared for myself physically. Remember that our assessment of ourselves is an ongoing process, yet so much easier once we are Awake and aware.

After I was out of my abusive situation you will see I was tired. I was very, very, tired. I could see how my career and my life were all about pleasing, respecting and honoring authority. Everything was about making sure I rose to any occasion that might be presented to me by them. I did this because I believed, most powerfully, that if I didn't rise to the occasion, something bad would happen.

This belief was quite a heavy burden to carry. No matter the self-sacrifice, no matter the pain, the driving beliefs in my life were that I could do better, I could be better, I could work harder, I could give more, I could go without breaks, I didn't need vacations, I didn't need much food, I didn't need much water. I did not take care of myself. I was realizing that I was actually not capable of taking care of myself. I had never tried. Instead, I took care of everyone else so that nothing bad would happen. Even if solder was burning holes in my leg, I knew I should never let go, or something bad would happen. That pain was nothing. It was just my body. But something bad did happen; I harmed myself. I produced a life largely absent of joy, and filled with chaos and despair. This was my reality whether I had acknowledged it or not.

I had always hated taking the time to eat. What a waste of time. This denial of food never led to weight loss. Though I was not starving for the purpose of losing weight, I was often amazed that even as I suffered and denied myself, I still didn't get the favorable side effect. Or perhaps, more importantly, that was the lesson. Through my own suffering and denial, I would never get the favorable result.

I have learned that when we feel abused, most of us abuse ourselves. When we feel others are abusing us, we respond by abusing ourselves further. It is likely that in times that we feel hurt by others, we respond by hurting ourselves. Sometimes we do this by overeating, or overindulging in drugs or alcohol. Maybe we even work out to an unhealthy extent, or curtail our food intake completely. We diminish ourselves when we feel diminished by others. We become the cruel parent punishing ourselves for our "misdeeds."

Consider this possibility: **When we feel abused, we abuse ourselves in return**.

Isn't suicide a paramount example of this truth?

How do you abuse yourself, what *distraction* do you use to avoid feeling?

I believe that sometimes we are looking for a way out, and even if we don't have the willingness to commit suicide or we can't bear the guilt of doing so, if we truly want to die, we will neglect ourselves, and the illness will be manifested. Sometimes illness is responding to our conscious, or perhaps unconscious, invitation. Since my focus was always on my service to others, I always neglected my body, and I subconsciously awaited the illness that I was certain would come.

We can neglect ourselves to death; and that decision is a choice. And at some level when we are making that choice, we know we are choosing death. Perhaps when we neglect ourselves we are subconsciously hoping we will die—dying because of an illness that may actually be suicide in disguise.

Once awake, I wanted to choose life, but I was not yet ready. I was still dealing with the realization that I had been deceived. I was still reeling from the constant vigilance that was needed to end my abuse.

How can you keep treating your physical body poorly and expect to live?

Throughout my life I was choosing death by the way I was living my life. I created a pattern that taught me that if I misbehaved, didn't act perfectly in accordance with my rules in any way, something bad would happen. Not just something bad, something tragic. Allow me to give you a history of evidence of what I discovered about my thoughts and fears relative to my health across the years.

There were a few times that I made myself a priority, where I decided to meet my desires, bend my rigid rules, act with a little frivolity, and I had quick and painful consequences. I had perfectly created this truth many times in my life.

149

Many years ago, while still sleeping, I was looking to expand my sexual freedom. I wanted to release my restrictive nature. I decided to get my fallopian tubes tied. I felt this would remove my debilitating fear of pregnancy that had led to my excessive sexual caution throughout my life. I believed anything good would lead to what I feared becoming true.

After the relatively simple procedure, I had dreadful pains on my next menstrual cycle and although I went to the doctor, I was too busy living life to go take the recommended tests. The pain subsided until my next cycle. Two months later, when my pain was unbearable, I went to the hospital and ultimately I was diagnosed with Streptococcus pyogenes (group A streptococci), a flesh eating, deadly bacteria.

This bacteria had gotten some attention when it was found to be responsible for the death of Jim Henson (creator of the Muppets), but it was totally foreign to me prior to my diagnosis. In an effort to diagnose my pain, exploratory surgery was performed. That surgery led to the removal of my appendix and fallopian tubes, to eliminate the spreading of the bacteria. When the pain returned a few weeks later, I was again taken in for surgery and my ovaries and uterus were removed. That bacteria was literally eating me up inside.

Shortly thereafter my gallbladder was removed. I was toxic and my body responded.

I claimed that I was finally embracing my sexuality by having my tubes tied, but I was doing so out of fear. I was afraid of pregnancy, and I had always felt that sex would lead to something shameful. I feared what society and my family thought. What if I got pregnant? In acting to eliminate that fear, I found myself now lacking my entire reproductive system. After this near death experience I decided to attempt to truly embrace my sexuality and femininity. I no longer had the fear of pregnancy, but the sense of shame remained. Something joyful will lead to something bad. In my very first sexual encounter after making this decision to tie my tubes to have more sexual freedom, I was given an STD (Herpes). I now understand this to be a solid testament to my shame, the shame I feared all my life.

Each of us has masculine and feminine energies. Because I viewed women as weak, I rejected portions of that side of me, and I operated from a far more male energy. I didn't understand then, how much of my illness was simply my rejection of my own femininity. I felt women were weak. I worked in a male dominated world and I was very successful. I failed in every feminine aspect of myself, I had tried to nurture my abusers into healing, and time and time again, I failed. They remained abusive despite my best efforts. I must not be a good woman, so I will reject that side. Who would want to be a weak woman anyway? I even rejected my middle name, Rose, having disgust for its femininity. Today I embrace it with all my heart. You can't reject any part of yourself, and expect that part of you to thrive and flourish. You can't live in incongruence, and expect to be whole and complete. These experiences were trying to awaken me. What will it take for us to finally honor and love ourselves?

Ending my external abuse brought about the realization that *I* might just play a key role in my physical pain. I had the constant thought that I was going to have health problems. Why would I choose to think that? My whole life had been about chaos. Now that I had removed my external sources of chaos, I assumed that I would find chaos from within myself. This drama was the only indication I had, that I was in fact alive.

I had lived a life filled with rules of how I would take care of myself physically. I felt that if I didn't follow those rules, I would die. Now, since I had no drama for the first time in my adult life, I broke several of my rules. I had been addicted to the drama, and now I was subconsciously trying to create more of it.

I didn't know how to live in peace. Even in the moments that I wasn't breaking the "rules" I held so dear, I perceived I would die. I was determined to restore my fear, the horseradish I was comfortable in.

One such rule was that if I was drinking more than two glasses of wine, I believed I was going to die of liver disease. I had begun to allow myself to violate my belief about drinking. I began to consistently break my rule and have more than two drinks. I had routine blood work done and my doctor had not expressed any concern about these results to me. With no concern or consideration, I had sent this blood work into an insurance company looking to get a new health insurance policy. I received a letter back stating that I was declined and that perhaps I should consider the state's high risk pool to gain my coverage. Unbeknownst to me my blood work indicated liver problems.

This response that I needed to consider a high risk pool, played into every fear I was trying to manage. I became terrified. A surprising reaction from someone who wanted to die, I suppose. But of course, my fear was not a rational fear of death, my fear was more about the shame I would be met with. If I had liver problems, I must be a drunk.

Since at this point in my life I was the only abuser left, I was prepared to suffer at my own hand. I was now in overdrive, creating a reality that would confirm my belief that something bad would happen if my rules were broken. I needed something to hang my fear on; I chose my health.

My fear pushed me and I immediately stopped consuming alcohol. I remember a quote I heard once that *action cures fear*. I was definitely moved to action. I stopped taking over the counter medication and I began to pay more attention to my food intake.

I felt anger that I was finally letting loose in some ways, finally stepping a little outside my rules by letting myself drink more, and I had an immediate, negative, ramification supporting my every belief about life. It was exactly what had happened when I began to let go in my sexual life. If I do something pleasurable, something outside my rules, something bad will happen. However, I had no peace in breaking my rules. I felt constant guilt, constant shame. I was unable to accept myself when I engaged in this behavior that I had for so long deemed unacceptable. My guilt became a self fulfilling prophecy.

I also felt deprived of something I enjoyed. For the next three months I abstained from all alcohol, and anything else that I felt would potentially have an adverse effect on my liver. In spite of the high risk pool scare, when I contacted my doctor she expressed little concern about the slight elevation in my liver enzymes. Regardless, I asked for rigid guidance to rectify the situation. I was obsessed. I wanted it perfect. I followed her guidelines to the letter.

My fear that it was too late and that something bad would happen was with me every day of that time. After carefully disciplining my behaviors; after restraining myself and avoiding all that I had decided was prohibited and forbidden, what were the results of my stellar effort?

Just four months later, I went in for new blood test results. My liver enzymes were reflected as follows: My AST was now 92 up from 60 (normal range was 5-35). My ALT was now 181 up from 97 (normal range 7-56), my Triglycerides which were low before, were now at the max acceptable range at 150. The results of my earlier blood work had reflected massive dehydration, which had improved slightly over the four month period. (My cholesterol was still quite high, although controlled by medication.) My months of deprivation and discipline had resulted in exacerbation of the most significant initial problems.

Now I was really upset. I had taken what I thought were all of the necessary steps in order to improve my health. I should have been moving forward, and my new set of blood work showed that I had simply taken a huge leap backwards.

I was beginning to realize that perhaps my health was more about my internal thoughts, than my external actions.

From where I stand now these realities are largely because we are the creators of our own life. Although I was seemingly making healthy choices by abstaining from potentially harmful things, I resented the choices I felt forced to make. To me it felt like yet another restraint, another control on me, another rule I had to follow to avoid something bad happening. My "healthier" lifestyle was the result of following guidance set forth by yet another authority in my life—my doctor, at my insistence no less. I wanted perfection.

Until I could release my doomsday approach to life, I was not embracing myself where I was. I had resentment first that my breaking my rules caused

153

an immediate negative consequence in my health, but then further resentment that when I jumped back in line and followed every rule that was designed to supposedly make me healthy, my health deteriorated further. I was angry. I was really, *really* angry. And I was sad at the thought that I could never be free.

In my life I had never known how to cut myself some slack. For more than ten years I was teaching my perception training, teaching people to be aware of how they treated themselves; yet I wasn't living it.

Every word that I had allowed to enter my mind about myself was negative. Just as I had tolerated from my intimate partners, I continued to abuse myself. I had nothing but negative self-talk about all my failings. I had always had negative self-talk about my body, but now it was escalated.

The reason I never binge ate, or ate that whole bag of potato chips or ate a gallon of ice cream, is that those behaviors would make me bad. I never would allow that. Worse, I would define in my mind what is acceptable, two cookies are acceptable. If I had three, then voila! I had a reason to view myself as bad and the world made sense again. If I was bad, everything was in perfect order, in accordance with my beliefs. So I continued to break these rules to justify my "badness." It is not that it would be good or healthy to do those things. It is that the compulsion of the rule begins to drive us to break it. It is the rules that create our tug-of-war. If we could accept ourselves, these things would melt away.

I believe this very incongruence is what leads to lack of joy in our life. This incongruence creates our health issues. We are bad, fat, unlovable…while longing for love and acceptance. It is our unconscious quest to harm ourselves, and see ourselves in a negative light that keeps us from shining. It is our unwillingness to accept ourselves as we are; our unwillingness to love ourselves as we are. What I know is true, is when you love something you treat it well. Imagine then what would happen if you fully loved yourself?

What if from that space, a space of love, healing can be almost effortless?

People who stop overeating, drinking too much, depriving themselves of food, over exercising, or whatever they do to abuse themselves, will not necessarily feel better about themselves when they stop. They may in fact replace the initial obsession, with another, or live feeling denied of the pleasures they seek. I believe we must heal from the inside out, and the rest just falls into place.

We have to be *willing* to *release* those things that we feel are our security, our crutch. If we don't, their hold on us gets tighter and tighter. The more we grip, the more control *it* (whatever "it" is) has. The *willingness* frees you, the acceptance of its lack of importance in your life; *allows* you to be free of these addictions. This does not pertain exclusively to our physical lives, this is a Universal truth.

Until I was willing to Wake Up, focus on myself, and see how I was in my own way, the reality that I couldn't step out of line from what *I defined* as perfect behaviors, or something bad would happen, would be an infinite presence in my life. I believe we all have beliefs that keep us in our own way. Your life is the evidence. Look backwards over your life and what do you see?

Don't wait until your choices are death or life. Choose life now. The choice of a joyful life was available to me at any time. It is available to you now as well. No matter how trapped you feel, that trap is just an illusion. The experience is real, the hopelessness is not.

On my journey to healing and getting in touch with my physical body for the first time, I went to the health food store. I asked the Universe to guide me to a cookbook that would help improve the quality of my eating. As I entered the aisle of books, it was almost like a neon glow drew me to a book.

This book's title implied that our bodies were constantly asking for water.

The moment I saw the title I had one of those moments when you know the message is for you. No matter how hard I then went to look for a cookbook, nothing resonated—just this book. I am not looking to make a statement of the truth of the testimonies made in this book. I only know that I asked for guidance and this book blatantly appeared. Once I was open to see, once I trusted a bigger Universe to lead me, answers arrived. You have the power to be guided to the right message for you, if you are open to it.

What I knew when I saw the title is that I had completely denied myself water. I almost prided myself on never having to stop to use the restroom! I prided myself on this, because it meant that I could work longer without a break. I never even stopped to consider the fact that perhaps this was because I was constantly in varying degrees of dehydration. I had been depriving myself of one of the most basic things that I needed to sustain life—Water.

Instead of depriving ourselves, what if we were always seeking to respond to the needs of our bodies. In fact, what if we responded to the needs of ourselves as a whole? Why not just grant our bodies the simplest of its needs, without it having to ask? Water, food, nourishment, breath, and love.

I have teased my clients that we don't breathe deeply because we believe we are unworthy of the air. Breathe deep. Become aware of how often we shut down our breath. Bring your breathing to a conscious level until you can recreate a healthy breathing pattern, and until caring for yourself is safe to become unconscious.

I remember at first being frustrated when I would try and increase my water intake because when I did, my body seemed to demand more of it and that was a hassle. Plus, then I would need to use the restroom more which was terribly inconvenient. After all, I was a doer. I couldn't take the time for myself that would enable me to do something as simple and vital as use the restroom. So, inevitably, I would stop drinking water.

What I didn't understand then, was that my body had been trained to operate with insufficiency. As I gave it more, it started trusting there would be more and would utilize it for my sufficiency. This is why you are hungrier earlier in the day if you eat breakfast. It kick starts your metabolism. If you don't eat, your body assumes it must conserve what energy (calories) it has, and your metabolism stays slow. Remember that throughout most of human history, food and water came in bursts. It was feast or famine, and our bodies know how to conserve what we give them, when they need to. Satisfy your

156

needs often enough that your body knows that next meal or next glass of water is coming. Teach your body that it can trust you. This journey is about teaching every part of yourself, that you can be trusted.

I have gone from drinking little to no water each day, to the often recommended 64 ounces a day. This may need to be a gradual process for you. In my experience, that first day drinking 64 ounces, I remember having terrible pains in my head. I literally thought I was going to die. Beginning to embrace all of me, all of the more expansive me, I stated out loud *I am finally considering living, I don't want to die...what do I do?* I heard audible words from within myself. Take a shower.

A therapist of mine suggested that I may have had an over expansion of blood vessels in my brain. After all, our brain is roughly 73% water. That shower may have saved my life. Imagine if it was always that easy—being open to something bigger than ourselves and listening to that still small voice.

To those of you who have health issues, I in no way mean to minimize your situation or your pain. My belief that we can control more than we realize about our bodies, does not mean that we can't *fall victim* to an illness. Even the most diligent person, cannot have positive thoughts and take perfect care of themselves at all times, and, I realize other causes can contribute to illness as well. The human race is known for many things, perfection certainly isn't one of them. I only hope to help you become more aware of what your beliefs are, and ask that you consider if they are serving you.

I also am not saying that no one should take medications or seek medical help that is available. What I am saying is that we cannot ignore, abuse, and have constant negative thoughts about our bodies, and expect them to remain healthy. We must listen to our bodies. Connect with our oneness with them. Feel that inner guidance that is leading us. What if we do that? Might that help us in our healing? It certainly couldn't hurt.

One of the best books that I have found to help you discover what the emotional cause of your physical ailment is, Louise Hay's *You Can Heal Your Life.* If you know that book and the messages it sends, then you were not surprised that I had high cholesterol, a full hysterectomy, liver issues, or for that matter, Herpes.

Allow me to share her wisdom:

Cholesterol—Clogging the channels of joy. Fear of accepting joy.

> New Thought Pattern: I choose to love life. My channels of joy are wide open. It is safe to receive.

Liver—Seat of anger.

> New Thought Pattern: Love and peace and joy are what I know.

Liver problems—Chronic complaining. Justifying fault-finding to deceive yourself. Feeling bad.

> New Thought Pattern: I choose to live through the open space in my heart. I look for love and find it everywhere.

Herpes—Mass belief in sexual guilt and the need for punishment. Public shame. Belief in a punishing God. Rejection of the genitals.

> New Thought Pattern: My concept of God supports me. I am normal and natural. I rejoice in my own sexuality and in my own body. I am wonderful."

I am not a doctor. The key is not to shun medical treatment. The key is to take care of yourself, and sometimes medical treatment is a part of that. However, a healthy lifestyle and thought process can go a long way in bringing us to healing, and that peaceful place of healthful living. We must acknowledge our role in our physical condition. Doctors may be able to cure us, but perhaps with proper attention to ourselves, we will have less of a need for treatment.

Learning to feel leads to healing. Just sucking it up, or denying your feelings after you experience such suffering, I believe, leads you to death, not life.

Since honoring the messages, the inner promptings I hear, I am healed in all areas.

I am no longer on **any** medication, not even hormone replacements. All of my medical issues are resolved. My blood work is now normal; this includes my liver enzymes, and cholesterol. I have chosen to create my healthy life from the inside out.

This improvement was not created by denying myself in any way; instead it was created through my decision to heal my life. I now love myself, exactly where I am. Once you fully love yourself, you naturally do the things that make you healthy. As I changed my beliefs and began living by healthy principles, instead of steadfast rules, I naturally moved to more organic eating. I began to accept eating what felt right to me. I broke all my patterns that were instilled in me by "society," a "society" I knew, and now freely acknowledge I do not agree with at many levels.

I seldom if ever have any incidence of Herpes. When you care for yourself and release your inner guilt and shame, your body responds accordingly. We cannot disown parts of us and be whole and complete, so I have learned to embrace all of me. I embrace my masculine and my feminine energies. I embrace my capacity for good and my capacity for evil. I embrace my physical body and my emotional self, even with my literal and figurative scars. I love myself.

I have decided nothing will have power over me. This is not a decision based on fighting, but one based on peace. I simply accept where I am and follow my own intuition if I need to change something. I am led in all areas by my inner knowing. My diet, activities, exercise, my being and my doings, are all determined by my intuition. If I feel incongruent, if I feel a pang of guilt or shame, or something arises in my health—I evaluate. I recognize now when I am not at peace, and honor the message in that lack of peace. When I evaluate, I decide if I need to change my behavior, or perhaps just the belief that I have in relationship to that behavior. I choose to do what feels healthy and right for me in any given moment, regardless of what anything outside of me directs.

I choose to not engage in behavior simply out of habit. If I do something habitually, it is because I have deemed that behavior as something that I would like to have in my daily routine. If I begin to feel a "bad habit" forming, I address that behavior. Then again, I do as I please. If in that process I choose to do something that is an over indulgence, or pushing the boundaries that I may have, I forgive myself. Even in my imperfections, I am exactly as I should be. I am at peace.

Sometimes we must make mistakes, so we know what we do not want. Always keep learning and life always keeps improving. Be willing to change.

Remember, when we have exhausted all of our other options and we find ourselves at the get sick, go crazy wall, we really only have two options:

Choose to change and live, or choose to die.

It is *us* that must change. It always was; it always will be.

Know that every time, the glory is that once we go through the final wall, the Change Wall, we get a bigger box, and will grow to fill that up. Then one day we may be frustrated yet again, looking to be free from our confinement. But ideally next time, we will simply know where to start; the Change Wall.

If you look carefully at the circumstance of my life, the real truth is, it was my insistence to deny every truth and control every outcome, that lead to my chaos and pain. I needed to release all those strings that made me jump. I needed to resolve these conflicts. I had to surrender. I could not stand the turmoil I was in.

I had to release my grip. I needed to accept that taking care of myself was not about strict boundaries and limitations; it was about peace, and trusting myself. I needed to understand that in taking care of myself, I would be empowered to help others. I had to realize it was my time to choose life, or choose death, and it was in fact a choice.

Mentally (Mind)

"Mentally" refers to your thought process,

and what power you feel those thoughts

have in the creation of your life.

While seemingly simple, your mentality is one of the most powerful areas to examine. Our mind is where we begin to actually examine the components of our belief system. The critical thing to realize is the power of our thoughts in the creation of our lives. As I have said, alignment is absolutely a given. This means that my thoughts created my reality and if I changed my thoughts, I would have changed my reality. It is not simply your thoughts on the surface; it is the whole of it. The thoughts you have consciously and perhaps more importantly, unconsciously, at the core of who you are, will manifest themselves in some tangible physical way. Your thoughts control your actions and inactions.

We must decide to treat ourselves with love and journey to discover peace. We must acknowledge the depth of our self-neglect, and the need for us, perhaps for the very first time, to deeply turn inward, and discover what we need to change about our life to live a happy, healthy life.

Discovering who we truly are and how we want to live has always been up to us; once we became adults, freedom was available. Yet so many of us choose to stay in a hell of our own making; asleep, trapped by the chains created by our childhood experiences. We often choose never to evaluate the resulting beliefs that we have come to embrace, and the outcomes those beliefs keep us expecting from life. We expect certain outcomes and receive them, providing the evidence that our beliefs are true. Now is the time for us to realize, it is in fact the inverse that is true. It is *because* we believe so assuredly, that those outcomes continue to assuredly appear. It is a self-fulfilling prophecy.

My message is to deeply and fully lead you to know, you **can** create the life you want to live. Begin to believe it to your core, and know that it will appear. Certainly, you have believed and experienced the other "truths" you created. Deep down, you had the distorted belief that you were worthy of abuse, and the abuse appeared. This is not a coincidence.

You are free, it is okay. You decide what is healthy for you. You decide what is right for you. Once you truly, consciously decide, once you believe, you will attract it to you. "It" being whatever is for your greatest good. Whatever you need to experience to *know* you are free. For many of us, we must think this freedom before we can feel it.

A dear friend used to remind me, "It is your illusion of invulnerability that makes you vulnerable." He was right. In our strength, in our illusion of invulnerability, we never let ourselves fall and never ask for help. The help was always there, we simply needed to admit our vulnerability so it could enter our life.

Our minds are constantly working to correct the perceived wrong of our lives. *I could have done this differently... I should have made this decision.* Some of the things that we replay time after time may have been in our control at one point; others never were to begin with. Either way, replaying and overanalyzing does nothing but focus our attention on the negative instances of our past. Our negative thoughts give these instances life in our present. We dwell on and fear the shame that comes with our mistakes. We relive our guilt. We hide in our minds, overanalyzing, when we should be verbalizing, even if initially it is only to ourselves, so that we can release the hold these thoughts have on us.

What does the fear and shame we hold inside tell us about ourselves as a culture? We encourage silent suffering. We encourage people to retreat into their own condemning minds. People feel so foolish about the predicaments they have created or various truths about themselves that many choose to remain silent. The people that harm us cultivate that feeling in us to help quiet our voice. They remind us we will look foolish. People are raped, robbed, abused, threatened and these acts so often are never reported. Why? Most often it is shame for their perceived role in the event or fears that they will be further harmed by the perpetrator. They may fear losing their standing, job or position, or fear having their image sullied. Yet in all these instances, in choosing to hide, we allow the perpetrator to be free, unaccountable, and often continuing to inflict pain and suffering on others, while we remain in our conditioned silent suffering.

As I relinquished my role as protector to the perpetrators and disclosed my truth to people that truly cared about me, my truth was received in love. Isn't it possible that help was always there? That God already had everything lined up waiting for me to admit I needed help?

Through clients, friends, and people I work with, as well as my own experiences, what I know is that many people live with terror and abuse from people that they thought loved them. I also know that they hide this truth so they will not be embarrassed or ashamed for the life they are living. Keeping it secret blocks their pathway to freedom. The shame is what keeps us in our self-induced hell. Instead, only choose environments where you can safely live transparently. You do not need to isolate yourself in the confines of your mind, too afraid to share your truth.

Shame is created in the mind. This is where we judge, where we analyze. I tell my clients to see themselves literally stripping the shame off of them, and placing it on the other person, the perpetrator in their image, as they recall their suffering. The person that raped you, beat you, stole from you, and/or lied to you, whether you were a child or adult, the person inflicting the harm, is a more appropriate place for the shame to be worn; not in or on you. Although that exercise is healing, know that ultimately any animosity toward another will harm you, so express your anger, release your shame, yet know that most often this is a private matter for your healing and you need not involve or address anything with the person who harmed you, especially if these events were in the distant past. Ultimately to be truly free we must release all negative emotions toward another, including that shame we may have initially redirected on them. Holding negative emotion only attaches a chain, a heavy burden, to you. That heavy burden weighs you down diminishing the quality of your life. We should not judge another, for when we do, some day we may be faced with a condition under which we gain a new understanding. One we never thought we would be faced with.

We hide our secrets of the harm bestowed on us to avoid judgment, which we fear, would only enhance our shame. Children are, unfortunately, innocent victims and rarely can they stand up successfully for themselves in childhood. As adults though, we have the necessary power and ability to Stand Up. We must use that power; the power that you will see, resides in you now.

Just as you should not judge others, remember that you should not accept judgment blindly. You may take the words of another as an opportunity for self-reflection, but if you feel that their views are not warranted, do not be afraid to cast those words aside. Choose to decide that those who would judge you harshly for your mistakes, differences, or shortcomings, are simply not the people you need to surround yourself with. You can love them, wish them well, and leave them. Surround yourself only with love. Their judgment

164

is often a reflection of their own fears and truths, the mirror for what they are unwilling to see in themselves.

Life isn't about what happens to you, it is about how you behave once it does.

Admit your truth first to yourself, in your own mind, then feel the consequence of that truth in your heart. Do not be afraid to speak this truth outside of yourself, even if only in your own journal. There are people you can trust; seek them. I am not suggesting we all wear our suffering on our sleeve, nor am I suggesting that we must disclose all our truths to everyone. What I am saying is that the sanctity of our lives deserves honor and love. There are many sources, people and organizations that can help. To be free though, you must first embrace your vulnerabilities in your own mind and heart, then reach out and expect that the Universe will provide precisely what you need.

The most powerful thing to understand about our mind is that where we focus our thoughts, our energy, is where our reality can be found. However, we cannot forget the other functions of our discriminating minds. When examining ourselves mentally it is important to realize that we are, in fact, intelligent human beings. We are capable of critical thought. We can make reasonable decisions for ourselves. We exercise this power by critically examining everything that is presented to us as a fact.

We live in a world where we are constantly bombarded with information. We are receiving information via people, printed word, television, radio, and the internet. We hear all of this information and we must choose what to believe, and what to ignore. This is not an easy decision to make. The easy thing to do would be to completely take every bit of information at face value. "They" said it, so it must be true. This passive absorption of information is what I would argue much of the world chooses to embrace. In doing so, we remain asleep. If you haven't done so already, I encourage you to move away from this way of thinking.

With every piece of information presented to you, examine the source. Question who it is that can benefit from your acceptance of this information. Might there be an agenda?

I am not encouraging the promotion of radical conspiracy theories. That kind of life can be exhausting. I merely encourage a critical eye. Just as you have been deceived by an individual, you must consider the possibility that you are being deceived on a grander scale as well. In so many of our families the truth is swept away. Can you honestly say that your family didn't "sweep' things they viewed as shameful under the rug? Someone getting pregnant as a teenager, molestation that happened between family members, someone contracting HIV (Human Immunodeficiency Virus), marital affairs, homosexuality or having an addiction…I am not saying all these things or any of these things are shameful, I am saying that people often hide what they fear will be viewed as shameful. No one wants to experience humiliation. That shame, the feeling that others view our circumstance as disgraceful, can turn inward. This existence with humiliation at its core can become a deep self-loathing, a hatred that can then transfer to others. A desire to retaliate can be ignited, or it can seem too heavy to carry and lead to depression and suicide.

This is why so many of us fear disclosing our personal truth; we don't want to be ashamed. If our own families would hide truths so that their "image" remains intact, shouldn't we consider that authority or those "in charge" might do the same? Often realities are hidden so no one will know. On a small scale of family, and a large scale of the world, we must consider that such hidden truths exist. So few of us question what we hear, what we are told by people in *authority*. We must begin to question. We must begin to doubt.

When people have a position of authority we tend to attribute credibility to what they say, but what they say may not always be true. What is the real truth about wars, oil, the stock market, extraterrestrial life, mass acts of violence, weapons, welfare programs, immigration, cures for diseases and elections? Do you really think you know? What if everything you think you know is nothing more than an illusion that we were made to believe intentionally by these "credible" people, so that they can benefit in ways you never imagined at the harm of people in unthinkable ways? I cannot say what the truth is, only that we all should consider the possibility that it is not always what is being spoon fed to us.

It is difficult enough to begin to accept that we may be being deceived on a personal level and perhaps even more difficult to consider it may go deeper. We may be dealing with people who could comprise the foundation of corporations, political forums, countries and even the World…but in the end, they are just people, and you need to awaken to those with the intent to harm at the core. We need to awaken to those who operate largely from their shadow.

When you Stand Up against what "credible" people say, what happens? Just turn on the news. Often, you are positioned as if you are crazy. Being crazy is the leverage that is used against you, in the hopes of shaming you into silence. The goal is to completely destroy your credibility, regardless of how credible you might be.

Earlier I mentioned a book that touts the health benefits of drinking water. I found the guidance in this book to be utterly life changing. Of course we have all heard that drinking water is beneficial, but how often is it posited that many health issues could be eliminated or avoided if we simply remained hydrated? Research led me to discover that some people have attempted to discredit the findings of the doctor who wrote this book. Is it possible that the attempts to discredit him were a result of his assertion that many of our most pervasive health issues, are caused, or exacerbated by, dehydration? Remember, there is no powerful water lobby in Washington.

If this belief that water is the medicine to keep our body healthy was broadly accepted, what would happen to the pharmaceutical and medical industry, and the massive profits that are obtained through the synthetic cures that they develop? Isn't it possible that there are people who could benefit from discrediting this idea, or better stated, at least not promoting it? Perhaps these thoughts about possible hidden agendas are right, perhaps they are not. That is for each of us to decide.

Of course we know medications and our medical community save lives. This is not about discrediting these necessary and valued individuals and the services they provide. I am grateful they are available. However, could we stunt our need for these resources if we simply took better care of our bodies, beginning with simply our water intake? Prevention and self-care through diet, hydration, exercise and positive self-talk may go a long way to limiting our dependence on curative measures. Certainly there are many out there looking to lead society in this direction. I applaud their efforts.

War is another difficult area to examine in our quest for objective truth, free from proposed or hidden agendas. Our true heroes, our soldiers, are motivated by their desire to serve. Most are devoted to the improvement of our lives as individuals, and as a country as a whole. They devotedly fight for our freedoms, deeply and dedicatedly believing they are fighting for those who cannot stand up, or defending against those who wish to harm us. Their efforts are for a virtuous endeavor. They are willing to pay with their lives to serve others. Overall these men and women fight for our Constitutional freedoms. All military personnel, including the President of the United States, take this oath, make this stand, to support and defend our Constitution. There is a slight, but perhaps monumental variance, in the oath of those who are enlisted and the oath of the officers. Enlisted men and women must swear to obey the President of the United States and orders of officers appointed over them, whereas officers swear to disobey any order that violates The Constitution. Is there ever a time an enlisted individual may feel in conflict with directives and what they believe is for the highest, greatest good? Might there be a time when their orders violate what they believe is constitutional? Are they free to confront this concern?

Are we all confronted with these conflicts from time to time? What is for the highest, greatest good as we see it, versus how we are being told to see it? It would seem then, the necessary courage to Stand Up varies by predicament. To stand up to a teacher, boss, parent, officer, or spouse certainly can have negative consequences, yet just how negative a consequence is dictated by the power that the individual or group of individuals has over our life.

In so many ways we are bound to listen to authority. It is demanded of us sometimes putting us in precarious scenarios. Nearly all of us are taught we MUST do as authority directs. Further, aren't we taught to not question authority? Perhaps that is where a great deal of our trouble begins. How often are we asked to violate our own principles to satisfy the demands of someone outside of ourselves, whether by a true or perceived leader, or simply someone who has been dubbed authority in our mind? Depending upon the environment, making a stand can be life and death. The circumstances drive just how much courage we need to Stand Up. In making a stand, are we willing to risk the consequences which could be as severe as death? Our mind certainly has a great deal to contend with, in knowing what is real, and what is not, and the resulting appropriate action.

In all realms of our lives, there are those who have good intentions and those who do not. Many studies have proven that we are such good followers that we often comply with any directive by authority, even if it leads us as far as to harm another. We do so, even if we think it is wrong. Even if we believe we would never harm another, under the directive of those that we deem authority, it may be true that anything is possible, until we Wake Up. Has a leader ever required you to do something you disagree with? Look no further than the work environment. How often are we told to institute a consequence on someone based on mere leader direction, or instead to turn a blind eye to behaviors we deem as "wrong?" In any circumstance, should we really choose to violate who we are and what we believe in because of a direct or perceived order? Should we have to choose between being our definition of a good person and being a good employee, soldier, student, citizen, spouse, son, daughter, parent, parishioner, and so on? Can we decide that being a good person shall always prevail, regardless of the depth of the consequences? Do we have the courage to Stand Up to authority both on a small scale in our personal world, and in the world at large?

If we choose to never stand up to authority, never demand the truth, never get in alignment with our values, what might the consequences be?

The challenge always is to distinguish between truth and deception. Is it possible, that at times there are interests other than those explicitly spelled out to us? Could there be agendas underneath what we are being told? I think now is the time we, as a people, are readying ourselves to awaken. We are beginning to make a stand against deceit, deception, and directives with ill intent. My goal is not to make a political stance, my goal is to encourage us to entertain various ideas rather than accepting whatever we are told, sometimes blindly. We should be safe to believe authority, but are we? We must each decide for ourselves.

How extensive is deceit, and how can we begin to know what perhaps we do not know? As your self-awareness increases, so does your awareness of the world around you. So the more self-aware you become, the less likely you will be fooled. The more you begin to be open to knowing, the more you will realize there is so much you may not know. Once awake, you are willing to doubt what you see or hear. When you are willing to doubt, you can stand back far enough to see if it is altruism, honor, caring, or love, that is at the root of the cause, or money, hate, power over, or control of. My hope is we, as human beings, will move toward worthy, truly humble causes of compassion. My hope is that we will honor what we know inside, not what we are being encouraged to believe by those in authority. We will not just be obedient servants, but instead follow our hearts, follow our values, instead of just compliantly acting on what we may have previously accepted as truth. The best way to live in your own integrity is to examine these "facts" and come to your own conclusions. Broaden your knowing. Then, you decide.

Never forget how powerful your thoughts and beliefs are. My inability to doubt those that I perceived were my authority, and my inability to lie to someone I deemed as being in an authoritative role, almost destroyed me. Assessing myself in all these areas—spiritually, financially, emotionally, physically and mentally—helped me to see who I really truly am, my oneness, and the Truth of the greater realities of life. My mind, body, and spirit, are a unified force that is creating my life. I couldn't ignore these elements and compartmentalize my life, and still find my wholeness. I needed to unite these powerful forces for one common goal—my happiness and joy; total inner peace. As I healed, I became conscious of each facet of my life. I awakened as to how to put all the pieces together to experience the full powers within me. I began to accept the joyful life that was always waiting for me to acknowledge and experience.

Self-Confidence & Self-Esteem

Your power and strength have remained dormant in your life if you have allowed yourself to be beaten down, judged, belittled or made to be small, in any or all of these areas we have been discussing. Perhaps the abuser was someone outside of yourself, or merely your own self-talk or your own treatment of yourself. Regardless, it is time to embrace ALL of you, all of your aspects of yourself. All capacities you possess.

By now I hope you are clear that you have always had both the capacity for good and the capacity for evil. We don't like the word evil, and since we choose not to act in an evil manner, we don't acknowledge its existence within us. However, perhaps by now you are beginning to see that rejecting that we have this capacity, leads us to be unable to see it in others. We judge others by who we see in us. We believe that we cannot harm no matter what someone does to us, and we do not expect to be harmed—even when we are under the cruelest attack, we simply excuse it away.

Instead, we need to embrace all capacities that we have so that we can be safe. When we give someone power over us, as I have said, at first they just put a string around our wrist. A string that if we realized it was causing us to allow harm in any one of the areas discussed here, we could simply break it. A simple tug.

However, in avoiding causing harm to another, fearing being seen as mean, we leave that string which then becomes a rope...and over time that rope becomes a chain, a heavy burden to carry. There are potentially many ropes and chains attached to you now. Once these ropes become chains it will require that we find our power to remove them, but often we are too exhausted from carrying the chains...so we tolerate our circumstance. We treat ourselves poorly by allowing our suffering to continue. We are too beaten down and drained.

Decide to no longer be violated. Your thoughts and feelings create your beliefs, your rules. It is your job to make sure your boundaries are set to protect those rules. No one has to live by your rules, and no one should be granted permission to violate you in regard to them. Be prepared. You must not allow others to violate your boundaries. Stand in your right to be honored. You have the right to say no. "No," needs no explanation. Practice saying no. Remember, being firm is not being mean.

As you stand for your rights and begin to uphold your boundaries, you begin to experience this sense of power that comes with being your own authority, the only ruler of your life. Even in what you might define as healthy relationships, at first, your new found comfort in your skin becomes difficult for those around you. It is natural that they long for you to revert to the behavior they knew and expected; the behavior where at various levels, you allowed them to control and manipulate you. Remember, not all manipulation is intended to harm. Everyone enjoys getting what they want, and they may be unconsciously using guilt to achieve it. This is true in all relationships. Yet, it is always up to us to determine what we will allow. Be aware that as the dynamic is changing, it may separate you at first from the other party. Remember our relationships have often lasted for years, decades in fact. It is impossible not to become experts in the reactions of our partners!

We have watched them year after year. We know when we do this, they do that. In this awkward new environment, initially, they attempt to get you to "change back." Oddly, those around us want us to change back, even if our new behavior is not only better serving us, but better serving them as well! We all like the comfort of what we have always known. However, in your wisdom you will know to keep forging forward; any person that wishes to maintain a relationship with you will have to learn the new terms. During the early stages of our strides toward freedom, it may feel as though we are being frequently tested to see if we are really going to stand in our new found power, or choose to resume our time-tested failing ways. It is as if the Universe is saying, *Are you sure you are truly committed to changing your life?* We must continue to stand. We mustn't fold when those old weapons are directed toward us. The only power they have, is the power we give them. You are in charge of the quality of your life and what you will and won't do.

I tell people to see themselves, standing side-by-side with the person they are presently in relationship with. Imagine you are standing on a circle. As you begin to show up differently in your own life, the other person will feel off balance. It may begin to separate you, and you may each move away from one another on the perimeter of this circle. As you continue, you may move further and further apart. If your partner is not ready to end the cycle of abuse, they may leave that circle, or you might. However, in relationships with a goal of having a healthy love, your partner will observe your freedom, peace, and power and may want to learn how you have become so secure in yourself, and join you. Then as you continue traveling around the circumference of the circle, you reunite on the other end of your circle. Here, your relationship will be beautiful, deep, and most importantly, free.

As discussed, within us all is both masculine and feminine energies. Our masculine energy is brought into balance through validation of the things that we do, or praise. We tend to seek this from our father or the more masculine authority in our life. We want to be told that our actions, our doings, are acceptable and good. This builds self-confidence. Our feminine energy is brought into balance by validation of our feelings, or nurturing. We tend to seek this from our mother or the more feminine authority in our life. We want to know it is okay to feel what we feel. We long for compassion and acceptance of our feelings, and to know we are lovable, no matter who we are, and what we are feeling. This builds self-esteem. We tend to seek these things from our parents when we are young because they are our primary relationship; in adulthood we tend to seek these validations from our romantic partners since they become our primary relationship. However, in order to find true peace, our primary relationship should be with ourselves. We must be able to offer ourselves all of the validation and nurturing we need. It is only then that we can begin to attract another who is also at peace with themselves. When we serendipitously connect with that person, we know we can travel together in peace and companionship if we so desire.

When there is genuine love, peace exists. If your life has seemed devoid of these feelings of peace, devoid of nurturing or validation, you are looking in the wrong places to discover it. Seeking wholeness outside of yourself leads to destruction. Don't beg for these cherished emotions; find them in yourself. Then, unite with someone who genuinely and freely offers them. Embrace all of yourself and be free. No one *completes you*, you are complete.

To help you better understand yourself and others, let's first evaluate and connect the association between:

Self-esteem: feeling

and

Self-confidence: doing

First, I will lay a foundation for the information I wish to build upon.

Self-Confidence: What we show the world. This is our outer shell, the physical. Self-confidence is about what we *do*. This is our more masculine energy and is built in childhood by validation of our doing, usually from a masculine authority (keep in mind women can be our more masculine authority if they operate from a place of *do*ing rather than *fee*ling).

High Self-Confidence means that you believe in your ability to decide and *do*.

176

Low Self-Confidence means you don't believe in your ability to decide and *do*.

It is possible to be confident in some areas of our life and not others.

The higher someone's overall self-confidence, the more willing they are to take risks, because they believe in their ability to accomplish any goal.

Self-Confidence largely drives us in business, sports, and tasks. Self-confidence is injured when we are met with a disregard for our accomplishments; especially from those we view as an authority, such as our parents. Depending on our level of self-esteem, this can leave us feeling neglected, hurt, or small.

Self-esteem can impact self-confidence but they are not the same. Self-confidence can also impact self-esteem, but often to a lesser extent.

Self-Esteem: Acknowledging and experiencing our feelings. This is our more feminine energy and is built in childhood by validation of our feelings or nurturing, usually from a feminine authority (keep in mind, men can be our more feminine authority if they operate from a place of *feel*ing rather than *do*ing). This is more complex than self-confidence. Your self-esteem is determined by (1) your ability to recognize and accept your feelings and allow yourself to experience them, and (2) your knowledge that you are worthy of love just as you are. While this is received externally as children, remember that we must look within ourselves to find this in adulthood.

People with High Self-Esteem do not need external confirmation that they are loved and accepted because they already genuinely love and accept themselves, honor themselves, and experience inner peace. They recognize that others are also worthy of love and they are open to allowing others in their lives. However, in the same way they recognize that others are worthy of love, they also acknowledge their own worthiness and are not tolerant of abuse. They tend to be giving and willing to receive. While they may have nice things and believe they are worthy of nice things, they are not particularly vested in those things and would not mourn their loss. They believe love is what matters most.

People with Low Self-Esteem do not acknowledge their own worthiness or their own feelings. They often feel nervous or uncomfortable, that they are an inconvenience or even that they are in the way. Internally they feel they are unimportant and believe clearly that their feelings are even less important. Low self-esteem is often a product of victimization in childhood, and not receiving acceptance or compassion for the pain of victimization. The depth of this lack of validation and the severity of the harm decide whether or not we will fragment. Victimization may be something obvious and difficult to ignore, such as physical or sexual abuse, or it may be something less obtrusive like a lack of validation. Either way, this victimization must be compensated for in any one of a various number of ways, *if,* it is not acknowledged and repaired by an authority—our care givers.

To further illustrate, once we are victimized as children, and remember we are *all* victimized in one way or another, it is the job of the parental adult to validate our feelings and love us through it. In extreme cases, when we do not receive this validation we make one of two choices.

1. As a result of being victimized we choose to disown our power, our capacity for evil, and only embrace our innocence, which is in essence our capacity for good. We disowned this capacity because we experienced the pain caused by the "evil" in another, and never want any part of us to be capable of that. In doing so we fragmented ourselves and lost our wholeness. We tend to victimize ourselves by allowing others to abuse us, or by engaging in self-destructive behaviors manifested by our relationship with a romantic partner, food, money, sex, drugs, etc.

2. As a result of being victimized we chose to disown our innocence, our capacity for good, and only embrace our darkness which is our capacity for evil. We disowned this capacity because we experienced "evil" and felt so powerless to overcome it that we embraced it, so we do not find ourselves victims once again. In doing so we fragmented ourselves and lost our wholeness. We tend to victimize others.

Either decision brought us to low self-esteem. In effect then, when our perception of the pain is deep enough, then, we become fragmented. The fragmentation is our coping mechanism for our low self-esteem. This fragmentation can occur even due to one event. One act of sexual abuse for example, especially by someone that was supposed to love us, might cause us to lose ourselves, detach from parts of ourselves. The victims who become fragmented will always become the victimizers; the only distinction is whether we victimize ourselves or others. Fragmentation is both a reaction to our low self-esteem and a catalyst for its continual decline. In our fragmented state we continue to deny the presence of our feelings, which further chips away at our self-esteem.

Sometimes, if our perception of the pain is not intense enough to cause a total rejection of a part of ourselves, we are not fragmented after our abuse. We are merely wounded. We will not operate from solely our capacity for good or our capacity for evil. We may simply build a wall and refuse to let anyone in to victimize us again. We chaotically swing our sword, but with no real target or strategy. Those that do get hurt are simply in the wrong place at the wrong time. They are just unlucky to be in the path of our swing. We simply want to ensure that others keep their distance. We fear letting them close enough to love, but we also do not allow them close enough to harm us, in the deeply personal way that a victimizer will harm. We will spend our lives stuck in the purgatory between good and evil, while longing for love and acceptance.

Remember, this is not to say that those who fragmented experienced "more" or "worse" abuse than those who are not fragmented. The thing that dictates whether or not we are fragmented is our *perception* of our pain.

If someone is foundationally whole, they are less likely to have a fragmentation later in life. While a death, divorce, or other tragedy may still result in a lessening of our self-esteem, it is more likely to present itself as a wounding. A wounding may be a temporary setback, but is less destructive than a fragmentation. However, keep in mind that if the perception of the pain is intense enough, a fragmentation may still result. We unconsciously determine our own threshold for fragmentation vs. wounding.

179

When we fragment in a manner that causes us to operate only from the innocence, we often find ourselves the victim. In situations where we do not perceive ourselves as the authority, as is often the case in our primary relationship, we do not defend from a place of power. We may yell that we deserve respect, yet we continue to endure abuses. This incongruence proves to our abuser that we do not feel we are worthy of the love and respect we claim we deserve. Our innocence, our neglected and broken child, is running our emotional life. Living from only our innocence, we are unarmed and unarmored, unaware of the sword of protection within our grasp. We refuse to embrace our capacity for the shadow, evil. We will experience great pain, but deny it. We tell ourselves our feelings are wrong, and in doing so, we change our view of the world and deny the pain in our experiences.

**The feeling I have that this is wrong
must in fact be what is wrong. My feelings are wrong,
not the act of what is happening to me or being told to me.**

Remember, our inability to see the capacity for evil in ourselves also blinds us to this capacity in others. If we have denied our capacity for evil, we deny the evil that is being bestowed upon us. We are mistaking our unwillingness to protect ourselves from harm, as compassion. Since we do not feel we were offered compassion when we were hurt, we are willing to offer it unconditionally to others. When we do this for our abusers, it is to prove to them our innocence, our goodness, in the hopes of receiving love and acceptance in return. The fact that the love and acceptance is never received does not thwart our efforts to heal the abuser through our own self-sacrifice. We are giving what we have always longed to receive: Compassion. We think, *This poor soul has been hurt before, just like I was. I will show them compassion so that they will see my innocence. Once they see my innocence, they will know that I won't hurt them, and they will offer me love and acceptance.* This is what we wish we could have done as a child; showed the evildoer our own innocence, and in response received love and acceptance. We are trying to right the wrong that was done to us. However, time and time again we feel as though we have failed to help another see our innocence; the innocence which is all we are willing to see in others. We cannot see what we deny exists. Those who operate from their shadow are incapable of seeing our innocence, just as we are incapable of seeing their evil. They have denied their capacity for good, and therefore they deny the good that is being done or bestowed on them. When our desperate attempts to receive the love and acceptance that we so willingly give are not met with reciprocation, we are left feeling numb to our own emotions. Empty.

We may also choose to victimize ourselves with self-destructive behavior. This often manifests itself in substance abuse, indiscriminate sexual encounters, or the acquisition of things that we do not need and cannot afford. This is our way of saying, *I am obviously not worthy of love and acceptance, so I will let this outside substance or experience give me the illusion of love and acceptance.* However, we will find ourselves still empty. We are numb even to our self-induced pain, we are still the victim.

When someone fragments in a manner that causes them to operate only from their shadow, the result is still feeling empty and numb. Unaware that largely their dark side is leading them, at some unconscious level they have a sense that, *Well, it was always done to me so I will do it to them.* They are bestowing their evil, forcing their power over and control of, on the innocence, as a reflection of what happened to them. This is what they wish they could have done as a child, showed their evil, their power to protect themselves, and as a result maintained their innocence. This fulfills their desire to be the perpetrator. They believe that the best way to avoid being the victim is to become the victimizer. They are living from their shadow or their evil, because they refuse to embrace their capacity for good, their lost innocence.

Those who operate from their capacity for good, see these people, and wish to offer them compassion. After all, those operating from their shadow are likely victims of old pain. It may not be that these people are unworthy of compassion or love; it is that those operating from their capacity for good must offer these things from a distance, if venturing too near will cause them to become a victim yet again. You should not endure pain in your quest to help another.

In all cases, what we are looking for in those things outside of ourselves is our wholeness. We tend to attract to us those who have the "piece" we are missing. We are a magnet drawing them in. The shadow seeks the innocence. The innocence seeks the shadow. Our quest is NOT for that person, it is for our wholeness and we unconsciously believe they can give that to us. Wholeness does not come from outside of us. No person, drug, food, or anything outside of you, will ever make you whole.

Whereas, those of us who choose to live in the light of our innocence, victimize ourselves, and wrongfully seek wholeness in abusive relationships or self-inflicted pain; those living in the depths of the shadow, seek power over or control of objects, in order to find their perception of wholeness. To them, people are nothing more than objects. They are prone to ultimately destroy these objects, especially when they sense they might lose control of the object. These shadow dwellers are often sociopaths. We can argue whether all sociopaths have low self-esteem or no self-esteem as some have argued, but rest assured that they are confident in their ability to do one thing: win. They want to appear successful to the rest of the world. Their image is vital. It is the only thing they can cling to, being unable to feel any true sense of love and unconsciously denying their lost innocence. A trait of a sociopath is that they want to appear to have it all—big house, nice car, perfect family. If you could see where these things came from, you would find a trail of deceit and destruction. They want the air of professional success, and some of them may very well achieve it, but if they aren't able to hold onto the professional title or monies they seek, you will hear story after story of the ways they were wronged, or how they gave it all up to be a better father/husband/son, daughter/wife/mother to those who came before you. Regardless of whether it is their professional success that has funded their extravagant lifestyle, or their personal manipulations, they ooze a hollow self-confidence. They know how to choose their victims and manipulate them. They apply their charm or power wherever it is necessary to gain power over and control of the objects of their choosing. Empathy and compassion do not exist in these relationships, no matter what might be presented.

In the end, all they want is:

Power over and Control of

In intimate relationships, all abusers are going to look for someone with low self-esteem, because only someone with low self-esteem would tolerate abuse. All abusers want a target.

Consider though, a very important distinction. A sociopath is looking for someone with **low self-esteem and high self-confidence**. What good is having control over a chess piece that has no power? And who has more power than the Queen?

I am now aware of the dangers of high self-confidence and low self-esteem. It is our high self-confidence that enables us to present ourselves well, we present an air of credibility; we are the rule following, honest, "get it done" folks. We present the perfect challenge for those living in the shadow. They lure us in, swoon us, capture us, hook us, and trance us under their spell.

What isn't so obvious to the outside world is that we have low self-esteem, as our high self-confidence acts as a mask, which makes us easy targets. We are desperately in need of love and acceptance for who we are in personal relationships, we want our feelings honored and we want to know what we feel is real. To win us over these predators give us exactly what we perceive we need, and we become hooked. In our fragmented states, while we reject our shadow selves, we attract those who live from the shadow, and believe they will make us whole.

Furthermore, those of us with high self-confidence are not used to failing and not used to quitting. We make things work, we have **stamina and endurance**. If it is not working we can fix it, we know we can. We will work harder, we will do better, and the abusers know it. It is our high self-confidence that drives us to willingly and confidently take charge of their piece of the jigsaw. Our confidence allows us to take control of their responsibilities. And our confidence and refusal to fail cause us to stay in longer and give it all we have, just like we gave to everything in our life—

completely. In reality the only true failure is to continue tolerating the intolerable.

The bonus round for the sociopath is that they know no one will suspect we are a victim of constant abuse, we are too confident for that. Recall the disconnect I spoke of between my professional success and my personal hell. We often thrive in business while being dismantled and capitalized on at home. What the abuser knows, what that sociopath knows, is **we do not want to feel shame**. We are successful and don't want to fail. **We will avoid shame at all cost**. When we are whole in ourselves, when we have high self-esteem, we will no longer fear shame. Awake, we will no longer attract or tolerate abuse.

So what is the first part of the secret to ending abuse?

Recovering Our Self-Esteem and Self-Confidence

Self-esteem drives us most significantly in primary relationships. It is what we feel on the inside as we interact with others.

We are born whole. We are nothing but love. We are connected to the source that is love in all things—God, the Universe. We are very aware.

Upon birth we are the observer. When we are first born we seldom focus on one thing. We are taking it all in, we are observing our environment and we love that feeling of being connected to source. We are congruent. Then we observe and experience things that are in opposition to the love and acceptance we know when connected to source, and we begin to wound. We feel pieces of us are being rejected.

As our life progresses and we have our experiences, loving experiences help us continue to own all of our capacities; stay connected to this energy I call "God." When we have negative experiences, we begin to disown the parts of us that made us feel unaccepted. As we create our "adapted selves," we become what we believe we need to be to gain the acceptance of others. We disown the emotions that are perceived to be unacceptable in our environment. Where there is control or power, the voice of our authority telling us which feelings are acceptable, it is our negative emotions that we feel are rejected, and so, we will begin to hide them. The more we hide them, the more repressed they become, the deeper our loss of self-esteem. As we observe conflict we often feel we are at the cause, so we attempt to do better and be better hoping that our environment will heal, that we can heal it. Where there is love and acceptance of who we are in all of our emotions, we will feel embraced, and we will thrive—we will remain whole, connected to the source and all parts of ourselves.

How many people take drugs or other mood altering substance to avoid feeling? This is a compensation for low self-esteem. We become numb to the pain and lose our compassion for ourselves.

We may not feel the pain, but it still exists. It is now buried within. Once we have harbored our emotions, our reactions tend to be much more intense. Our reactions may be bigger than the present circumstance, or we may have no reaction to a circumstance where an expression of significant feeling might be appropriate. Sometimes the absence of emotion can be just as intense as our overreaction. Either way, these are indicators we need to release our harbored emotions. Many people fear this release. They fear that if the floodgates open, then all they have repressed will come out at once. They fear that if this happens, the pain will have no end. This fear that they have is simply false. Initially, it may feel you moved from the safe shore into the thrashing of the river, yet know, that the safety of the shore was an "illusion." As you thrash in the river, you may be fearful that you have made a mistake, longing to turn back, longing for the safety of the numbness on the shore. Keep your eyes forward on the goal, the freedom on the other side. I cannot emphasize enough, the only way around is through. You cannot jump to being healed without first acknowledging all that is repressed. Once you have released all that is harbored, the easiest way to avoid an onslaught of harbored sadness, anger, hurt, etc. is to feel, and thereby release each emotion as you experience it.

The negative energy vibrating in our body clouds our view of the world. We see most things through that negative lens. All emotions long to be acknowledged. When they are acknowledged and released, clarity and awareness follows.

The level of repression of our emotions will affect all aspects of our behavior.

Parenting, then, is a pretty big job. We need to teach our children that all emotions are acceptable. If we acknowledge the emotions we see, or perceive that our children might be feeling by labeling them, there will likely be less negative behavior in the extreme sense, when they experience these emotions. Acceptance of their emotions leads them to acceptance of themselves.

Rejection of the emotions, teaching or declaring some emotions are bad, is what is bad! We need to acknowledge and experience *all* emotions, not just the "good" ones. We must teach not that the emotion is bad, but that certain behaviors or means of releasing that emotion are inappropriate. The important thing is what we *do* with that emotion. Stuffing it deep inside will not lead to peace and healing.

Validating emotions, or nurturing, begins to build self-esteem.

Validating actions, or praise, begins to build self-confidence.

If a child is learning how to ride a bicycle and falls off...

In order to build self-esteem, label the emotion, "That must hurt." Normalize the emotion, "Anyone would be hurt if they fell off of their bicycle," or "Anyone would cry if they were hurt like that," and continue to offer love. Encourage the child to try again, and when they finally ride the bike without falling tell them, "Wow! Good job!! I knew you would get it. I'm so glad you didn't give up!" This builds self-confidence.

Even in a situation where perhaps the emotion is one that we would rather discourage, the same principles can be used.

If a child is certain there is a monster in the closet...

186

In order to build self-esteem, label the emotion, "That must be scary." Normalize the emotion, "Anyone would be afraid if they thought there was a monster in the closet," and continue to offer love. However, explain to the child that even though it would be scary if there *was* a monster in the closet, there is not a monster in the closet. Then assist in whatever way you see fit. I might offer to check first, and encourage the child to check with me, and when they finally are able to overcome their fear I would tell them, "Good job!! I know it was hard to face your fear, but I am so proud of you for checking the closet with me and sleeping in your bedroom."

If they attempt to release the emotion in an unhealthy way, encourage them to find an alternative. Again, I do not claim be educated in parenting beyond personal experience. What I do feel knowledgeable in, is the important reality that everyone wants to be loved and accepted as they are, and at an early age we make decisions that will stay with us for potentially our whole life. Therefore, even as we discipline, we must do so without diminishing the spirit. This is true for children, employees, spouses, everyone. Representative of this concept "Johnny stole my toy, so I punched him!" should not result in, *What is wrong with you, are you an idiot?* That voice, those words, will ring in their head for years to come. They will be asking themselves...*Am I an idiot?* Or worse, they will determine they are an idiot, and those words will be uttered inside their head anytime they deem they have made an error in judgment. Perhaps respond by labeling the anger felt, and providing an alternative release. "I understand that you are angry with Johnny. Anyone would be angry if someone took their toy, but no one should ever hit to express their anger. Take a deep breath and count to ten to help you control your actions when you feel anger. Use words to ask for your toy back and express your feelings, not violence." Obviously each child's needs are different and in extreme cases you may need to change your approach. The important thing for the child to understand is that you love them, even if you don't like their inappropriate behavior. Address the behavior, while loving the child. When we discount them and their emotions, it is confusing, and begins the terrible act of repression and denial.

"Oh that doesn't hurt, get over it," translates to, "Your feelings aren't real or right." In our heart we feel as children, *But it does hurt.* Over time after continuous discounting, we deny our feelings. We decide, *It doesn't hurt. I am not angry. It is no big deal.*

We hear, "Don't be such a baby, you are not that hurt." We believe we did it wrong, our feelings our wrong.

> **The feeling I have that this is wrong**
> **must in fact be what is wrong. My feelings are wrong,**
> **not the act of what is happening to me or being told to me.**

And the discounting and invalidation of self begins.

Numbness begins.

What's funny is that as we get older, after years of our emotions being discounted and invalidated, if we get honor, we discount it!

If we say to an adult, "Wow that must have really hurt," what is often the response we receive?

"It wasn't that bad."

Or if we compliment, "Great tie!"

We are told, "This old thing?"

How about instead, "Thank you!" Acceptance. We must be willing to receive in order to experience complete happiness.

There is no such thing as a perfect parent but one concept is easy:

No matter what mistakes they may make, we must love and accept our children through it. Always embracing where they are, not where we think they should be or where we would like them to be.

Anyone who knows without question they are loved has already what most of us spend our life seeking; Wholeness. Love of the whole of us is the biggest secret to peace.

Now, as you know, this is not a parenting book. Each of us was likely denied this nurturing and validation in some way as a child. There are no perfect parents. Even those parents who work hard to praise and nurture their children will likely fall short of perfection. This does not make them bad parents, it only makes them human.

In order to rebuild the self-esteem and self-confidence that we have lost over our lifetimes, we must begin to be the parent to ourselves. Who knows what we need better than we do? Remember, we are each holding the hand of the little child inside of us. We must nurture this child until this child knows that we, the adult, can be trusted to take care of him or her. We must build our toolkit and learn how to offer ourselves the love and acceptance that we have been denied. We cannot expect to find external love until we have found it within ourselves.

When our feelings become too much to bear, we stop *feeling* them and start *thinking* them. Our emotions move from our hearts to our heads. We feel only our numbness in our hearts. We operate in our mind because of fear. This has been our defense, our default. This is how we "keep it together." We think our feelings by overanalyzing. We replay situations in our minds over and over. We try to strategize, try to control. We end up being frenetic and anxious. Feelings are not meant for the mind, they are meant for the heart.

Allow me to provide you with a useful exercise in moving from your mind to your heart. Sit quietly, inhale and exhale slowly. Release all the tension in every part of your body, your "happy place" can help. Once you do that, imagine a very small version of yourself coming down a ladder from your brain or mind, to your heart. See a little door in front of your heart and consider stepping in.

Some people are too terrified to step in. Pretend there is someone with you, anyone you'd like, even if they don't really exist, and attempt to walk in. Meet your heart. As you see the contents of your heart, just pour love, however you envision love, on everything you see or feel. Begin to once again embrace the feeling power of your heart.

This is not to discount the power of our minds, they are powerful and necessary parts of who we are. Our hearts are as well. Obtaining congruence between your heart and your mind leads to a congruent, healthy and flowing body, mind, and spirit. If we only use our minds, it is as if we are only using our left hands. We can get things done, but it is difficult with only one hand. Let the other hand join, and our power exponentially increases. Use both hands...mind and heart. Over time, you can use the whole of you, mind, body, and spirit. There is no shame in feeling our emotions in our heart. We no longer need our facade of invulnerability. After all of the time that we have been numb, we may have forgotten how to feel. We may not be aware that we are feeling anything, let alone what those feelings are. We must regain access to our hearts by beginning in the place where we currently are, our minds.

A simple action to begin rebuilding your self-esteem is to imagine you have sticky labels, and throughout the day, label your emotions. Sad, angry, hurt, afraid, label the positive ones too. There is never a "wrong" emotion. Any emotion that shows up is the right emotion to lead us to the truth about ourselves. Don't argue with your feelings. Through allowing yourself to acknowledge your feelings, you begin to be more self-aware. By consciously and actively labeling our emotions, we are forcing ourselves to be introspective.

If you don't journal, think of starting. I recommend it as a daily activity preferably in the morning. There is no wrong way to journal. Just write freely anything that comes to mind or heart. To release harbored emotions, name the emotion that might be harbored. *I feel sad, I feel angry, I feel ashamed, I feel _____ because*...stick with one emotion until you feel you have exhausted those feelings. Literally keep rewriting *I feel _____*, filling in that blank with the same emotion, and a new thought after it relative to that same emotion until you can really *feel* that emotion. Then write, scream, cry, hit a pillow on the bed, or talk until that "negative" emotion has dissipated. Then, feel which new emotion emerges and continue this procedure. Of course you must not harm yourself or others in this process, this is solely a private matter that you resolve in a healthy way. Do this as often as you need to, for as long as you need to, until thinking of that event or memory stirs no feeling. It has been released. I realize many of you may now, or as you progress, feel numb. Numb can be placed in that sentence as the emotion you are feeling until another one comes to light. *I feel numb because...*

By labeling and recognizing your emotions, at least you are beginning to acknowledge that you feel. You also begin to see what and how you feel. Acknowledging that you feel begins to evidence for you that you exist. Through honoring your emotions you begin to restore your diminished or destroyed self-esteem. This is crucial to creating a happy life. We have disregarded ourselves for far too long.

When we begin to become more aware of our feelings, sometimes we may be unclear why we feel a certain way. Often, when an unexpected emotion shows up it is due to some unresolved issue of our past. Generally, the past emotion is one that we experienced involving someone very close to us, in our inner circle, those that occupy the parental role; but the present emotion may be directed at someone who is a practical stranger, someone in our outer circle. When this happens, we find it easier to direct our emotion toward the person who is in our outer circle. We find it easier because it is too scary to stand up to those who are in our inner circle. Many times, we have never really made a legitimate stand against them, and now we find ourselves unable to do so, even if the confrontation is only theoretical. However, it is important to acknowledge and release the root of the emotion. This may mean journaling or writing a letter that will never be sent to the person in the inner circle who caused the original anger, sadness, or pain. You must express every emotion that has remained unspoken and unexpressed. It isn't always easy, but the emotion will continue to pop up unexpectedly until the original pain is addressed. Use your childhood experiences or current experiences as the tools to trigger the emotions. Once you have released your pain, you will find your way to forgiveness. You cannot think your way from acknowledgement to forgiveness. You must feel your way there.

If you pay attention, you will know when emotions want to get your attention. You will feel something even if you don't know what the emotion is; you will know what it is not. It is not, for example, joy or happiness. Investigate the feeling, knowing that it is likely some unresolved pain that recent events are reminding you of again, likely from within your inner circle. Like maybe you feel abandoned or neglected in a situation but it may not be about that situation, it may be that someone else is being the mirror so you can see your pain about how a sibling or parent neglected or abandoned you. As you pay attention to your feelings, you will begin to know the deepest parts of you.

Sometimes releasing your emotions helps you see that emotions you had directed at another, were really related to an internal issue. In contrast, sometimes as you release your emotions and gain your clarity, you may realize that the person you felt the emotions toward has mistreated you. Once you are clear, you can and will decide whether you need to address the situation, or if releasing the emotion was enough. You may realize that perhaps you need to release the person, and as you find your strength you will be willing do so. Cut the string, or break the chain. No one holds your lifeline except you.

Bottom line:

Turning inward always gives you the wisdom regarding what you need to do to be free.

There are several techniques to release harbored emotions. One is to alter the movie that you see in your head by either writing or imaging those events, only this time, defend yourself in the image you have recalled. Go back in and figuratively say and do what you wish you would have done at the time, but you were too small or too powerless to do it. This is a very empowering exercise. Even if you have no recall of childhood events, understand that recurring issues in your adult life probably stem from childhood issues. Be aware and utilize those current experiences to recognize the patterns, it will better help you uncover and resolve the lingering pain. The patterns represent the common conditions in your life that repeatedly compel certain emotions or responses to be ignited within you. As you examine the patterns of the circumstances and your response, you may begin to discover a common theme overshadowing your life, such as, *I am not good enough* or *I am not loveable*. These experiences, which are being created in *congruence* with your thoughts, validate your sense of being powerless. The goal is to rediscover your power, rather than allowing these perceived conditions to further diminish your power. Although you lost your power as child, you can use the current events and your image work to reclaim it.

I have learned that even while imagining these events and attempting to stand up to authority, we are afraid. We commonly feel the need to keep our distance, sit while they stand or avoid eye contact. We know at some level that parent or perpetrator of some abuse against us is not physically in the room, yet we often still get immobilized by gripping fear to stand up to authority, or as I prefer to say it, to take back the power that we left behind so. long ago. We often feel we are too helpless to act, too helpless to stand up and be free. Raise your voice, shout, and don't hold back. This is about *your* healing, not about harming them. Bang a pillow on the bed, cry. Release those emotions now heavily stored in your body creating pain.

Recognize too, that once we have reached a level where we feel resentment toward another, it is easy for us to translate all that they do and say into something with vile intent. As a coach, I will often take the story, letter, or email that someone is reacting to with deep hurt or anger, and suggest that we switch roles. I will then ask them to breathe and come to a place of calm the best they can. Then, I tell them I am going to tell "their" story, only I am going to make it *my* story, as if the events they outlined occurred between my family member(s) and me. Then I tell them that when I am done with "my" story, I would like their advice. Inevitably, the client sees the message in a new light. All the hate and vileness they were experiencing seems lessened. They are suddenly more objective. They discover that their years of resentment towards this person, has distorted their objectivity. It may be true that someone isn't treating them right. It may also be true that their inability to let go of what has occurred in the past, blinds them. As I have said when you believe something assuredly, evidence will assuredly keep confirming *this* truth, even if this perceived truth is in fact, false.

As you begin to release all these harbored emotions, as you express the fullness of your emotions and begin to reclaim your power, you will gain some new clarity. Once the emotions are no longer harbored in the mind, the "mind clutter" is gone. You no longer find your mind flooded with racing thoughts. Your heart is also now open to feel, enabling you to better intuit. This new clarity will be available to you always. In this clarity you more readily move to forgiveness. If you look closely, you will likely also discover that all the worst parts of your authority, the parent or other guardian of your early life that you harbored the most disdain for, created the best parts of you. Simply write a list of three of four characteristics that you despised in them followed by three or four characteristics you love about you. Take a moment and thoughtfully consider what you discover. They taught you what not to be. Have gratitude.

As we come to know our emotions, we will not need to cognitively label them in our mind in order to feel them in our heart. In time, we will feel and accept the emotions right where they are, in our hearts. As your heart restores, your intuition, what I call the *voice of God*, will strengthen. Eventually, we may even allow our hearts to guide the actions of our minds. When this happens, all of our actions will be from a place of love, love of ourselves as well as others. To begin to feel might seem scary, but ultimately it is less painful then a life void of joy. If you can't feel the intensity of your pain, consider that you also can't feel the intensity of your joy.

Rebuilding your self-confidence is a little different than rebuilding your self-esteem. To do so you must acknowledge and praise yourself for the things you *do* well. You may have to start small, *I did an excellent job making my bed.* If you have been diminished to the point of nothingness, you may find that you criticized yourself even for these small things in the past, so it is time to start praising yourself for those small things. You may find it difficult to acknowledge your successes in these areas, even if you felt no discomfort in ridiculing yourself in these ways. Pat yourself on the back or give yourself a gold star, whatever you need to do to finally recognize that you *are* competent. You are capable of doing things well.

Once we have high self-confidence *and* high self-esteem, no words can hurt us. We need nothing from the outer world. We know that all we need for wholeness is already with us. We do not need the validation of our emotions or actions. We recognize low self-esteem in others and acknowledge when they operate from their shadow to compensate for their fragmentation. We see all this, and we may feel sorrow for these people, we may offer love, but never again will we allow ourselves to fall victim to their predation. It is in our wholeness that we recognize that we no longer need to sacrifice ourselves, to save those that operate from their shadow. We are finally free from deception. We are awake to the truth. We can offer healing and assistance in the right ways, at the right times, for those who are truly in need.

For those of us who are used to "fixing" others, the hardest part lies in allowing others to feel their emotions without our interventions. When those adults around you experience their emotions, don't try to fix them or change them, just silently label them. Just label it. *They are angry, sad, happy, lonely...I will just let them have their anger, sadness, etc...* This is especially important when you are healing. You do not need to worry about helping others regain their self-esteem until you have become comfortable in your own. Once you find your personal comfort in the presence of all of you, your inner knowing will boldly be your guide.

In abusive relationships the emotions of the abuser are likely to be extreme and erratic. As you are learning to label your own emotions, you will likely be compelled to help them see what they are feeling. This is simply continuing to engage in the abuse. They are not willing participants in their healing, and vocalizing your identification of their feelings is only inviting in more abuse. It is not your responsibility to be their parent. You must only parent yourself. I found this very difficult at first. It was my job to make everyone happy, it was my job to fix it, but to wake up I had to begin to simply observe their emotions and silently name them; that is all. And as I healed, I gave up all desire to control.

Clearly, in loving relationships to acknowledge and validate the emotions can lead to greater depth. This is true only once we have reached a level of

195

cognizance of our emotions and our partner has as well. In all relationships it is important to let the other person have their emotions without feeling the need to fix or remedy what someone is experiencing or feeling. How often do we allow someone's sadness or sense of being overwhelmed to create discomfort in us? To relieve *our* discomfort with *their* feelings, we often feel the need to act, to do something to ease their discomfort, only to harbor resentment over time for having to close the gap or carry the weight that they seemed unable to handle. Each person must find their way to resolve their wounds and all we can do is love them through it. Try not to own their pain and act upon it, instead, observe, as a means of gaining understanding of who they are, as they are, not as you want them to be. When individuals seek continued growth and healing, then the conversation is not about parenting, but about love and support. Emotional connection is part of our soul connection, the oneness that connects us all. Our heart and soul; Our spirit of God.

All emotions are good. It is what we do once we feel them that defines us. Any unacknowledged emotion remains harbored in our bodies longing to be acknowledged and accepted, just as we all have been longing for. If you reject it, deny it, or ignore it, it doesn't go away; instead it festers in your body until you will notice it. The more it festers the more your behavior, health, and life will be negatively impacted. We may overreact or become increasingly vile with our words or our actions. We may lose all patience and have a lack of acceptance of ourselves and others around us. We often feel anxiety and ultimately our health will be where the anxiety manifests. This is why it is vital to continue to acknowledge and experience your emotions as they continue to present themselves, even after your self-esteem has been restored. In your wholeness, this task will not seem daunting as it once did.

Your body, mind, and spirit have been working together to keep you aware and leading a happy healthy life, if you would just honor what you feel, rather than running or hiding from your emotions.

When you embrace all of you and get in alignment with who you really are, negative emotions simply don't show up very often. When we are living in alignment, we will almost never experience the pain associated with abuse by ourselves or others because we no longer tolerate abuse. Our higher sense of self and the healing of our wounds, enable us to see and feel things more clearly. When an emotion appears, we label it and let it flow through us. We no longer take things personally. We realize the actions of others are about them, about what they see in the mirror, not us.

This is what we may need to remind ourselves as we experience the floodgates of our harbored emotions opening. As I indicated, often times once you begin to experience your emotions, you feel as if you are treading water in a raging river. You fear you will never get to the other side, but you will. You must feel your way through. As we return to wholeness even in painful situations we recognize that we are not living a life of pain. We may experience something that once again makes us feel sad or angry, but it is much more tolerable knowing that we will not be experiencing that emotion indefinitely.

*I feel angry, anyone would feel angry if this happened to them...**and this too shall pass**.*

In my world now I embrace every emotion and I do not deny them. I don't need to hold that little girl's hand anymore because in finally taking care of myself; she is also taken care of. We are free to experience life joyfully together as one. We are free to play. I am able to embrace relationships that nourish me, and eliminate those that are destructive.

Through rebuilding our self-esteem and self-confidence, we will find it easier to implement what we have discovered in our assessment. We should set guidelines for what we expect from ourselves and from others regarding ourselves. Those guidelines are our boundaries. The existence and placement of our boundaries is driven by where we are relative to our self-esteem. Where we are defines our willingness to offer love and nurturing, and how far we will go in the hopes of receiving the same. Boundaries that are too rigid or too loose can cause unnecessary stress in our lives. Knowing that we get our self-esteem and self-confidence from within, we will find it easier to establish boundaries as we establish our beliefs about our worthiness.

Boundaries

Do you have behaviors in your life that you want to stop but can't seem to?

I want to stop drinking, I know I need to exercise, I don't want to work so many hours, yet I can't seem to change it; I have no choice. If you have felt guilt your whole life, you will continue to engage in behaviors that make you feel guilty. You create justification for your guilt. Otherwise you would walk around feeling guilty, and not know why! The more we dwell on these behaviors that we no longer want in our lives, the longer we will find ourselves engaging in those behaviors. It is only once we accept ourselves in our "flawed" state and begin to love ourselves, that we can move past these behaviors. Release the adamancy of these behaviors (*I **have** to work out three days a week, I **must** give up drinking*) and they will be much easier to change. As long as you are holding steadily to your false beliefs, or your condemning, harmful thoughts, very little will change. Permanent change requires a permanent extinguishing of your negative beliefs and self-talk, and the creation of boundaries that are truly acceptable to you; who *you* really are. Sadly we struggle to change our behavior. It is as if we want to stand up, but our belt loop keeps getting caught on the chair. We feel stuck, gripping and focusing on what we no longer want in our lives.

It is up to us to build our self-confidence and self-esteem. The sooner we release our grip on the things we want to change, the easier it will be to move to living free. Often, recovering our self-confidence and self-esteem and building our boundaries happens simultaneously.

Until we alter the programming, the beliefs that are harming us, those outer experiences will not permanently change. As with all areas of our lives, the change must begin within. Our self-talk is the easiest thing for us to control. So start there by accepting those things that you perceive as bad behaviors for now, embrace them. No longer condemn yourself for them. Remind yourself that you will better care for yourself moving forward. No longer be that harsh, judgmental parent to yourself. You deserve nurturing and compassion. Like raising a child, you must embrace yourself where you are, not criticize yourself. Begin to believe that you can move to a better place. Rejection of any part of yourself will create more negative emotions, and more negative emotions will likely lead to intensification of those behaviors. You can't reject part of yourself hoping to arrive at wholeness. These behaviors will melt away once you begin to live in alignment with who you really are, and love and accept yourself in every step along the way. It is so liberating. It is so freeing. Trust the process, trust yourself.

If I had healthy boundaries, I would have understood and adopted the beliefs I have articulated:

- ❖ **Always honor yourself.**
- ❖ **Honor others as long as honoring others doesn't cause you to dishonor yourself.**
- ❖ **If someone is asking you to dishonor yourself for them, that is not okay. Say no.**

Boundaries begin to allow us to fulfill our own needs and create our own safe environments. Some people have fluid boundaries, others have rigid boundaries. The boundaries themselves were created as a perceived way of keeping ourselves safe. Boundaries are about safety. Becoming conscious of our boundaries and redefining where and how they need to be, helps us have the most fulfilling and productive life. It is an important part of learning to live free.

Boundaries can be complicated and there are many angles and views. I want to encourage you to think of your boundaries as part of the means for you to create the life you want. You do not need to be able to categorize your boundaries. You simply have to begin to realize that it is your responsibility, and only your responsibility, to keep yourself safe and surrounded in love and acceptance so that you can live free.

In order to better understand boundaries, think of them as the banks of a river. We are the water flowing within this river, but often times we allow our banks and our course to be determined by external forces. Perhaps we are following what we perceive to be our natural course, unaware that it was dictated by societal or parental expectations. When our banks are too narrow and too rigid, we become chaotic and stressed. The pressure builds as our mass of water attempts to flow through this narrow space. The confines of our rules, our banks, act as a prison. Most people refuse to venture into our river, fearing that they will drown in our rushing waters. When we look for others to help us loosen our boundaries, the only ones willing to brave our waters are those who know how to deceptively destroy our banks. We seek out those who we feel have freer flow than our own. As always, we are erroneously seeking those who have what we perceive we need, to be whole. We need instead to embrace these abilities hidden within ourselves. We see their lack of boundaries, a lack that we envy at some level, and oddly, we try to build their banks to control their flow. We are so busy worrying about their banks, that we don't see that we are allowing them to destroy our own. If that happens, if we allow our boundaries to be destroyed, we will overflow our banks. When we allow this to continue we become nothing more than a stagnant swamp. We have no form, we have evaporated. We are invisible. This all happened as we stood immobilized in their boggy quicksand trying to build their banks. You cannot control the river of another, without their permission. It is only once we recognize the power of our own river that we gain control. *We* can dictate our boundaries, our course. Once we do, just as the Colorado River created the Grand Canyon, we are a powerful force flowing effortlessly through the path we have determined. When we recognize our power, the river moves at a calm and peaceful pace, etching as it travels a beautiful formation, our peaceful life. When we recognize our power, we allow ourselves to guide our path.

In the past we were incapable of nurturing ourselves, and also incapable of receiving nurturing from others, but we were extraordinary at offering nurturing to others with no protection of boundaries for ourselves. So we offered nurturing to build others up, which in turn destroyed us.

To be safe in the oneness, you need to be able to distinguish between true need and deception. I see the potential glaring conflict, to say that we must embrace our oneness, while simultaneously saying we must put up boundaries to distinguish where one person ends and another begins. There is not a conflict between Universal connectedness and protection. To be safe in the oneness, you need to be able to distinguish between deception and truth, fear and love, control and freedom, those who seek power over and those who offer compassion. You have to back away to distinguish these attributes accurately. As it is said, *you cannot see the forest for the trees*.

To be safe, you need to be able to identify the people kneeling in that metaphorical puddle who have every ability to stand up, but would rather manipulate and control you for the sheer pleasure of draining you of your life force, your power. In contrast, you must also be able to identify those who are in the puddle unaware that it is a puddle. These people feel that they are drowning in the depth of the water and as a result, they need some support and help to build their confidence and stand. There are also those who are unaware that they are not standing, and are oblivious to the fact that if they remain in the puddle, the ground beneath them may soften and they may sink in the quicksand and disappear. We were these people. We couldn't see our own predicament and therefore we couldn't save ourselves. When you Wake Up to all your capacities you become wiser and much more able to see. The more you know of your heart and your truth, the clearer you can see the heart and truth of others.

202

To wake up, you need to back up. Sometimes this comes in the form of physical distance. If you can, remove yourself from the physical presence of the person or situation that is keeping you from peace. This distance will allow you to examine things more clearly. Sometimes physical distance is unattainable or you are not ready, either way you need to distance yourself emotionally, financially, or in any other way that you can. This may not be as simple as it sounds. It is done gradually. Sometimes the person or situation is so much a part of us, that if we were to rip them away completely we fear we might bleed to death. We need to slowly begin to pull away. Once we reach this place of physical and/or emotional distance, the process of waking up becomes easier. From our new vantage point it will be easier to apply the knowledge we have begun to acquire on our path to waking. Awake, we can more easily see where our boundaries are, and where they need to be. To arrive at wakefulness you become the observer.

Realize now that the "loving one another" principle requires that we begin with loving and protecting ourselves. Setting up boundaries is vital to our protection. Once we are in our comfortable boundaries, all the rest becomes a natural outpouring of that love. Through embracing all of our capacities, we understand that we do have the strength and ability to build our boundaries, to swing our sword of truth, and to protect ourselves and those we love. Those who idly watch evil being imposed upon another are part of the abusive circle themselves. Wake Up and Stand Up against abuse…even those abuses imposed directly upon yourself. You do matter. You are worthy. To Wake Up and Stand Up is on a small scale in just *your* world at first, then in the world at large. You see, once we hold firmly to our own piece and find ourselves, we begin to experience inner peace. In short order, we realize we no longer need hold firmly, for we will understand the path to Living Free. As we all begin to hold our own piece, and find ourselves, there will be more peace in the World. We can save the world by having the courage to wake up to the true reality of our circumstances, rather than continuing to eat the porridge, blindly believing that which we are "fed."

As we become comfortable with what we will accept as a person, we join with others to determine our boundaries as a family, community, society, or world. If you can't say no, or you are tired from dancing to the beat of everyone else's drum, you do not have good boundaries. Boundaries that are too rigid keep us striving to control not only ourselves, but those around us. This can be isolating. Others may find it difficult to operate within our narrow limitations. As we begin to back up and examine our boundaries, the first thing that we must determine is if our boundaries are being set by ourselves, or by forces outside of ourselves. The key is to operate from within our own belief system. If our boundaries are in alignment with our belief system, we will be at peace knowing that no one can move them except us.

We should express our needs and desires, and then it is up to the other person to change or not. It serves us to decide that we are powerless in getting others to change, and instead realize that once we place our desires and needs out into the Universe, we simply observe the other person's response to our disclosure or desire. As the observer rather than the controller, we see who people really are, and then observe whether or not we feel they are in alignment, whether or not they act from a place of love, from their light. Then, if we don't like what we see, we can move on. We can act when we feel our boundaries are violated, we do not have to wait until the pain is unbearable. It is easier to cut the string then to break the chain.

For now, just begin to be aware of when you are feeling violated, and start to consider that you are allowing this violation and you do not have to. You can live free. Any perception of a marionette string or chains controlling you is just that—a perception. You have the power and ability to cut all strings that bind your life.

Boundaries are vital. Back Up, Wake up, Stand Up, Live Free!

We believe that we are invulnerable. We often believe we don't need any help; we can tackle it all on our own. We believe we can not only hold our piece of the jigsaw puzzle, we perceive we can hold everyone else's also. Actually, at the most important levels, I was not even carrying my own piece, no one was. I carried others' pieces out of what I thought was love; however, they were manipulating me, using my fear of shame and guilt; I simply wouldn't see. It was always my choice. There was always that little voice in my head telling me to stop. It just seemed so impossible, impossible to let go. Carrying their pieces is all I knew. I thought it was my responsibility.

**Control less, observe more, focus on you,
and be surrounded by only love.**

It was letting go of those pieces, releasing the pieces of the men in my life that I held onto so tightly, that was absolutely necessary to wake up. A key step to waking up is releasing. I began letting go of the pieces while in my final abusive relationships. Once I let go of their pieces, I really began to see the true colors of my abusers. Colors that were obstructed from view, as long as I saw myself as the person who had to keep them safe, keep their affairs in order; assure that they never got hurt; hold tightly to their pieces. While I was carrying their pieces I was too tired and distracted to see the need to carry my own. Once I let go of their pieces, my path to freedom became visible.

So, to step closer to freedom you must wake up. To wake up, I recommend you let go of everyone else's piece to the extent that you can, remain safe, and start focusing on you. This sounds so simple but it is not. At first you will likely feel much like you may have felt when you first saw your child fall. You will want to run to their rescue, feeling an obligation as if it is your responsibility to save them.

If their intentions have been disingenuous, any contrary illusion has been by their design, and you were willing to take the role. You need to release it. Release their piece. Know that when you do, just as they have each time their manipulations fail to work, you may see them escalate. They may appear to need you more than ever. Remember, it is not about love, it is about chess.

Holding someone's piece means that you are letting yourself be responsible and accountable for the things that they should be caring for themselves. You do this, in most cases, because you don't want them to fall. You may fear the guilt and shame associated with their falling. Further though, you may perceive that their falling will hurt you in some way. You may need to be okay with that.

For example, my obsessive devotion to the boundary that dictated that no bill was ever late, that nothing could harm my credit, was part of the compulsion that kept me carrying their piece. I never wanted an indication anywhere that I was irresponsible. The most irresponsible thing I did was letting that fear, the fear that something bad would happen, be a trump card that people could leverage to my destruction.

Let go of your desire to control outcomes. We can only control our actions and thoughts, which will lead to outcomes. When we focus on simply doing what is right from moment to moment, and stop dwelling on the outcomes, we will be in essence eliminating all trump cards. If you are acting from a "right" place, the outcomes will take care of themselves. To exemplify, my daughter and I both love to cook. I nearly always use a recipe. My daughter on the other hand, never follows a recipe. When I ask her how she knows how the meal will turn out without a recipe she tells me, "I know if I am cooking with good, fresh ingredients, I can do almost anything with them and it will be delicious." This is the same concept. If you act from a place of goodness and integrity as defined by your belief system, then you are using only the best, freshest ingredients. You are bound to have a good outcome. While I have reasonably mastered this concept in life, apparently I still need my daughter's push to embrace this truth in the kitchen!

You see, while asleep, we care about what people think, how things appear. We generally want to have good credit and pay our bills, take exquisite care of our belongings, anything reflecting how we are perceived in the world. We make everything a priority except ourselves. When I began to wake up I realized that I might now need to compromise some of those things that seemed important before. I needed to decide they were not of paramount importance so that I could get to the greater outcome, safety for myself and my family. I needed to release my exhausting need to control the outcome and maintain appearances, in order to begin living in alignment. I had to stop allowing others to violate the belief system I claimed to have. I claimed to value independence and self sufficiency, but I was enabling their parasitism. My belief that I needed to protect my image, and my credit, was being used to my detriment, and was causing me to violate other more valued beliefs. Remember, all of my beliefs about financial scarcity came out of fear that I would have to go on welfare. This belief, this boundary, was not my own. Our beliefs and boundaries should not be rooted in fear.

To release the power of my trump cards I had to be okay with no longer trying to control what happened financially. Previously, if they didn't pay the debt they had racked up in my name or a bill that was in my name, I always felt I had to run to the rescue and pay it to protect my credit. As I was waking, I was backing away from this belief, and anything I was manipulated into paying due to that threat, I simply stopped paying. I no longer worried if I had a blemish on my credit, thus taking away their ability to manipulate me to act. There were multiple entanglements, not just one person or circumstance, and I was waking to all of it simultaneously. Interestingly, when I backed away, taking care of these things on their own became a priority to them. They feared my playing the *game-over* card. They never want the "game" of the relationship to end, especially ***not*** on ***someone else's*** terms. They knew the dangers of harming me in my most critical area, financially, so they did what they had to do to keep the game in play. You see, in releasing my control, I actually obtained better outcomes.

You may have to move some boundaries that you are comfortable with today. You have to begin to release your desire to control and your fear of shame. These boundaries, or perceived rules, that you have, may be harming you. To live free you need to remember that you decide where the banks of the river are placed, and as a result where the flow will lead. I encourage you to release all the laws of society, your family, or your work. Start to live by your own moral law, what is right for you on a higher plane. Let yourself advance to a higher ground where decisions are about the greatest good. Your greatest good, the greatest good, cannot come from being manipulated or harmed. To me the greatest good always has a foundation of love; and that love includes a love of yourself.

**Control less, observe more, focus on you,
and be surrounded by only love.**

Remember, an abuser is an excellent observer. He or she is watching how we treat ourselves and is learning how to best manipulate us. They assess what the rules are that you live by. The rules you have adopted as your creed that you would never, ever, break. And that is how they play you. This is why it is so important that our boundaries are placed in such a way, that they protect the one thing we never seem to worry about protecting—ourselves.

I am hoping that you are beginning to consider that the reason you were able to be controlled is in part because you wanted to control the outcome in many cases. In essence then, it was your desire to control the outcome that lead to your suffering. By analyzing yourself in all the areas we discussed, you can begin to learn who you really are, and observe in a similar fashion who they are.

In the past, and perhaps presently, you didn't want them to die, fail, or be hurt, so you acted to control the outcome. You wanted to keep the peace, for no one to be harmed. You wanted to be seen as good and not mean. Your actions were your decision, and may have been designed to keep *them* safe, but if you look back you will see your actions or inactions to protect them were **harming you**. This is true on the small scale of life and the grand scale as well. We want to believe, respect, and protect those we deem as our authority, or that we deem we have a responsibility to serve, even to our own hindrance.

As you begin to focus on caring for yourself, you also choose to become more of the observer of the people and circumstances of your situation, and less of the controller. When you are observing, more than rescuing and thereby controlling, you begin to see patterns.

Realize too that guilt may have been your driver, whether self-induced or manipulated, it draws the same outcome; your sacrifice and pain. Guilt is what we experience when we feel we are misaligned with the "rules" or what is "expected" of us. Evaluating who you really are redefines all those beliefs that have held you in such pain.

Allow others to operate within their own boundaries. Do not try to change the banks of another's river. As you attune to who you are, and reset your banks, you are on the pathway to awakening and enjoying the peaceful flow of the river. Others may tell you where the banks of their river lie, but examine their flow, their actions. You will be able to tell if their words are true. As you decide their words are meaningless and look only at their actions for the truth, you are quickly approaching awakening. Their words will act only as the yard stick against which you measure their actions to detect incongruence.

Observe the responses and behaviors of the people around you and decide if they are who you want in your life, rather than deciding if you can change who they are, so that they can become who you want in your life. Take care of yourself, make yourself a priority.

Only allow loving treatment of yourself; embrace this thought:

Control less, observe more, focus on you,
and be surrounded by only love.

As the observer, rather than the controller, you are able to more readily see who someone really is, not who you imagine them to be, or who they tell you they are. From the position of observer it is like you are gathering information in a barrel. Think of it like rain. Each drop of rain that drops in the barrel accumulates with the rain already in the barrel. Eventually, the rain will overflow the barrel, and you will be Awake. You are waking as you are observing, listening, learning, and caring for yourself, more than caring for them. All information is leading you to awareness. That moment in time when you are fully awake, you are on a new platform from which you are likely to never fall.

Arming the Abuser

As you know, the trump card that had power over me was that I didn't want anything bad to happen. This was true in all areas, but especially financially. My fear of welfare, of failure and shame, drove my every move.

Shame. If something bad happened, I would feel it was my fault and I would feel shame. The shame was what controlled me.

In order to manipulate me, my abuser never even needed to explicitly threaten me with shame, although at times they certainly did. They knew if they presented me with a situation, I could get to the potential for shame all by myself. If they said, "The IRS is demanding that I pay, and I don't have the money," I would immediately decide that they would go to jail, lose everything, or the IRS would come after my money. All of this would happen unless I stopped it. So I did. Every time.

As I said, the abuser is a good observer. They knew I was a "good girl" in this regard, and they played on that truth to make me act.

Somewhere on my journey of life I recall being introduced to the concept that there are three "yous." The "you" you want people to believe you are, the "you" you fear you are, and the "you" you really are. I challenge you to reveal the "you" you really are, above all else, to yourself. In assessing your belief system and accepting your "flaws," you are well on your way to finding comfort in who *you* really are, and there will be fewer weapons to be used against you. Right now you may have misplaced inhibitions or rules which are harming you.

Bottom line: Your inhibitions create opportunities for you to be exploited.

In essence, it is our own inhibitions that make us susceptible for dreadful pain from those who wish to harm us.

I am not saying we shouldn't have inhibitions. What I am saying is we just may need to take a look at the ones we are carrying around and decide if they are valid. By valid I mean, how did we draw those conclusions and are they really true?

We instill rules, inhibitions, forbidden actions, on our lives. We set the confines of our behavior. We build the banks of our river. There are so many ways to articulate this, but the important thing to take away is that *we* set up our own boundaries. We create these rules that we believe we must adhere to in order to be good. Each of us decides individually what these things are; what we are prohibited or forbidden from doing. The important thing to realize though is that we created this rule or we allowed someone to create it for us. Armed with this rule we make a mental note to live by:

If we do these things—we are good.

If we do those—we are bad.

The truth is our morality is defined by us. Our morality is defined only by us. We decide what is appropriate and inappropriate. And frankly, if we are honest, our view of those things may be constantly changing as we learn and grow. If we are willing, new perspectives come all the time.

We are so busy building boundaries to restrict our own behavior, or deny the flow of our river, that we forget what we should really be using boundaries for: to protect ourselves. Boundaries, when executed properly, are first and foremost about ensuring that we are not violated, not by any outside force, and certainly not by ourselves.

We have these inhibitions—things we are forbidden from doing. Then we apply restraint, generally as a harsh judgmental parent, disciplining ourselves to stay within these behaviors as we define them, or perceive they are defined.

Your abuser watches what your inhibitions are. They see where you exercise tremendous restraint and those are the areas they criticize you most harshly. They learned this from you.

To gain some insight into my inhibitions, allow me to share the following perceptions I had:

- ❖ To me a "good girl":
  - o Makes the man happy;
  - o Is not promiscuous;
  - o Does not drink too much;
  - o Is not fat;
  - o Is kind to others; and,
  - o Never lies.

Who created this for me? I don't know; society, books, parents, school. It doesn't matter. We have the rules that we have. We have boundaries we cannot cross, for if we did, something bad would happen and it would be shameful.

To define your own list, look at the behaviors or attributes that bring you shame. Your boundaries lie where your judgment of yourself begins. What are the boundaries that you hold yourself to?

Each of these concepts can be broken down or defined as specifically as you choose. Each of us has our own unique list. However, even if your list looked identical to mine, the meaning behind your rules are unique to you.

I already shared with you many of my beliefs but let us look a little more closely:

- ❖ Makes a man happy, which means:
    - o Does not betray them;
    - o Does not shame them;
    - o Honors and protects them; and,
    - o Changes her behavior to satisfy their wants and needs.
- ❖ Is not promiscuous, which means:
    - o Wears appropriate clothing;
    - o Does not cheat on their partner;
    - o Does not flirt; and,
    - o Does not have casual sex.
- ❖ Is not a drunk, which means:
    - o Never has more than two drinks;
    - o Never loses control;
    - o Remains well spoken; and,
    - o Does NOT get silly or playful.
- ❖ Is not fat, which means:
    - o Should not gain any weight from her high school weight;
    - o Should not indulge in desserts;
    - o Eats very little; and,
    - o Should exercise.

What is important to realize here, is the list of beliefs I wrote about good girls, I actually still broadly believe. What was wrong with my list was the impossible guidelines I placed around them. I made the path so narrow, that one wrong move would make me plummet into the depths of despair, guilt, and shame.

If two drinks was my limit and I had three, I would have so much burden of guilt that it was killing me. This guilt kept me from being free. My rules kept me from being free. When I would tell someone, when I would confess my sins if you will, relative to any of my "bad" behaviors, people who knew me and loved me didn't get it. "What are you so hard on yourself for, Diana?" It didn't make any sense to them. That is because my definition of bad was distorted. I knew why I felt so bad. It was because I broke **my** rule.

Our struggle is our desire to do the noble thing, but until we can embrace all of ourselves and discover who we really are, we often feel in absolute conflict with ourselves—we battle with shame. This conflict we experience is based only on our internal rules, which are driven by our beliefs and our inability to embrace all of our capacities, including the necessary capacity to wield our sword. I needed to engage in a battle to protect the highest moral good; and in doing so, I needed to realize I was going to break my own rigid rules that in reality had harmed me long enough. When my abuser would tell me I should feel guilt or shame about something, some way I had broken my own rule, I would believe them. If I was told I was dressing inappropriately, I felt guilty no matter what I was actually wearing. I got so used to feeling the shame, that I would feel it without any accusation. It is almost like we draw the unconscious conclusion that if we are going to feel bad about ourselves, we might as well do something that will justify our badness! For me I would engage in behavior, like having three drinks where I knew I "should" feel shame for, simply so I would be able to justify my shame!

In the throes of my guilt and shame, I would share my feelings of guilt with my abuser. This is how they learned my rules, the code I lived by. They used my rules as ammunition against me. To wake up you must stop sharing your vulnerabilities with your abuser. You must stop loading their gun of destruction. Once they know what is important to you, once they know who you are and who you are not, they work to label you as those things you strive to avoid. They provide evidence, real or conjured, for this "truth." Their goal is to trap you in shame, so they have power over you. Don't hand them your trump card. Only allow yourself to be vulnerable to those who offer you love and acceptance, not those who will use your trust as a weapon. Save your intimacies for those who deserve your heart. In the hands of the abuser, your inner most "truths" will be used as artillery to their benefit, and the pain of their rapid fire is unbearable. It is not that you should avoid sharing your intimate feelings for the sole purpose of avoiding them being used against you, it is that those who *would* use them against you are not worth the energy of telling these details of your vulnerabilities. You must construct healthy boundaries. The more you are clear on who you really are, the more you will know where to place them. As you uphold your boundaries for your protection, and you experience the abuse in your life diminishing, you will begin to trust yourself again. As you begin to trust yourself, you can stay in the chess game without uncontrollable emotions, and win—which means escaping and Living Free. You simply need to trust yourself again.

Do you have the courage to trust yourself?

I am now able to share the fullness of my vulnerabilities. I am safe to live by a code of full transparency. This is not because I trust every person who may know what my vulnerabilities are, but because I trust myself. I feel no shame for my life, and therefore there is no gun to load, no secret to fear being revealed. I am free. I have reached a point where even my most intimate flaws cannot be used against me. This is true because in healing my wounds I have found my wholeness. In addition, my boundaries do not allow people who would use the vulnerabilities I trusted them with as a weapon to remain in my life. When you reach a state without wounds you will no longer feel defensive at accusations. If you feel defensive, that is your signal to name the emotion and look inside to find your wound.

I remember when I taught my perception training I would say, "If I was always skinny and never felt that I was an ounce overweight, and you called me fat, I wouldn't bother defending myself and assuring you that I exercise and eat right. No. I would just think you were crazy for thinking I was fat."

214

So when you are defensive and feel the need to worthlessly defend yourself; stop. All that has happened is someone has poked your wound. Someone has found your perceived weakness. Someone has reminded you that you may not be living up to your own standards.

As I was learning to be free, in response to those accusations, rather than defend I adopted some one-liners to place the boundaries. Perhaps these thoughts will assist you as you devise your plan to keep yourself safe.

As you consider utilizing one-liners, don't leave the words open as if you are waiting for their pending brutal response. I have observed that I would answer with a subtle pause, waiting for the attack. That pause allowed the situation to escalate. That pause is the invitation to engage in an abusive encounter. The pause seems to say, *Is this response acceptable or do you need more information? Are you going to attack me, question me or accept this?* That pause plays right into their hand. In that pause, they hear your doubt. It was as if I had painted a big red bull's-eye on myself as I stood their shouting, "Don't shoot!" In using one-liners or responding to questions, you must state things with conviction and not doubt. Be clear that you believe yourself. Using these one-liners I was beginning to stop wasting my time defending myself. Eventually I was able to see that the accusations being hurled at me tended to more accurately describe my abuser.

The more matter-of-fact you are, the more you don't pause expecting a negative outcome, the less questions you will likely get. When questioned in any accusatory fashion, respond succinctly and move on to another topic.

For example, if I was asked, "Why are you late?":

> I would respond, "I stopped at the store. What would you like for dinner?"

Do not offer an elaborate explanation of every stop light, every turn, everything that made you late. Don't defend yourself or try to prove you were not doing anything wrong. Don't apologize. Just speak your truth, and whenever possible respond with a one-liner. No pause.

If you are accused of cheating:

"I am trustworthy. What are we doing tonight?"

No matter how many accusations would fly; I would just repeat those words. "I am trustworthy," in a calm and repetitive way.

Start placing boundaries.

If I was called names I would simply say:

"It is not okay to talk to me that way."

"It's sad you feel that way."

"That hurt."

"That was cruel."

With the proper tonality, these responses do not engage the abusive play. As I was waking, I was learning how to avoid engaging. When people say cruel words, do not take them personally, do not engage, do not be afraid to stand up if necessary and stay safe.

Use your judgment, you know your abuser. If you think this disengagement will provoke a physical attack and threaten your safety, **don't do it.** Remember disengagement can lead to escalation on the part of the abuser. Perhaps the safest thing for you to do is to simply sneak away. That is a call that only you can make.

Make it clear that you will not stay engaged in any discussion or relationship that is abusive. If you state you will leave, hang up, or leave the relationship, you actually have to do it. Otherwise *your* words are meaningless, just as theirs have likely become. Anyone can speak words. **It is your actions or inactions that tell the truth about where your limitations are.**

If you choose to begin to stand your ground, decide that there is no explaining necessary.

I learned that if I answered the question precisely and with as few words as possible, there were fewer attacks.

Remember, your pleas of innocence will never convince them, just as they never have in the past, so why waste your energy? Abuse victims are used to being questioned to the nth degree. I remember constantly fearing the consequences if I had allowed too much time to elapse between "check-ins." It was demanded that I call at frequent intervals throughout my work day. If I had back-to-back meetings and no time to call, an intense battle would ensue. Accusations of my infidelity would be hurled at me. He would stalk my every move. I was constantly defending myself. It was exhausting. If I were to go out to dinner or to socialize, I would be bombarded with phone calls throughout the entire experience. Once such time after dining with my daughter, we emerged from the restaurant to see his unmistakable truck, which quickly sped away upon catching our eye. His assertion that it *must* have been someone else, with the same vehicle and same distinguishing characteristics, was met with disbelief, even by me in my asleep state. These nonsensical discussions were a constant presence in my life. Once I adopted the one-liners, things became easier and this insanity diminished.

Note also that a long explanation can also be the voice of a liar, trying to convince you; sometimes less, truly is more.

We tell the whole truth believing we need to convince them of it to keep ourselves safe, however, they see in us only their own deception glaring back at them. Liberation begins when we stop taking responsibility for how they see us, and focus on who we are instead.

As an example, if you and I are standing outside and I say to you, "It is not raining outside," would you expend a lot of energy convincing me I am wrong? Probably not. You might simply say, "Yes, it is. I'm getting wet, I am going inside."

If I want to stand out in the rain denying it is raining, so be it. If that person wants to go on a tirade about how it is not raining outside while they are drenched, we will just think they are crazy. Speaking something with conviction doesn't make it so; it is just intended to convince others it is so.

Often we are trying to convince people of things we do not believe ourselves. Sometimes we have been abused for so long that we doubt our own convictions, since we have never been believed by our abusers. We want to be believed and trusted, because we *are* trustworthy. However, we are communicating with someone who isn't. It is *them* that they see, not *us*.

Stop acting like a small child who is going to get in trouble. You are stronger than you realize. To reflect that the principles you are learning here apply in other areas of your life, consider that this is true in your work environment as well. When you free yourself from the rules and live by a moral law, when you realize that your security is you, and not your job or anyone else, you will not allow anyone to have power over you, even in the workplace.

On the threshold of waking, one by one the realizations of your reality sink in, and it can be overwhelming. When waking up to work abuses, I remember the first time I stood up to my boss. I remember the fear experienced when you first begin to set strong boundaries and stand up to uphold them. I recall vividly, typing my one or two sentence email telling my boss I thought he should cancel his scheduled flight to see me because it wasn't good timing. *I* was telling *him* he should change his plans because it was inconvenient for *me*. I remember shaking as I typed and thinking there would be a terrible repercussion; something terrible would happen. Contrary to my fears, as I stood up, I was honored. He didn't come on that trip. It was never even an issue.

The liberation when you become your own authority is exhilarating. Cutting the perceived strings that bind you to the control of others is the best thing you can do for yourself. Live by your rules, and trust that you create your own security. If they don't like how you play, they may ask you to leave, giving you the opportunity to live in alignment with your values. Or better yet, you can just pack your bags and leave. In personal relationships, this is a

218

little harder. Remember, although my focus is waking up in intimate relationships, being free is a broad scope of all the areas of your life.

Know that you can never control what people will believe. Choose to only surround yourself with people who see you as you are and accept you that way. You do not need to get anyone to see the truth about you; except you. You will learn that your abusers presented you with the best opportunity to see all of you, if only you were ready to see it.

To me; I was invisible. This made me invisible to others. I never chose to truly take care of myself; spiritually, financially, emotionally, physically, or mentally.

I left myself out, and the Universe, in its wisdom, had been trying for years to shake me awake. Eventually, I had no choice but to begin to look inward for my peace.

Eventually, I accepted this code that had always been hidden from me:

- ❖ **Always honor yourself.**
- ❖ **Honor others as long as honoring others doesn't cause you to dishonor yourself.**
- ❖ **If someone is asking you to dishonor yourself for them, that is not okay. Say no.**

Waking up is a process. For me, I realized that I may need to end my last abusive relationship before my true moment of awakening. You may have a similar experience. As I became more aware of my reality in small doses, I gained strength, and it was that strength that enabled me to cast my net of awareness further and further.

Even when I knew I had to get out of the abusive world I created for myself, I was still asleep. I believed that there was love. I still had hope my abuser would change, and all would be as promised. Even though I believed this could happen, I knew I couldn't wait. I could no longer bear the pain. Once you are awake it will instantly become clear to you, that it wasn't love, it isn't love. In fact, it was never love. We were told it was love and chose to believe. Today, just accept where you are.

You are still asleep if you want to trust them, if you still believe they can change, if you still want to believe they will become or are becoming what you long for them to be, the loving soul they told you they were; the partner in the cocoon. You are still asleep if you are unwilling to place your boundaries in a manner that protects yourself. A truly loving and respectful partner would honor those boundaries.

I hope I have already emphasized that one of the most critical factors is that your abuser does not want a game-over card. The one thing they fear is the word, "Goodbye." "Goodbye" is the game-over card, the indication they have lost. They fear losing. If you show your game-over card you are very likely in danger. What level of danger is determined by the depth of the violent behavior of your attacker; something I simply cannot know. Nor can I know your best exit strategy or what particular thing will be the precise catalyst to wake you. What I do know, is that as you back up and raise your awareness of the truth of who you are deep within yourself, you will awaken. Design a plan for your freedom, and know that the more awake you become, the more you will be able to see and utilize the tools, organizations, and people around you that are waiting to help you be free.

You must begin to take exquisite care of yourself. If you use alcohol or drugs—stop, or at least diminish your intake, you need your full wits about you. Numbing yourself is the strategy you may have chosen to keep from waking up. This is because at some unconscious level you dreaded waking. You fear waking because you recognize that it may be a long road of work ahead of you. You may be right, but it is worth it. This is why caring for yourself is so very important. Realize what you have endured already was the hardest part. Do not numb your intuition, your feelings, or your mind. You will need all of these things now.

In the process of waking, when you are separating yourself and changing some of your patterns, they sense the change and may jump into their best behavior. In this phase when you are distancing, they may seem kinder, more tender, and much more attentive. They may start wanting to go on dates and begin engaging in dreams of the future. They feel your distance and want to reset the hook. They are confused, and they are now observing how this new game is being played, so they can re-calculate how to win.

You and your partner have been engaging in stimulus response patterns for some time. Each of you knows precisely how play to the weak side of the other to get a reaction. Your abuser has mastered this game. Now though, you seem to be playing differently. You are instilling some boundaries. You are having new reactions. They are not sure how to play in this new game. They know though, if they want to continue to play, they need to learn, or at least seek, how the game is now being played. They want to lure you back in so they can learn.

In my case, a vacation to see my parents was planned. What better way to rekindle our love than a vacation…or in sociopathic terms, what better way to learn the right cards to play to keep the game moving. Although I was separating, constructing my boundaries, and beginning to take care of myself, I still was willing to trust him with my intimacies, which still allowed me to be manipulated with shame. I was still asleep. I didn't know I was dealing with a sociopath, or even that such a thing existed, and I certainly didn't realize the level of my danger. All I knew was, I wanted my relationship to be loving and I wanted to help it become that.

My decision to back away or separate enmeshments was made before I knew I needed to leave. I felt it was a way for me to gain artificial autonomy while staying in the relationship. However, the act of doing so was making me more aware, stronger, and less vulnerable. I was backing up. I was more cognizant of the manipulations. I became clearer on how I needed and deserved to be treated…but still I carried hope. The one emotion they want to keep instilling in us is hope. That is the purpose of their empty promises.

When you are dealing with a sociopath they are often quite subtle. All their abuse is behind closed doors where no one can see. There are so many examples of this. Those of you who lived it, or are living it now, know what I mean. They will present love to you for all your friends to see, and as they lean in to hug you they will whisper words of hate in your ear. They want to keep up appearances. They want to make you think you are crazy. The mind games are intended to lead you to believe you are off balance, unclear, or confused. They love making you think you are unstable. For years men tried to convince me I was imagining their hatred, their cruelty, and given that they never allowed others to witness their cruelty, it was hard not to question myself.

When you are with them behind closed doors you are defenseless at many levels. You know enough to not let your fear show. You never want them to discover you are unarmed, but you see they have known all along—that is why they chose you. You qualified as a target. You act invincible, you ignore your pain. You cannot be free, until you first acknowledge you are vulnerable. From our place of vulnerability, our truth is revealed and all healing begins. The series of events that catapulted me into my awake state began to unfold on this vacation to visit my parents.

Again, I had misbehaved, contacted someone deemed inappropriate by my abuser's intense guidelines. I had placed a toe outside of the suffocating, restrictive rules that had been set for my behavior, and now I was being punished. I was being called names, as was customary, only this time I stood up more boldly. I had an advantage; I was in my parent's home. With the home field advantage I unconsciously felt safer. I was in my family surroundings. This abuse was not as extreme as what I had become accustomed to, of course, now I understand that when the relationship is nearing game over, the abuser is on his best behavior to lure you back in.

This was the first time I had witnesses, and those witnesses were people who loved me. Things escalated, my family intervened. Once they entered the room, unconsciously I knew in that moment, I wouldn't die. While I was in their home and they were there, I would be safe. I felt safe enough to reveal all my fear which I had always had to hide to stay safe. I don't mean my fear just with this man, I mean a lifetime of fear that I could never show, even as far back as being a child. It was cumulative and huge. It was immeasurable and indescribable. Remember, I discussed the evolution of fear. Feeling the depth of our fear is a sign we are ready to wake up. I was ready. It was in this moment I released my illusion of invulnerability, and moved to reality, I was vulnerable. My parents were there to protect me, the still frightened little girl, but I was growing stronger by the minute.

I was trembling; literally shaking. I could not control my physical body. For the first time in my relationship with him or any man, I felt fear. True fear. This reaction of fear was a response to an accumulation of a lifetime of torment under which I could show no fear...I was absolutely terrified. I realized I *was* defenseless, and I acknowledged for the first time that I believed my abuser was capable of killing me.

I would feel more terror as I woke up. As I have said, this is why we choose to sleep—to avoid the reality of our fear and pain. It is seemingly easier to stay asleep than wake up and feel the reality of our life.

That fear in me was becoming more real...shocking even me. I felt the tension building inside of me, like all the pain that had been hidden all those years was bubbling to the surface. The terror I was feeling did not seem commensurate with the circumstance. It appeared that we were just having an argument. My reaction was much bigger than what was happening in that precise moment. However, given my life, it was in fact an appropriate reaction. I was waking up.

That night I finally had the courage to let go of this man. I told him to leave and that I did not want him back in my life. I knew I meant it, however until you are completely Awake, you will still vacillate. When you begin to feel that fear and find your strength, you are almost there.

The road at this phase becomes scary, but on the other side is freedom.

Although scared, you begin to see things as they really are without making excuses. This leads to being fully Awake. However, I was still in the groggy stage of waking at this point, the stage during which I was beginning to see pieces of the truth, but I was not yet fully in my power. You stand up, but you are still not awake to fully see. This is why I emphasize that to be free you must fully Wake Up. Once you do, you **Stand Up** on a whole new platform.

Immediately, I discovered that in spite of his agreement to let me fly home first to get to the home safely, he had boarded a plane ahead of me. He had forgotten his ID at my parents' home, but as a testimony to his powers of manipulation, he was able to board the airplane without an ID. He had managed to manipulate security. I would have been impressed if I wasn't so frightened.

I remember being terrified of what might await me at my home. While driving home from the airport I was so afraid that I called the police. I was compelled to act by remembering the concept that it was my job to protect the child, which was me. Trembling I gave them a little detail of the circumstances and asked if I could get an escort home. They asked me, "Has this man ever physically harmed you?" I immediately saw flashes of all the harm, and then felt my accompanying fear of his abuse being discovered. I stammered, "…Uh no, I am just afraid he might." I met an officer and he followed me home. At my request, he came in the home and waited as I walked in each room. The home was indeed empty, but I knew my abuser or someone had been there. All the guns were missing, except one. I walked into the kitchen and actually said to the officer, "Well, it is kind of strange that several guns are missing, but, um, I am sure it is no big deal." The officer left. Once again, no police report. I was terrified. I knew those weapons were taken so I *would* be terrified. I felt utterly trapped and alone.

Later, as I listened to various recordings of 911 calls made by my abuser, I understood that leaving one gun behind was a strategy. There needed to be a weapon supplied, to assure that a claim of my being an undiagnosed bipolar with a concealed weapons license, could be leveraged to get multiple cops to my home at will. Intimidation and fear will always be a constant methodology of those that wish to control.

Although you may feel that you are stuck and there is no way out, I want you to consider that your belief is false. Believe that when you decide, truly decide, that you deserve to be free, the Universe will begin to create perfect synchronicities on your path to freedom. You have always had the power to take care of yourself, now you simply must decide it is time.

No one has the right to control where you go, what you do, who you see, or the right to instill fear, or hurl painful and unfounded accusations. Those are boundaries that need to be set. Until this moment you may have chosen to tolerate it, but I hope you now see we all have choices. We all have the ability to Wake Up, Stand Up, and Live Free.

We are in love with the dream they promise us, not them.

We wanted them to see our innocence; which was all we were. We experienced their darkness but refused to acknowledge it. Our longing for wholeness, the wholeness we always had, but refused to embrace, is what enabled us to be under their spell. Continue to ask yourself, would you inflict the abuse that you are tolerating on another? Start to realize you must find your power. You must decide to no longer incessantly defend yourself to no avail. Instead, you must protect yourself with the degree of vengeance necessary for your safety. You must find your shadow self which has been imploring you to embrace the power it grants you.

Typically, leaving your abuser may best be handled as a gradual process. They have a hold on you and the best way to break that hold, is by backing up first, readying yourself to release them. Trust yourself. You will know what to do if you start to believe in yourself, and listen to what your intuition guides you to do. To get out you need to start setting up boundaries. As I said, start by separating yourself from your abuser in as many tangible ways as you can; begin to draw a clear dividing line between yourself and your abuser. Akin to not being able to see the forest for the trees, you must Back Up so that you can adequately see the truth. Use this same strategy if you are leaving your job, your church, whatever is mistreating or controlling you. You have to pull the hooks from yourself to be free. You want to move slowly because if you just pull the hooks out in one move, as I said, you may fear you will bleed to death. Those abusers are in us. They are part of us, they made it that way. They completely isolated us in an attempt to become our whole world. This was by design. Now that you have alienated, or should I say *they* have, everyone who was close to you, you really believe that they are your whole world. It is hard for you to see that there is a great big beautiful world that is available to you once you can get free.

225

Once awake you can freely release those hooks. However when you are asleep, even if you leave, either their hooks will still be in you enough allowing them to manipulate you from a far, or the pain from the sudden withdraw will have you wanting those hooks back, so you can stop the rush of blood that feels like it is exiting your body. Like an addiction; they will still have a hold on you. Leaving is right. The more you awaken the easier it will get. Just start with the separation of the places you are adjoined.

Until now, it is as if you are both sharing one life force. You have been working now to develop your own belief system, your own self-esteem, your own boundaries. This in essence ensures that you will recognize that you have your own identity, your own life force. In spite of how it may feel, removing the life force of your abuser will not kill you. You will be alive. You will be whole. You will be free.

You have to cut those strings one at time. You do this by first deciding that these circumstances do not have full power over you, even if you feel they do. Once you realize that this thing outside of yourself does not have to possess a hold over you, you begin to experience freedom. No one holds your lifeline except you. Look for what the trump cards are that are keeping you in the game. What is the reason you believe this situation has a permanent hold on you? What are you afraid of?

I understand there may be a threat that lies before you; a sense that if you leave, you cannot afford to live, or you fear being alone, alone for possibly the first time in your life. As long as someone else, or something else, is holding the trump card, you will lose, you have been losing and you will continue to lose. You can never be winning if you are not free.

You are not helpless, you are not small and it is the illusion of your insignificance that has caused your torment. The sooner you realize this life is a reality of your own creation, a life that you are allowing, the sooner you can instead live in the hammock, swaying in the breeze, the sooner you can float down the river wherever the path will lead, or be the eye in any storm. The sooner you begin to be safe in your own life, the sooner you will know freedom, know peace. Acknowledge you are free, then start to cut the strings.

Wake Up and Stand Up, it is within you, start now. Some risks are scary, yet I tell you, nothing is worse than the life in constant abuse, fear, vigilance, control, and manipulation. To me, even death would not be worse. Seek assistance if you feel you are unsafe, the resources are available.

Leave behind your adapted self, and recognize that we are responsible for the banks of our river. We can decide where and how we want our river to flow. In other words, we can decide as adults what to say "yes" to and "no" to. This realization is incredibly empowering and leads to a happier, purposeful, and generally better life! We can put our banks up and control the flow of the river. There are no marionette strings controlling us. Once all the strings are cut, there is no one to blame. When you think of that marionette, you can be the puppet or the puppeteer; both roles however are ultimately unfulfilling. Whether we are the controlled or the controller we are not free. The controller can only act through another. When the controller can no longer control the people or the circumstances around them, they lose control. They have no identity or sense of purpose. Control is an illusion. Ideally, you learn you are the river, and you can ebb and flow wherever life takes you. We are free. Decide now to live this truth.

What if once we learn, *really learn*, that we are the creators of our own lives, we can freely let go of the confining boundaries we imagined, release our illusion of control, and realize that we have, in essence, *become* one with the river and can truly trust the flow of life? Once we have established the comfortable banks/boundaries that serve us, then all that remains is to allow ourselves to simply float down the river, while enjoying the scenery and serving the oneness that is all of us in total peace! We can enjoy our lives no matter what is happening on the outer banks; Living Free, Awake to any deceits that pretend to be true.

Moment of Awakening

The journey I have shared with you thus far is intended to give you guidance as you find your way to what seems like that elusive "Awake" place. As I share with you the precise moment that I *awakened*, you will see how I instinctively began to use the power within me to keep myself safe. This power, this free reign that I was now using, was always mine. I had mistakenly refused to acknowledge it. We repeatedly allow harm to be bestowed on us because we often feel as though protecting ourselves is wrong, as it might harm another. Once awake, we see the distinction. We realize we are not inflicting harm merely for harm's sake. We are instead, properly defending and protecting ourselves *from* harm.

Once awake, I may have been afraid at first, but ultimately I knew how to turn the tables in the right way for my situation because I chose to listen to myself, to trust myself, and to recognize and use the details of the abusers' patterns, that I had learned, as the observer. I was finally able to use my power as Queen. I finally learned it was okay to protect. It was necessary to defend with conviction. I finally acknowledged it is not mean, it is right.

Do not be threatened into submission by their intimidation tactics. Intimidation is a cheap parlor trick, the true power lies in awareness. Awaken your dormant power, by being courageous enough to see and utilize all your capacities.

Perhaps your abuse has not been as intense as what I have described. Perhaps my stories are mere child's play compared to what you are experiencing. I ask; why should you be abused at all? I have chosen to cut all marionette strings. I cut those strings so that I might Live Free, and I do. Wake Up, Stand Up, Live Free.

Once you take the power of their trump card away, the game is almost over, except for sweeping up the mess. This is easier said than done. Whether they live or die, go in debt, or lose relationships, is not up to you, it is up to them. Let them hold their own piece of the jigsaw puzzle.

Once you embrace your own capacity for evil, you can more clearly see their capacity for evil. Once you can see their evil intent, you can wield your sword. The more you embrace all of your capacities, the more you can see every one of theirs.

Do not forget the role we have played in our situation. We strive for control. We fear shame. We *allow* the trump card to work. We never want to feel as though we have harmed another, we always strive to do the "right" thing. We never want to be seen as mean, and our distortion of its meaning destroys us. It is our desire to control everything so it will be perfect and right that creates so much of our pain. We don't want to get in trouble, or let someone down; that is the leverage that is used against us. Our opponent instills in us the fear that we will look bad, get in trouble, or have some negative consequence and it moves us to action. We fear the shame, but do we not also feel shame when we violate our own belief system? You see shame is appropriate if we violate another, but shame can also be a learning tool to help us recognize who we want to be. Shame is not something we should own based on another's actions or inactions, only our own. We each only own our responsibility to act in non-shameful ways. Protecting ourselves is not shameful, and it certainly is not mean. It is necessary.

**Control less, observe more, focus on you,
and be surrounded by only love.**

Our desire to control, to make sense of things, contributes to the insanity of our situations. Abusers love it when we get "crazy" as they put it, when we are desperate from allowing ourselves to be under their control, or when we begin to doubt our own sanity. Often these abusers will even engage in what I call "Crazymaking." This is an extraordinarily painful experience. Those that have experienced this methodology will validate the agony it induces. This "Crazymaking" is exactly what it sounds like. The abuser will send contradictory messages, or claim that we do not remember events as they actually transpired. They work to get us to doubt ourselves, to think that perhaps we really are losing it. They want to break us.

For insight into how the crazymaking is played let me give a little detail.

Eventually, you tire of their manipulations and you begin to find your strength. They sense you pulling away. They fear that you are gaining the awareness that you hold the "game-over card" and that once it is played they will lose their reign as controller of your life. It is important that you recall, that when they sense a game-over card is near, the first approach is generally to present to you the behaviors they know you *want* to see. They know, because we have vocalized them in full detail. Suddenly that love, compassion, and acceptance we have been longing for, appears. They know that those things will lure us in, just as they have in the past.

One instance that illustrates what I am describing was in the moments leading to my full awakening. After returning from the vacation to my parents' house, I was on the phone with my then abuser who I was looking to end the relationship with. As established during that trip we were no longer living together, and of course he was looking to manipulate his way back into my home. Remember, this is always a ploy. They will try endless techniques to get in, or get you physically to be near them, which is often how people end up dead. I was not letting him in, a strength that illustrates just how close I was to fully waking. I was *finally* beginning to trust *myself* instead of *him*.

He had been working tirelessly to prove to me how he had changed. He was being the picture of the man that I had longed for. The behavior was impressive. However, as he sensed that I was still pulling away, he became harder to predict, and more confusing.

When he saw that his *act* was not being as effective as it had been in the past, he tried a new strategy. He moved to accountability. During a memorable phone call, he took ownership for his failings in the relationship. One by one he emotionally listed the ways that he had damaged our relationship. He listed the many ways he had harmed me and let me down. I was stunned as I listened. I was moved to tears at this admission of guilt, and his longing for redemption. I knew I had to leave him for good, yet so much of me wanted to believe, still, I was suspicious. Unconsciously though, the incongruence of his words and the behavior I had always known, was so apparent that I asked if he was alone, or if he was taping the call. I wanted to know whose benefit this ownership of his failings was for. Suspicion was part of the evidence that I was on the verge of waking.

In that instant, he switched. He now turned the tables.

He began to accuse me of all the failings in the relationship. He began to say that I abandoned him. Each and every accusation he owned just moments before was being calculatedly hurled at me. One by one, in painstaking detail, I was being diminished and destroyed. Suddenly, everything wrong with our relationship was my fault. He denied any claim he had made just moments before. I couldn't breathe. I dropped to my knees. I was in sheer agony over the head game. I screamed, "You betrayed me, you betrayed yourself! How could you? **Who are you???**" I was crying, screaming. I thought I must have been having a nervous breakdown. My scream was not one of anger. It was a scream of destruction; of uncontrollable pain. Just as it began to dawn on me that this insanity is what he had wanted all along, I hear him say, "Do you want me to come over and hold you?" I still couldn't breathe. I thought, *Oh my God! What? What did he just say? He is offering*

232

compassion? Comfort? What is he doing? The insanity stops me dead in my tracks. I went silent. I was in absolute confusion and pain. I am not sure how long I held my breath. I guess I hung up.

I was stunned and confused. I didn't understand his mixed signals. Which was it? Was he apologizing or blaming? My head was throbbing. The incongruence was taking its toll on my body. My head and heart were experiencing intolerable, excruciating pain. This pain left me on my knees unable to breathe for some time. Finally, I inhaled. I tasted the sweet breath of life. I then considered how that tape of our call would harm me. I was now confident there was one.

That encounter was "Crazymaking". This is what they do so that they can call you crazy and you will believe it. This is not you acting or being crazy. As a new friend that I met days after this experience would repeatedly remind me, "You were having a sane reaction to an insane situation."

This new friend, who I was provided with in perfect timing, helped carry me through my Standing Up process. He would constantly reassure me of my sanity. He told me that my abusers' incongruence was meant to drive me crazy. I am grateful for this friend, as he guided me to move from my emotions to my power. He guided me to Stand and indeed I did. Previously in the insanity of these types of crazymaking situations when I tried to stand before fully awake, it was not unusual for me to leave long, desperate voicemails and emails to those who were causing me harm, trying to get them to see the error of their ways. At times I would even reach out in my broken, tearful state to "authorities" whose help I thought I needed. I would outline all the insanities that had been inflicted on me by this other person and in doing so, I would sound crazy. People dismissed my claims allowing my abusers' plans to be executed successfully, perfectly by their design. The abusers claimed I was crazy and now I sounded like I was. Thankfully, this friend could see past my disorganized thinking, to the root of my problem. He helped me to see the logic through my heartache. He led me to truly Stand! We must Awaken before we can appropriately Stand.

After that grueling phone call, when I rose to my feet, I felt I was a totally changed woman; although I didn't know precisely why. I felt broken, but different. This crazymaking pushed me somewhere new.

However, I was still susceptible. As if to prove this reality, I answered my abusers' next call.

In this call, mere hours after the first, the usual empty promises were made. I was nervous but there was this new sense about me. I suddenly saw this man as a stranger, as nothing more than the predator he was, and always will be. I could see his promises for what they were. Empty. He spoke of his love and devotion, and as he made all his promises I interrupted him and said, "I am not going to talk to you anymore. I know you are taping these conversations." "No, I am not!" he exclaimed. I say effortlessly, almost instinctively, "Of course you are, just like you taped the other women in your life." He denied that as well, to which I replied, "Oh, but you have. I know because I have the tapes" and I hung up.

**In this single precise moment I Woke Up,
fully, unequivocally, and completely**.

I Woke Up! I felt the experience. I knew this was different. I knew **I** was different, and I liked it. I could, for the first time, see the monster I was dealing with, and what's more—I no longer loved him. Mere hours before, I was devastated when thinking of a life without him, and now I could not get him out of my life fast enough. You are Awake when you see the truth of who they are. You see their behavior as pathetic, deplorable, even disgusting. You are Awake when you can see them for the "bad," perhaps "evil" person they are.

I knew I was Awake because my own behavior was unrecognizable. What was so powerful about my accusation, what was so astonishing about my insistence of those tapes, was that I lied. I knew nothing of tapes. I lied because I was ready to protect myself. My shadow and I were ready. I was suddenly capable of playing chess. I was on the path to *truly* becoming invulnerable. I was in the game, and I now had no interest to serve or protect him. I was suddenly on my own team. All that pull, that sense of love, all of that was instantly gone. I had finally embraced my shadow. It is like we have our power waiting in the wings, longing for us to accept it, so we can come to our own rescue. That denied part of us; our shadow, was there all along, if only we were ready to embrace its power. I was ready. Our shadow longs for us to know it is not mean to use our power to protect ourselves, it is essential.

I must tell you though; the reality of that moment pushed me into Awake **fear**, remember our evolution of fear! I could see the truth about this man, the truth I never could see before. I felt no freedom when I first woke up. I felt trapped. I felt hunted, deceived, watched and vulnerable. Above all else, I felt threatened, yet I felt a new sense of power too.

Gavin DeBecker speaks about this in his book, *The Gift of Fear*. He states that "fear summons powerful predictive resources that tell us what might happen next. It is that which might come next that we fear—what might happen, not what is happening now."

Immediately as I hung up, I was conscious of my fear. In real fear, my "shadow self" kicked in. Without thinking I spoke those words about the tapes. I spoke them because I instinctively knew what I needed to do to protect myself. From that precise moment, I was now able to operate from a whole new level; I was forever changed. I was able to do what was necessary to protect myself, even if I had to lie to do it. I was Awake. I now was able to play chess, a game as it turns out, I am exceptionally good at.

Those of you who have been in abusive relationships know that if you hang up on your abuser, they call back relentlessly. I awaited the call, but the phone never rang. I took the fact that he didn't call back as clear confirmation that he was caught red handed. I felt certain that I was right, he was taping the call. I knew this because I know how he plays chess. I have been experiencing abusers' behaviors for years. I now knew that the rules of the game only changed, when I changed how I played it. The fact that he wasn't calling back was a confession, perhaps not evidentially, but I knew intuitively.

Awake, I trusted that I was right. So I picked up the phone again, not really thinking, just acting from some source within myself. My call went straight to his voicemail and I said, "Before I was assuming you were taping the calls, now I know you are. You really should be more careful who you trust." I hung up.

It wasn't the pleading voicemail I might have left in the past, begging that he communicate with me and not tape the calls, or imploring him to get help so we can make things work, as I had done so many times before. It was calculated. It was brief…and it was the beginning of my power.

Where did that idea come from? It was as if I knew he would believe I called someone in the silence, in the pause after I hung up, and I felt certain he would believe I confirmed that he was taping the call. It was as if I knew he would start to wonder who might have betrayed his trust, it was as if I knew he would start to doubt his players, he would start to lose stability, he would have uncertainty and I would have more power. I believe your inner knowing and your understanding of the reactions and patterns of your abuser will lead you through. It was amazing to me how once I was Awake I could predict with alarming accuracy my abuser's next move, to the disbelief of many around me since some of my predictions were so outrageous, and yet accurate. The more I realized my feelings about their actions were right, the stronger I became. Each correct prediction heightened my knowing that I could trust myself. Once I knew I was in a game of chess, I could use all the wisdom from all the years of watching them play, to put them in checkmate. Awake to the truth I now had knowing.

Keep in mind, I do not feel that it is appropriate to lie to harm others, that makes us no better than the abusers who torment us. However, sometimes we must lie to protect ourselves or others, like the fact that there are Jews in our attic. In this instance, I needed to show that I was strong, even though I wasn't fully there yet. I needed him to begin to lose control over me. I believe this small lie led him to believe his grip was loosening.

Remember, they have choreographed the dances we were doing while asleep. The best way to move forward is to trust yourself, and don't try and convince anyone of anything. Trust your knowing and create your own dance.

We have to stop seeing ourselves as children who have to justify our behavior and make people believe us. We are adults, we do what we want to, we follow our moral standard and no one has the right to question us, or perhaps more aptly put, try to force us to doubt ourselves. If they doubt us, that is about them. If they don't like what they see in us, they can leave, as you can, if you don't like what you see.

A great Dale Carnegie quote is useful here:

"A person convinced against their will is of the same opinion still."

Once you deeply and truly know who you are, it will never matter to you again who others see you as. You answer only to your own belief system. You are whole and complete the moment you accept all parts of you and heal your wounds. Whole and complete, you will forever Live Free.

My life had been about integrity, full disclosure, transparency. Once I awakened, I needed to change all that. I started to see I needed to learn to only give all of myself to those who I could trust. I do not feel that I need to hide who I am, I like being an open book. However, I refuse to be read by those who look to do me harm. I could see the truth, where I was safe and where I was not. I needed to masterfully embrace my power, my sword, and I had to wield it.

And I would. And it would work.

- ❖ **Once awake we become courageous rather than compliant.**
- ❖ **Always honor yourself.**
- ❖ **Honor others as long as honoring others doesn't cause you to dishonor yourself.**
- ❖ **If someone is asking you to dishonor yourself for them, that is not okay. Say no.**

I was awake—I was finally embracing the existence of my shadow side.

Me and My Shadow   Diana Rose Iannarone

<u>Awake and Standing Up</u>

Once you wake up, it is as though you step back from the small portion of the mosaic that you have been looking at, and the seemingly chaotic and haphazard pieces come together to form a complete image. It happens in an instant. However, when you see the whole picture for the first time it is often terrifying, and too overwhelming to attempt to deal with the whole image at once. Gradually, you begin to see the structure of your chaos. Structure allows you to begin to trust yourself, thus overcoming your fear. All the wisdom that you had, but did not own, comes into view. The more of your wisdom that comes into view, the faster your fear begins to subside. Then suddenly, you are no longer overwhelmed by the whole image, you know how to get to your freedom, step by step, piece by piece, you are aware.

Having journeyed this far with me, you have watched as I excused away cruel behavior. How I believed the perpetrator over myself. How I allowed myself to be brainwashed into doubting my own knowledge and sanity, in favor of the influence of people that wished to harm me. I was unwilling to accept that people who claimed to love me would intentionally do me harm. You have listened and observed how I ignored my intuition at every turn, the very intuition that is intended to protect me. In DeBecker's book, he shares that the root of the word *intuition, tuere,* means "to guard, to protect." It is only in shifting the focus from the abuser to ourselves that we begin to understand how to establish that protection.

For me standing up meant fighting. After years of blindly serving the needs of others, the needs they told me they had, that I chose to believe, it was time for me to stand up. I needed to stand up and fight for myself, for that little girl who had been left unprotected all those years, holding my hand enduring intolerable pain.

Abusers are dangerous. Sometimes walking away with your life is the way to stand up. It is not always wise to stand up the way I chose to, by fighting. I knew what I had to do for me. To me, getting free through Standing Up was truly worth dying for. I was clear that the loss of my assets was not the largest priority that was on the table, it was the loss of myself I would not allow. I decided I would fight, regardless of the risks, I am not advising you to do that.

I felt I couldn't recover from giving any more of myself away. I only had a little of me left that I could see. I had to hold onto it and gather the rest of me, to begin to fully Stand. Then, I would need to heal my wounds.

"Give Me Liberty or Give Me Death," as Patrick Henry said, March 23, 1775, ironically on my birthday (though a few years earlier). That is where I stood from finally. That is what pulled me through.

You are intimately aware of who your abuser is, more than anyone else, and you should take the time to evaluate the whole of your situation. My goal is to help you find ideas that may help you, and I of course do not want to lead you into danger or harm. Instead, I want to lead you to have confidence in yourself, know that you are worthy, and know that you can choose freedom. Once you are Awake, you will know how to approach your definition of Standing Up.

Running away instead of standing up, only because you are exhausted may not be a good enough reason. Once you are out of the abusive situation, you will have to be comfortable with how you chose to stand up. Assess what will have you feeling that you made the best decisions for your health and well-being. Do what you need to do to feel the best about who you are. Your self-esteem is a critical component of you, you must live without regret. However, the most critical thing to remember, is that you must do all you can to stay safe. This isn't about revenge, this is about freedom.

I needed to trust myself. I needed to trust my feelings. Our feelings are what has been discredited, our knowing in our soul. Our intuition was our protector, trying to awaken us to the truth of our power which we had forfeited to these abusers. I needed to take care of myself. I needed to believe in my mind and my intuition. I needed to stop hearing any words uttered to me by my manipulators as truth; they were only words with an ulterior motive—to harm me. I needed to know that if my inner knowing made a prediction, I must trust it. No one will be allowed to talk me out of my truth again. What I believe, and have experienced in my own life, is that once you Wake Up, you are standing on a totally different platform, and true Standing Up naturally follows. All that magnetism, the spell these people have on you, disappears and a few other magical things happen. First, you become a magnet to what you need.

I promise you that as I decided, absolutely decided, that I was different and ready for a life with no abuse, I became open. It was as if I had a new energetic level and could now draw to me the help I needed. The resources were placed in my path, like the friend who reassured me after the crazymaking encounter I described.

It was very powerful to have someone who believed my words and fears. You may not have that person, but you have yourself, and now that is all you need. Believe in yourself and act upon your intuition to protect yourself from the real dangers that may be present. As I have said before, some people may think that you are simply being paranoid, but you know your abuser better than anyone. Who could understand this situation if they have never been in it? I was constantly reminded my intuition was right and I should trust it, and now I hope to remind you.

Regardless of people's reactions to your truth when you reach out for help, you must stay grounded in that truth. Give little consideration to how credible the people around you seem to be who are choosing to doubt you. You must continue believing in your truth, and you must find a way out, and must do so quickly and effectively. You must do so by listening to your inner guidance, it has been waiting for you for a very long time.

When you are starting to act from a new place, you want to take this moment to begin to stand grounded in your logic. You want to breathe and focus on your facts, like an analyst who wants to win a calculated game, not like an emotional person who wants someone to see all they have been through and have empathy and compassion for you. Remember, just because we began to stop solely thinking our emotions rather than feeling them, does not mean that we can't use our minds to strategize in our chess game. We must combine the logic of our minds and the intuition of our hearts. We need the whole of us to escape.

As I escaped my abuse, I found the concept of protecting that little girl who was holding my hand was a great tool to decide what to do. I would literally ask myself, *If my child was in the position I see, what would I do?* and I would always do just that; whatever I deemed wisest. Truly, I watched as she grew. My voice changed, my demeanor changed. I was finally becoming a grown-up. You need to let the child whose hand you have been holding know that you are ready to take over. I would encourage you to write her a letter of gratitude for enduring all these years of pain and letting her know that you are so sorry, apologize and tell her that you will take care of her forevermore. And you will. Ask for forgiveness and offer it to yourself. Let yourself feel the emotions. Avoidance will not get you where you want to go.

It is time to stop letting peoples' words overpower your own sound thinking. And, given what you may be up against, you need structure in your situations so you are not ranting and rambling. The more calm and well spoken you are, the more credibility will be granted to you. Evidence is undeniable credibility. Start documenting.

Amassing an arsenal of concrete evidence does not mean you should deny your intuition. Exactly the opposite. Your intuition is the most sound guidance you have. Trust it. Listen to it. It may lead you to some of the most powerful weapons in your arsenal.

Once you are awake, you will no longer desire to protect those who are harming you. In your battle to be free, you will only be concerned with your safety, protection of you and the things and people that are important to you. For the first time you will be your own warrior. We are our own heroes. We must act. It is us that must make ourselves a priority. If we don't make ourselves a priority, no one will.

As I have said, waking up can be overwhelming. The act of standing up can be as well. At first you may be afraid and shocked by what you can now see. You are looking with awake eyes, and in Standing Up you may find yourself looking in places you have never dreamed of going to discover evidence. As quickly as possible you must get grounded in your strength. Your reality may initially ignite terror. It's okay, be with the feelings as they show up. Whatever shows up is the right emotion, but never allow your emotions to stand in the way of your goal; your freedom. Experience the emotions, but do not dwell, there is no time for that now.

See the truth; that is the most important thing to help you get safe. Once the light is shining on all the darkness you refused to see before, you can see the exit, you can see the obstacles, and you will know you can get free.

Embrace the truth of what you see and all the capacities within you. At the moment of awakening, you picked up the sword that was available to you all along. Because you allowed your strings to become ropes, and your ropes to become chains, you will need to use your sword to free yourself. You will need to Stand, in **all** your power. You can do it.

Focus on yourself. Take exquisite care of yourself spiritually, financially, emotionally, physically, and mentally. Get in alignment with yourself. Stand in your integrity and not your fear. Fear was created by those who wanted to stifle our ability to love and nurture ourselves and to use our power.

No longer be so free to give out information. Learn to be vague in your language when up against your opponent. If they are dangerous, do what you can to stay away. See this person as a stranger, in reality they are. They are not who they showed themselves to be, and you have no reason to meet with anyone who could harm you. Never let them in any space where they will have you alone.

Build your self-esteem, keep increasing your awareness of who your opponent is and all your capacities; you are ready, a strong person who now knows their power. You are the Queen or the one with the most power, regardless of sex. It was your power that made you a target, and it is your acknowledgement of, and willingness to use, that power that can set you free.

I believe there is a path to freedom. The way to find your unique path is for the first time to know that you must remove the hook that is embedded in you and be free. Literally, see yourself removing that hook. Once Awake you will finally care about your safety! Until I awakened I was a pushover, wrought with fear and confusion, believing what I was being told, feeling emotionally for the others in my life who were harming me. Once Awake you have very little concern for their safety. Finally you realize that they are adults, and it is not your job to protect them.

Once awake we become courageous rather than compliant.

My abusers were used to the idea that I was weak and predictable, that they could manipulate me as they could a marionette. I had taught every abuser in my life that I would never use my power. So imagine their shock when I did! I was becoming the choreographer now.

Awake I could see that I always had the power of the Queen. I was simply not using that power; I was too afraid, too ashamed to bring harm to anyone but myself. They always told me that I was mean, cruel even, if I did not properly care for and protect them. I believed them. I promised myself at a very young age that I would never harm another. In order to begin protecting myself from harm, I had to realize that allowing natural consequences for another's cruelty was not the same as harming an innocent.

When we act from our empowered and awakened state we throw our abuser off balance. It is during these imbalanced moments that they are recalculating a new strategy and this is when your abuser may become the most dangerous. You must decide for yourself what the safest way to handle this situation is. What I know is, you can't keep doing what you have done and expect a different result. Before when they escalated, you likely gave in more, looking to appease, help, or calm the situation. That may not be the right way to play anymore.

In my instance, what I learned is that when my abusers played the normal trump cards, I didn't react. Over and over those same cards would be thrown at me, with intent to ignite my fear that I would get in trouble with authority. There were implications made that I cheated on my taxes, was violating an order that would jail me for contempt, was armed and dangerous, was drunk and unfit, even that I was a potential killer! Through all of that, I didn't react. The less reactive I was, the more confused they (my abusers and those who assisted them) would be. I didn't react because I stayed focused on the tasks at hand, rather than all the ancillary creation of drama and fear. I wanted out. I was no longer in fear of shame. I finally embraced that I had nothing to be ashamed of. I was no longer a little girl in fear, not embracing all of myself. I felt fear, lots of fear, but for the first time it was appropriate fear. Fear for my safety, for my life. **Not the petty fear of shame that had always guided me before.** In this fear, I was now courageous. I was not hiding. I was standing in my light. I was shining the flashlight on their evil behavior in ways that *they* feared. The one thing they vowed never to become was a victim. I knew they had that fear and I leveraged it when needed. I had power to expose who they were, and they prefer to stay in the shadows.

Once awake, I could see their shadow, which only became possible once I accepted that the shadow dwelled in me as well. Once this capacity is acknowledged, we can instantly begin operating from it. However, I wanted to rapidly find my fullest power, my ability to boldly wield my sword. I now understood, force is an acceptable power, when used to protect.

245

Wielding our sword is a foreign concept to us. We must use whatever level of force is necessary to be free from harm. Ideally, we should not exceed that level. Violence, if you will, is acceptable in self-defense. In my case, I feared that I didn't have the fullness of this resource and I knew I needed help. Remember, it is through embracing your vulnerability that help arrives. We must admit that we are not in fact invincible, as we have portrayed. It is in accepting this reality, that we finally reach for help and all the teachers arrive. We are now beginning to summon and unleash the true power within us. This announcement of our vulnerability leads to **truly** being invulnerable. Soon, our life and truths will no longer be illusions.

In an effort to gain my strength while beginning the standing up process, I arranged to do some EMDR (Eye Movement Desensitization and Reprocessing) and hypnotherapy. A powerful exercise that I was directed to do while in a hypnotic state was to see myself in an image. In this image I was asked to imagine me wielding my sword to protect myself from my attacker, to harm him just enough to get him to retract. I remember feeling the weight of my empty arms. I remember imagining the sword in my hand and I simply could not lift it. Even when I would summon the courage and lift my arms, they would drop right back down in my lap. I could not do it. I was directed to imagine wielding my sword just enough to draw perhaps a little blood so my attacker would leave; I simply could not. I could not lift my arms for longer than a moment.

I remember I was tearful at my weakness; my inability to do this simple task; wield my imaginary sword at my attacker and protect myself by inflicting harm. In the hypnotic state I believe I was acting in my real truth, not the surface truth where, of course, I could easily and powerfully wield my sword. In this state, I could experience **the** truth; I could not and would not yet cause harm. I could not be what I perceived as mean. I had lied, I had moved forward, but I needed a push to stand in my full power. My unwillingness to harm another, even to defend myself, left me completely vulnerable.

For me, in my hypnotic state, it was real. I would have told you that I could wield my sword given the right set of circumstances, yet when I tried to do it, in imagery designed to help me find the part of me that could wield my sword for protection, I could not. I don't know how long I was in this session before I could finally swing my sword, but I recall vividly the moment I was able.

With guidance, I called upon the strength in both my mind and heart, of any spiritual support possible (mythical, real, or imagined does not matter). It was as if I could literally feel my attacker sucking the blood from my neck; just like a vampire. Pulling my life force, bleeding me dry and yet, I was unable to retaliate. I can't tell you how real this feeling was. I could feel his weight on my neck draining me of my life force, and still I felt powerless. It was so hard to imagine that I couldn't stop my pain in this moment. I couldn't defend myself through harm in this powerful imagery.

I have always had an affinity for Joan of Arc. I feel although she was a bit haphazard, she was courageous and intuitive and had strength to Stand Up, even if she had to die in the process. I imagined that I had called upon her. As her force, which I perceived was greater than my own, joined me in my fight, I remember feeling this extraordinary power filling my body. I was crying and strengthening until the power was inescapably present. I remember being suddenly able to wield my sword. It was a life changing experience. I enlisted Joan's support and swung my sword. I asked for help, something I wasn't very good at doing, and then I wielded my sword. In that moment when I wielded my sword, I felt power. I was ready to freely, powerfully, wield my sword as needed to break those chains.

As soon as I wielded my sword and put closure to the image, as I drew blood from the attacker, I cried, and without conscious awareness, I brought my hands in a prayer like position in front of my heart. My position was in essence acknowledging that I finally had true balance. My masculine and feminine energies were finally united. I was able to defend myself. I chased him away in my image, and I would chase him away in real life. I could finally embrace and act from all my capacities, always.

I reclaimed the disowned parts of myself. I would find strength even in the fear I encountered during my journey to freedom. The more my strength prevailed, the smaller my fear would be. In the fight to be free while you are

247

Standing Up, you still maintain that vigilance you have known, but this time you are fighting for yourself.

Your job all along was to be the observer, to hold your own piece and live from your light, while embracing and knowing you have all capacities. Your sword is found by embracing your denied capacity for evil. Owning your shadow self, you will stand in the fullness of the light; you will finally stand in the full spirit of God. Aware of the truth of your power, you will likely have no reason to use your sword moving forward, since you will be able to see all truths once you get out from under the shadow of their darkness. Awake, others see your fullness, your wholeness, your power, you will be free.

As you stand on your journey to freedom, I want to make sure you are clear on the kinds of intimidation you can expect. I also want you to know it is perfectly normal to be terrified. Remember, this is a reality check about all you have denied in your life.

It may not be the physical threats that terrify you. Your trump card may be invoked to elicit that fear.

In the past, what was the biggest trump card that would make me jump?

Financial; it was the basis of what I mistakenly thought love was: providing.

My perspective was changing. Would it be worth being poor to be free? Are you really poor if you are free? It is my contention that in abuse we are starving, in abuse we are malnourished, in abuse we are denied, poor, isolated, and alone. Suddenly welfare was perfectly acceptable. I was starting to realize what little meaning the tangible things that money can buy had. Items of the "physical" world seemed to be of only incidental value. My sense of what was important was shifting, and my self-esteem was rising.

Awake, there are no trump cards. Awake you cannot be manipulated. So as you look to break free and they toss those trump cards on the table, you can simply tear them up. While I was Standing to break free, one of the abusers told me that a property I owned with them was going into foreclosure because there was no way they could pay the mortgage since the tenant had left. I simply said, "Do you want me to just call the bank and tell them they could take the building now then?" He paid the mortgage.

When I was told a building I co-owned in another state was being condemned, I contacted the county. Funny the inspector wouldn't call me back, until I said I would call his superior. I suspected the "condemner" was in cahoots with one of my abusers, the co-owner. The outer building was beautifully maintained, certainly not worthy of being condemned. Meeting with this "regulator" was, well, fun. He stammered as I brought to light my awareness of their likely shenanigans. It was yet another ploy to get me to give money to this abuser, so he could do the needed "repairs." I now suspected the money was simply lining his pockets. None of their leverage points worked any longer.

Remember, there are no boundaries. No lie they will not tell, no "set-up" they will not try. Be on high alert, and don't discount your gut feeling. You know more than you think you do.

Strength happens when you stay focused on your confidence in how the game has been played, so that you know how to play it now. Gather your facts, try to stay clear of the drama, get someone to stay with you if you can, get a dog...protect yourself. At all times, keep a camera with you, and try not to be alone. Those that slink in the darkness of the shadows, have one weapon they fear. A weapon that makes them run for cover even more than a vile threat on their life, one that will ignite their terror more than any other; cameras. It is hard to remain in the darkness, if you are captured in truth, by the light. They wish to never be caught; they wish to never have their true actions revealed. They so enjoy hiding behind the illusion of their innocence.

Your goal is to be free from this manipulation and chaos you have chosen. Depending upon the depths of the capacity for harm of your abuser, you may want to try to avoid the opportunity for them to set you up in some way. Don't underestimate who may be on their team. Know that they are likely watching you and have others doing so as well. In my case, on any given day there may have been 30 or more drive by's to watch, and even film, what was happening in my home…sometimes with abusers even renting vehicles to avoid being identified. One abuser would sometimes simply park in front of my home for an hour or more at a time, just in an attempt to intimidate me.

When we do not engage in their game, the game is ultimately more frustrating for them. As I have said, to engage us, they normally keep raising the stakes. What I can't predict is if your abusers' frustration and resulting escalation will lead them to harm you, lead them to troll for their next victim, or both. In my case, because my stand was so hard, because I had cameras everywhere, I believe I simply became too much work. They moved on.

If you try to Stand Up without first waking up, you can be embroiled in these battles for years. Why? When we stay asleep, we still apply compassion and reason. We continue to hope. We want to be nice. Wake up and play to your strengths. The person you thought you loved, does not exist. This person has only one goal; to have power over and control of—you, and anything that matters to you. Remember this truth exists in multiple arenas; all abusers, not just those of the intimate kind, have a hidden agenda.

In his book *The Gift of Fear*, Gavin De Becker, talks about "satellites." He describes satellites as unnecessary details or details that are seemingly not pertinent to the story that people disclose while being questioned. When he hears these incidental details, he gleans from them powerful clues that often lead to disclosure of who is the perpetrator of a violent crime.

To me this was an indication that at some level we almost always know more information about a concern or danger than we realize. I encourage you to look for "satellites." These incidental, seemingly unimportant details mentioned almost as an aside are, in fact, likely to be critical pieces of information that may help you see the truth you may need to see.

It was a "satellite" that led me to some pertinent information.

In one such instance, while awake but still at the fearful stage of standing up, my abuser was at my home, escorted by police at his request (he claimed *he* was afraid of *me*!). He insisted that he needed certain items for work and that I was keeping them from him. Not at all surprisingly though, all he took was

250

my set of women's golf clubs. He may have escaped with this plunder, but at my insistence the police caught up with him demanding their return. Women's golf clubs certainly didn't qualify as essential occupational equipment. His true goal was simply to intimidate me. During the time he spent rummaging through things in an effort to show he could still violate me, he casually asked the police officers if he would be able to come back at some point for additional property. As he spoke those words, I noticed that he glanced at a sack that sat on a pile of what seemed like disregarded property. I said nothing, but I noticed. I felt he had unwittingly disclosed something. He had given me what I accepted as a "satellite."

Finding my courage since Waking Up, and now Standing Up, I knew I had to investigate. I had always feared doing so. I never investigated the goings on in the life of my abusers. I had been taught what was off limits and what wasn't, and I never broke those invisible boundaries until Awakening. After he and the officers left, I approached that sack. I recall as I ran hurriedly to retrieve it, fearing my "wrong doings" would be caught by my cameras, as if there was a penalty for acting within my legal rights. I had installed these powerful surveillance cameras at my home, shortly after waking to assure myself greater protection. I remember feeling measurable fear as I "snuck" around my own property to grab this little sack and investigate its contents. Early on my trepidation was high, but you see the more you Stand, the more you face your fear, the more quickly your fear dissipates. Investigating this "satellite" caused me to discover substantial evidence that helped me validate all I had thought to be true, but feared believing. My hope for you is that you do not need to find the evidence in a neat little package as I did…instead you will simply trust your knowing, and then be willing to line things up well to support your claims.

That sack would just be the beginning of the evidence which led me to many revelations. I would be shown the depths of the lies I had been told, and that would allow me to garner undisputable wisdom to the real truth in every tale. These various pieces of information enabled me to stand grounded in my Awakeness, and confirmed that what I believed about these perpetrators was true. That truth, which was always right there at my fingertips that I never chose to grasp…right there, as it was from the beginning, the opportunity to Wake Up.

You do not need to find this little sack…you need to know the truth and choose to believe your own inner voice, even if you can't find the evidence. The sack merely confirmed for me what I already knew. As I said, in making a documented claim against someone, having the evidence is paramount. However, in simply living your life, your gut instinct can really be your guide, decide to trust it.

Do you recall that I made an accusation of tapes I had between my abuser and previous women at the moment of my awakening? They were among the items I discovered in that sack. At some level I knew. We know, we always know.

Looking in this sack provided so much information. You see though, because I was awake I did not have the compulsion to call someone and rant and rave about my discovery. I was simply playing chess. Since I was now open and awake, more information of the truth was revealed to me every day. Every day I moved away from fear and became more and more grounded. Every day I was acting stronger at my game until eventually I no longer had to *act* strong, I *was* strong. I would never again be unwittingly in the kinds of situations I had created all my life.

There were multiple turning points that reflected my power and ultimately caused the abusers to disappear. There were many times that my strength enabled me to act in ways previously foreign to me. As I said, in our Awake state, we can see lifelines we never could have seen while asleep.

My final attorney had come to respect and honor my crazy predictions about my abusers' behavior. I say "final" attorney because I had to be strong enough to release another attorney who didn't have my best interest at heart, which was very difficult. Remember in places of authority, sociopaths lurk.

During the battle for my exit, one of my abusers had managed to claim that certain items at my home were used for his business, and a judge had ordered that I give him access to these items when he *needed* them. He was required to give me very little notice. He would claim to need these items frequently, as an excuse to come to my home and intimidate me. In these moments, I found having a private investigator there to film to be very powerful. Remember, to these abusers the click in the chamber of a gun ignites less fear, than the click of a camera.

As my fear diminished, I could see more clearly every day. I decided this time when the notice was given, I would refuse to honor the legal agreement to the use of the property. This decision was vehemently against my attorney's advice. I stated I would rent a similar item for my abuser to use if it was necessary. The response from opposing counsel was that there would be contempt charges against me, which would likely result in jail time. I stood my ground. I wasn't afraid. I couldn't see a judge caring where the item came from as long the equipment was made available to serve the purpose of the "claimed" need. Authority just wasn't that scary anymore. I was my own authority now.

I was finally willing and able to file contempt or domestic violence charges as appropriate on them, as well as to risk contempt charges on myself. I was willing to take steps to protect myself, even if it meant that they would get in trouble. I was no longer intent on holding their piece. My focus was my safety. Their protection was of no concern to me.

It was clear to all parties, the game had changed.

Ultimately, cameras were my hero. They captured things that were too evident to run from. The key is to let the fear that you likely feel upon awakening, transition to adrenaline to keep you finding ways out and strengthening your self-esteem. Wield your sword of protection boldly and with precision. Seek help. If you have a gut intuitive feeling that the help you chose cannot be trusted, then keep looking for other help. Break the string the moment you see the person on the other end is operating from their shadow. The moment you see or feel that someone does not have your best interest at heart, simply tug that string and break it, don't ever let that string become a rope, more securely attached to you to your detriment ever again.

After all the battles had subsided, given some of the situations I had dealt with, I decided to involve the Office of Internal Affairs of the local police department. Awake, I was a force to be reckoned with, and I will be forevermore.

I remember that meeting because I didn't show up like a scared little girl telling them, "the authority," all the horrible things these "bad men" tried to do. I was Awake and they could feel it. I was brief, succinct and clear. I had a natural air of confidence. I was cool, calm, and collected. I didn't need to prove myself. I was relaxed. I knew the truth. I found all the peace and confidence I needed in that knowledge. I was certain that those I was meeting with also knew the truth. I didn't really feel compelled to convince them. I was a grown up now. I'll never know if it was directed or by their choice, but two of my biggest abusers moved away very quickly after my stand. I began to feel a sense of safety and power.

Once awake we become courageous rather than compliant.

Where I am today, I am fully aware of my ability to wield my sword, yet I doubt I will ever need to again. Now, I simply break the attachment to any abuser while it remains a mere string. No longer do I stay in the abuse until it becomes a chain. The difference in my life now is, I know, and "they" know, I have my sword, and I am not afraid to use it. I simply needed to embrace that reality, the reality that I could swing my sword. The power of protection was always within me, just as it is within you. We just have to tap into it. Embrace it.

The principles to freedom are quite easy, the courage and ability to Stand is much tougher. From where I sit now, I wouldn't change a thing. I am free. No strings, no manipulation, no control. I am the only ruler of my life, and my life is nothing but love. Of course people and circumstances happen and I address them as they come. I no longer tolerate improper treatment of myself, not even by me.

In your situation, a different path might take you to freedom. It is hard, challenging, scary, and ultimately invigorating and empowering—the path to freedom.

When you no longer trust your opponent, it validates that you are likely Awake. You will release your misdirected compassion, and you will observe their behavior in a new light. You will recognize that their calculating antics to win are not confined by logic or any set of rules; there are no limits or boundaries to them. Their patterns will remind you what they are capable of.

Once awake we become courageous rather than compliant.

My guess is that even in this moment, you can look across your life and remind yourself of countless times that if you had trusted yourself and not someone else, or trusted what you felt rather than someone else's words, you may have avoided unnecessary pain. Recall though, "should haves" will not serve you well. Most of us fold to the power of others, rather than trusting ourselves and doubting those things outside of us. We are so easily influenced that we often adopted beliefs without ever taking a moment to question them. We do this to our own detriment. Now is the time for you to seek your truth in all areas, and live by them, trust your Truth.

My life had a critical and complete pivotal change the moment I began to trust myself again. In the moment when I Woke Up I found my voice, I trusted my voice, and it enabled me to Wake Up *and* Stand Up and now we enter the beginning of the next phase, Living Free.

Sometimes, Standing Up is almost as exhausting as living in the abuse. Sometimes, Standing Up is even harder than continuing to live in our abuse. We are already tired from living in this way, full of torment and suffering, and now we must muster the energy to fight. As we are standing, we are dealing with sections of the mosaic in manageable pieces. It can still be overwhelming and arduous. By the time we are done, we have dismantled the entire mosaic in front of us. We did this step by step, piece by piece. Being blind to the image of the mosaic could have been life threatening, but examining the entire image at once initially left us staggering. As we grew in strength, we knew we could embrace the whole truth, and we knew how we could dismantle it. Now we are Awake, the abuse is gone. For some of us, this is where we begin to Live Free. Phew! One big sigh of relief and we are through. For others, including myself, we begin reeling as we see all the dismantled pieces and the damage our ignorance to the truth has caused. We feel a heavy emptiness, an echoing silence from our loud chaos. A silence that can be deafening. Still, do not be distraught. It is in that silence that we find our peace.

The Calm After The Storm

Perhaps you will feel discouraged after you wake up to see whatever you were choosing to ignore. You may find yourself looking back at all of the times you spotted a red flag, or had some kind of inner prompting that you were at risk, and chose to sleep through it. It may feel discouraging that it took you so much time, that you lost so much. As you now acknowledge those feelings of doubt, that were there but ignored, you may begin to want to badger yourself for your failing. I encourage you to not exacerbate your pain by beating yourself up, for the moment you awaken you can see, and that is all that matters.

Consider accepting the long standing idea that everything happens in perfect timing. It is not unnatural to have remorse and regret, but it is counterproductive to spend a lot of time being in that space, living through the "only ifs" or "should haves." Even if a different decision in the past seems as though it could have brought you to a more favorable present, you

257

will never know exactly how that decision would have played out, and you can never change the past. You must accept where you are today, and focus only on how you treat that nagging little voice moving forward. You have likely experienced enough abuse without wasting energy on those pesky little "should haves," as that too is a form of abuse. Those negative thoughts drain the present moment, and our ability to joyfully move forward armed with our new knowledge.

It's over. We are free from the abusive situation, now what?

There will be many things you will need to embrace and accept; things you may not want to see. In many ways, it will be like you can finally see the movie of your life without the distortions you allowed when you were asleep. Parts of you will likely wish you hadn't woken up. You may long for your slumber when you did not have to bear the pain you so skillfully ignored until now. However, know that waking up may be hard to do, but it is the key step toward standing and Living Free.

Now you are awake and you can clearly see the devastation you allowed in your life. It may feel as if you have been inside a tornado and were so busy being tossed to and fro, that you never had a moment to observe the destruction. Now, as you sit on the floor awake and look around you, you see everything is destroyed. You can see how you abandoned yourself. You can see how badly you let yourself be abused. You can see how you allowed your spiritual, financial, emotional, physical, and mental spirit to be stolen.

You totally neglected yourself. You had no time to notice this neglect in the past. You had spent so much time, weeks, months, years, maybe even decades, completely distracted. You were distracted by your abuse, and then you were distracted by getting away from your abuse. Suddenly, everything has stopped. You no longer live every moment in heightened vigilance. You are used to plotting your every step, walking the tightrope. You had to be quick on your feet to stay safe. This vigilance was in every moment of your life, both while in the relationships, and especially while getting out of them. A lifetime of chaos, control, manipulation and fear. Now suddenly it is gone.

It is an inexplicable feeling. Honestly, it is an empty feeling. No stimulations. Nothing.

All of your reality, everything you thought you knew, is gone. Now it is just you, and the remains of a life you thought you had. Just you, as you stand examining the debris of your shattered life, your shattered dream, strewn under your feet. Your memories and false hopes are the only relics of the fantasy that was constantly dangled on the horizon. All the potential you were betting on is shattered. And now from here, you know there was never any potential in those you built your life around. It was all an illusion— everything.

I can't know precisely what you feel at this phase. I can only share what the experience was like for me at the end of finally standing up and leaving my life of abuse behind.

Being free from the abuse, all I could see was that every noble cause and purpose I thought my life was based on was an illusion. I lived, at many levels, in a fantasy world, and now all the characters that I fantasized would bring love and family to my life were evaporated. In reality, they never existed.

How do you pick up the pieces and move on?

I not only didn't know how to take care of myself, I didn't want to. It was like sitting in a hole in the ruins of my life; a deep hole. I could even see there was a rope hanging down the center of that hole. I remember seeing that imaginary rope, but being unable or unwilling to reach for it. I would not climb. I had been climbing my whole life only to discover I never really left the hole. Given that, it seemed wiser and easier and logical to just sit there. No more throwing ropes, no more reaching for ropes. I will just sit. I was exhausted, and I was devastated. I had worked so hard only to find myself alone. Even though I wanted to be free of the abuse, I had forgotten that without the abuse I would truly be alone.

At the time, I recall being discouraged that recovery wasn't feeling like the easy part. I felt I had gotten free and now it should be easy. However, I had to see and feel the devastation I had so carefully ignored and denied. That part wasn't easy.

Thankfully, I would come to understand that compared to the hell I had already lived, this *would* actually be the easy part, although it didn't seem so at first. It is the easy part because now no one else is controlling you, no one else is beating you down, and no one else is manipulating you. Now, though, you have to contend with the person who caused you the most pain, the most suffering, the worst abuser of all—You.

Yes, the worst abuser of all was who I was left to contend with. A great healer and friend coined a term for my behavior: "self-sociopath." By self-sociopath, he was suggesting that I continually caused or allowed harm to be bestowed on me, without feeling the need to make it stop. Even at moments when I would decide to stop the abuse, and believed I should stop the abuse, I would go out and repeat the same pattern again. Not this time. I had finally broken the pattern. The "self-sociopath," was now Awake.

**Control less, observe more, focus on you,
and be surrounded by only love.**

I considered suicide most of the first year or so of this recovery. It seemed easier to just quit. I was tired. I had worked to hold so many lives together until mine had fallen completely apart. Although it was my job to simply hold my piece over my head, I was holding the pieces of those around me. In that, I lost my balance, my strength, my direction. Now, as all the pieces dropped to the floor, I felt I had nothing left; no piece worth carrying remained in my hand, not even my own. It is hard to get used to a life without chaos, when it is all you know. I imagine it is the same feeling that people have when released from prison. They are so happy to be free, but so lost without the structure of their confinement. It is no surprise that so many choose to reoffend, to return to the only life they know.

The reason I chose to live was that I couldn't bear leaving my daughter, parents, and friends to suffer through my suicide. I knew my death would make those who I cared about most in the world suffer. They did not deserve that pain. However, my motive was not purely to save those who I love from pain. I also wanted to believe that maybe there was a life still left to live, one that included family, grandchildren, joy and abundant love. I reminded myself of this possibility almost every day, as the thoughts of suicide repeatedly drifted through my mind.

I had to remind myself that I believe taking your own life just shortens the journey, and cheats the world of the fullness of your gifts. These gifts often have not revealed themselves fully, not even to you. I believe that if you take your own life, you only face those challenges again in the next. Remember, there is never a true way around—only through.

Wouldn't suicide be in fact the ultimate self-abuse; the murder of me, the murder of my own limitless potential? Potential was the main characteristic I chose to see in each of these men. I had focused for so long on helping them to reach their potential, I had forgotten that the same characteristic lived in me.

After my world collapsed in on me, I didn't care anymore. Let someone come and rescue *me*, throw *me* a rope. I didn't feel like I was kneeling in a puddle. I felt like someone had held my head under water for more than thirty years, and now I simply did not want to come up for air. I was done pulling, pushing, being responsible. I was done trying to fight for the right to breathe, the right to live, I didn't want to do either anymore. I was done trying to get the kneeling person to stand up and live their life to their potential, even if that person was me.

Simultaneous to finding it difficult to channel the motivation to live, I found myself overwhelmed with a large piece of property that my abuser had manipulated me into buying. He had also robbed me of the tools I needed to maintain this property. Not only did I need to find a way to drag myself out of bed, I had to find the motivation to maintain this land and all that went with it.

I would sit on my property and helplessly cry. *I can't do this. I don't want to do this. This is exactly what I didn't want.* I would, in constant repetition, recall my clear statement, my adamancy, that I did *not* want to move into this property because I did *not* want to have to manage it all by myself if the relationship did not last. Here I was; exactly what I feared and dreaded had become my reality. My energy had been focused on the very thing I feared, and therefore my fear became my reality. Fear is the invitation. Fear seldom brings you anywhere good, and fear, in my view, is not from God.

I felt I could no longer afford to pay someone to maintain my property, and I felt I couldn't do it myself, I felt trapped…I hated my life.

Wow.

I was a mess.

I struggled to want to live.

I wanted to die.

At the level of my mind, my intellect, I knew I was not truly trapped. I knew there were always options, but at the level of my heart, my emotions, I simply did not have the desire or strength to take any of the options that might have existed. I just wanted to disappear.

As I watched the movie of my life in seemingly endless clips, I was forced to see everything that was always there which I chose to deny. The painful revelations were also still trickling in. People were sharing information that I had not known. It seemed at every turn, another truth would reveal itself to shine the light on the farce of my life, and the deviance of the calculating players. At first I could not bear to see how all these people had betrayed my genuine acts of love with deception. In time, I would learn and accept, that I was the one who most brutally betrayed myself. I allowed it all and I had to embrace the truth and forgive. Just as I was the worst of my abusers, it would make sense that I was also the person who I struggled most to forgive.

I had spent my life working towards love and happiness only to find the path I had taken did not bring me to my goals. I had put so much effort into finding love, building a family, and achieving financial security. Now, I sat alone—no intimate relationship, my daughter had moved away to begin her own life, and most of my assets had disappeared into the pockets of those who wished only to deceive me. My entire life was just a series of chess games, and I never noticed, until now.

I felt so betrayed. I felt betrayed by them. I felt betrayed by myself. I felt I had failed on all counts. It was like my world, the one I created a whole dream around, was killed overnight. It was as if there was a plane crash, or a tragic accident and everyone and everything I thought was at the core of my life was gone.

There was no funeral though. There were no mourners circling me with awareness of this great loss. For the most part, understandably, everyone was just relieved that I was free from the life I was living. The many friends that have travelled on this vicious journey with me and stood beside me in my pain and my sorrow, offered compassion. They did what they could, but their compassion was not enough to fill the void of my lost dream.

Every day I asked myself how *I,* the woman who had spent decades working on herself through countless hours of therapy and a library of self-help books, how could *I* be such a mess?

I felt used beyond measure. I looked back on every kind word, every loving gesture, every tender moment that had moved me to joyful tears. Now I was able to see that what I had understood to be love and sincerity had merely been a part of the script. Every kiss was based not on love, but on what I could be manipulated out of, using my loving spirit for leverage. My trust and my heart had been mangled. I was devastated.

Knowing that I created that life was so hard to acknowledge and accept. That reality only intensified the pain. I now saw I had a path to freedom every moment of that time, and chose not to use it. All I had to do was look at myself. I simply had to love and embrace all of me. If only I had done that 20 years sooner. I imagined the life I could have had, the life I thought I was working towards. In time I would know everything happened as it was meant to.

I began to ache for the numbness that had once been mine. I started to drink a bottle of wine or more daily. I was becoming closer to what my abusers claimed me to be all along, a depressed drunk. I had trouble making myself eat.

Before my life fell apart, I was a Life Coach, most often coaching executives. Now with my life in shambles, how could I coach others? I stopped working. I couldn't even speculate as to what I should be doing with my career, or with my life. I gave more of my energy to wallowing in my sadness, I was completely disconnected. Nothing really mattered. I kept jumping in one direction and then another, trying to rediscover my career and my life, but I landed nowhere. I was lost in all parts of my life. I had no clarity, no direction, and no hope.

I realized that every single door I tried to open seemed to shut on me. Once every path I took left me with no evidence that I was right or headed in the right direction, I finally stopped.

At this time I had been reading a memoir in which a woman was trying to recover from the loss of a love. A friend comforts her with reassuring words and tells her to cherish this sacred time of grieving. As soon as I read the word grieving, I collapsed into tears. I realize now that it should have been obvious to me that I had been grieving, but until I read those words, I didn't really see. I was grieving the loss of the dream, and more importantly the loss of the family that was part of it. I was grieving all the pain that I had put myself through. Grieving how I had allowed people to treat me. I was grieving the fact that those who claimed to love me never expressed remorse for the vile pain they inflicted on me, nor did they ever want to make it right.

The loss of the dream was so traumatic because I felt it was what I spent my whole life chasing. I know now you don't chase your dreams, you live them. The loss of the dream would be the hardest of all the pain to recover from. The dream was the hook that my abusers had placed in the deepest part of me.

During this phase in my life, I began to seriously neglect my body. My neglectful behaviors were my efforts to die. At some level, I wanted to die. If I could pin it to something other than suicide, there would be no blame or resentment from others. I could die of an illness. They could accept my dying from a health issue, rather than from a suicide. They would have to accept it. If I was lucky, perhaps my illness would elicit the one thing I had longed for, someone to compassionately take care of me.

I was negative about my physical, my emotional, my financial, my mental, and even about my spiritual self. If there was that oneness I believed, if there was karma, if love comes back to you, how could I be in this space?

I woke up every morning only to review the day before and find those things that I needed to criticize myself for. What rule existed that I had broken? I was breaking my rules, the boundaries I had placed on my behavior, but I was wallowing in guilt and self-loathing for taking these liberties.

I now *wanted* to treat myself with love in every area of my life. I vowed to only allow those in my life who would treat me with the love I deserved, but the internal conflict I was experiencing was tearing me apart. I wanted so badly to be free, but I could not let go of the rules I had created for myself. My constant badgering of myself was overwhelming.

In the healing process I felt I was in a constant tug-of-war. I felt like pleasurable things would bring me pain. I felt so convicted in this belief that my life was a reflection of its truth. I understood I had created these rules about what perfection looked like relative to my physical self, the way I cared for my body, and the way I should behave. I would intentionally disobey these standards. I found a way to always feel bad about myself. It was to the point that this conflict, this cognitive dissonance, was consuming.

I was so used to feeling guilt and shame that I didn't know how to exist without their presence, so I engaged in behaviors to justify my feelings of guilt and shame. Without my "shameful" behavior I would have no idea *why* I was feeling guilt, therefore, I would just feel like I was crazy. Instead I was more comfortable carrying those emotions and deeming myself bad. I believed I was not good enough.

I was a harsh and judgmental parent to myself. I was unforgiving for any misstep. My vision of how I should be was in conflict with the way I wanted

265

to be. I wanted to be freer and yet I was bound by all these rules of my own making.

I could consciously, intellectually, see the conflict and I knew all I had to do was give up one or the other, the rule or the behavior, but emotionally I couldn't get there. I didn't know which I should do; or even if I could do either one. Obviously, I still had to adjust the banks of my river before I would be able to peacefully float downstream.

I also had that cruel voice in my head after all those years of hateful words being spewed at me. I spent a lifetime fighting against those words. I had spoken endless pleas to be heard, and for it to be seen, that I was none of those things. All those years it was as if I was a child trying to show them my reflection in a mirror and say: See me. This is me. It is different from what you see.

Consider for now the possibility, that until we Wake Up fully and embrace all the capacities within us, we can only see in the mirror the capacity we operate from, the one we choose to acknowledge, for we deny the other exists.

In their mirror I could only see the light/innocence; which was the part of me I was willing to embrace.

In my mirror they could only see the shadow/evil; which was the part of them they were willing to embrace.

I was going to have to learn to accept myself precisely as I was; where I was. I had to learn I could not be whole while rejecting parts of me. I would remind myself over and over, that the relationships seemed real to me, and I gave my heart and soul out of love. I had to remind myself about the perfection of the Universe. I needed to accept, all was as it was intended to be, even though I couldn't see all the purposes for my pain and path. I needed to trust that from this space, my life would transform. I couldn't possibly know the impact each event in my life had on this beautifully connected world. Kindness had always been my motivator. Maybe somehow my efforts to be kind and loving had a positive impact unbeknownst to me. Perhaps someday I would understand the greater reason for my suffering. A butterfly flaps its wings…the whole Universe is affected.

Silence can bring you through the pathway to healing.

As I began my recovery I couldn't be around people. I couldn't be around noise. It was like I had been a prisoner of war for twenty plus years and now I had been released. I didn't know what to do now that I was released. I was uncomfortable in my freedom. I wanted to be done already, get through it, get over it, and suck it up. Initially, I had no patience with myself in my healing. However, instead I had to learn to love myself right where I was, and allow myself to feel and heal. I think these feelings are similar for anyone who has experienced a tragic loss.

Anyone who has lived through abuse has lived in fear, whether they acknowledged that fear or not. This means they lived with vigilance. They could never really rest, not fully, as at some levels they didn't even feel safe closing their eyes.

Living in that kind of vigilance creates patterns for you that will keep your life comfortable, in a strange sort of way, when you are on high alert, waiting for the next person to capitalize on you or harm you in some way. That belief begets more of the same.

To find joy you have to begin to trust again, trust and honor your feelings and complete wholeness will arrive. You have to believe people will treat you well, and it all begins by you treating yourself well. You need to decide to be uncomfortable on high alert and know that it is no longer necessary to live with that pattern.

However, you will have triggers which will cause a cascade of old reactions to appear. These will diminish greatly over time. We are more prone to fall back into these old behaviors if we are neglecting ourselves in any way.

Post Traumatic Stress Disorder (PTSD) is often present in individuals who return from war. I am not trying to compare my life to the terror that combat veterans have experienced. I am suggesting that the vigilance and the flash backs may be similar at some levels. As the name implies "Post" Traumatic Stress Disorder, is not something you get while in the war, you get it when you leave the war.

While in the war, it is like we shut off or never awaken a piece of ourselves so we can survive in the hostile environment we are in. Then later, when we are no longer in that environment that requires constant vigilance, we can feel and experience all the fear and pain we couldn't risk feeling at the time of the war. In essence, I had been in a war that lasted 30 years or so, acknowledging it was a war of my own making was devastating. You too have likely carried these patterns a long time.

Triggering events can bring us back to that feeling of terror, even though there is really nothing to be terrified of in that moment.

I had a triggering event years after I thought my PTSD symptoms were over. Truly, I thought these symptoms were completely behind me. I had moved to another state inadvertently bringing with me a gun, which had been registered to one of my abusers. The gun he had left behind and never retrieved from me. I mentioned its existence in passing to a friend and I was promptly informed that it was a felony to bring a gun into that state; I had committed an act that was deemed a violent crime.

I did my homework and learned that if it was discovered that I had this weapon, which I was permitted to possess in the previous state, it was possible that I could go to prison for seven years. In the past I had never actually done anything wrong, I only allowed manipulators to scare me into thinking I had. This time, I had unknowingly done something wrong...it was illegal to have that gun.

I went back in time, back into that war zone. I feared one of my abusers would know I had the gun and would call the police. I imagined the police would come into my home and arrest me. I was terrified. I would be driving and looking over my shoulder fearing I would be pulled over and for some reason they would discover I had the gun at my home.

My reaction was hard for my friends to understand, but to me, it was real.

It was like being back in that world of deception. Emotionally, I was back in the vigilance I had needed to maintain for so long. Intellectually, I knew it was absolutely ludicrous! Once I could breathe and find my peace, which took me a few days, I was no longer afraid to have the gun, however, given it was not registered to me I sought ways to resolve the issue by choosing to relinquish it. Fortunately, a local precinct had gun amnesty. I went to the station and turned in the gun, grateful to be rid of one of the few remnants I had of my past abuse.

I had no fear as I entered the police station. I had no trepidation. I was no longer a little girl, and authority no longer terrified me.

When we can step out of the flashback we are not afraid. We know there is nothing to fear. However, while in the moment, we feel all the fear as if it is real.

It may be where you go emotionally, but it does NOT have to be where you act from.

I needed to accept myself precisely where I was in order to begin to take care of myself. A useful image may be to imagine there is a fountain flowing right in front of you that holds in it everything you need for an abundant life; however, if we are holding our cup to the left or the right of that flow, or in essence, in the past or in the future, we are missing the flow right in front of us. We are searching for what is right there in front of us available for us to enjoy, as we always have been.

I had to learn to be in the present moment. I needed to begin to feel and experience this space I was currently occupying. Any time we choose to not be in the present moment, we are forfeiting that moment, and we can never retrieve it. I have learned to be in the moment as I live my life. What would my life have looked like if I observed how I *felt* in the moment, and took a moment to honor that feeling?

I had to go into the silence and learn to be with myself each moment, embracing and accepting where I was. The first step in healing is to offer complete acceptance of yourself, in your frailties, in your addictions, in your negativity, in the exact place you are. Embrace where you are with love.

When have you ever known complete acceptance of you?

Get free and rest, end the life of vigilance. It's time.

Decide to live this. It takes courage.

Love and acceptance are what we have been striving for all along. We did so by trying to reel it in from the external, when all we needed to do was turn to ourselves. This is your time to give caring and compassion to yourself, so you will know what it feels like and recognize when you are receiving something to the contrary. And as you begin to love and accept yourself as you are, you will see you will receive an abundance of love and acceptance from others. You have always been the teacher of what you deserve. You are the magnet that brings just what you are asking for into your life.

If you have been in abusive situations your whole life, I feel confident stating you have never embraced where you are. You have always pursued perfection. You have always demanded more of yourself. You have always had rigid expectations. You repeatedly reminded yourself that you could be better, you cannot stop, and you cannot rest. You have carried the belief that **stamina and endurance** were necessary or something bad would happen. You have moved to your head, your mind, you were always thinking and avoiding feeling. We perceived it was safer in our mind than our heart, so we chose to live in that space. We must return to our heart to truly be free.

At this stage of healing, I reached out for help. And again, in perfect design I was introduced to a healer who led me toward living free. He utilized a wide variety of techniques, including acupuncture, reiki and discussion therapy. I was open to all things and followed where I felt I was led.

In our work together it was suggested that I do healing exercises:

1. Write down questions for myself and then answer them as I felt directed.

2. Get a box of Band-Aids and place them on the parts of me that were
hurting.

These experiences transformed into the most pivotal moments of my healing.
It is for this reason I choose to share them with you just as I wrote them then.
I would like you to feel the experience with me as I did in those moments.

I started by writing questions:

1. What am I supposed to do with my life?
2. Why did I have to go through so much pain?
3. Will I ever heal?
4. Should I move?
5. How will I make a living?
6. Will I stop "using" wine to help numb myself?
7. Will my fear of life ever go away?
8. Will I ever feel whole again?
9. I long for joy; will I ever be free to feel it? To live it?
10. What should I do?

I thought I would get profound responses from the Universe; I listened for a
message, an internal voice, a prompting; something that I could hear as God.
I awaited responses that would be in depth and profound. Instead the answers
I felt I heard were succinct and took only a moment to reveal themselves.
Perhaps I knew the answers all along.

1. Live it.
2. To learn.
3. Yes.
4. Yes (?)
5. Healing others.
6. When you are ready.
7. When you decide.
8. Keep Standing Up.
9. Yes.
10. Play and sing.

I didn't really know what to do with that. I expected so much more, yet I couldn't argue with the power of the answers. Perhaps it was God speaking directly to me. I wasn't sure what to make of the feeling of uncertainty on number 4, but for the moment, I just accepted it.

I realize it may be ironic that my biggest weakness was my perceived "soul" purpose of trying to heal the abuser, and now, I felt my calling was to heal others. However, there was an important distinction this time. This time, I would only heal those who wanted healing. The people I helped would actually heal themselves. I would simply be their guide.

Learning to play and sing would prove difficult for me. I had never been good at playing. I had to take small steps to learn how to really laugh again.

I paused for a moment and acknowledged, there were my questions, there were my answers. Feeling there was nothing else I could do with this exercise, I moved on to the next one.

The other healing exercise that was recommended to me felt rather silly at first. However, I was in no place to look down upon anything that might bring me to a place of peace. The recommendation was to take the band-aids and write on them the part of me that I felt was wounded. I started doing the exercise as directed, and then I really didn't know what to do with the band-aid, so I took the idea about the band-aids and put a twist on it. Of course I could place it on my body, but that didn't feel right.

I placed the first band-aid on a notebook specifically selected for these exercises and on it I wrote: My heart.

To add to the meaning of this exercise I had purchased *Sesame Street* band-aids. Even now, I smile recalling the many wondrous times my daughter and I had sharing the joys of *Sesame Street*. At that time I was grasping for any joy I could find.

I now began labeling the wounded parts of me and offering the band-aid as a testimony to the wound. First is heart, then spirit, then soul, then female organs, then liver, then digestive system, then femininity, then my endurance (stamina), my body, my mind, my trust, my intuition, my honor, my inner child, my throat (voice), my joy, my respect, my security, my finances, my self-worth, my daughter…

I felt guided to return to each one and add to it:

My heart—for the pain I allowed it to endure;

My spirit—for letting it be crushed;

My soul—for burying it;

My female organs—for denying my value as a woman;

My liver—for all my swallowed (repressed) anger;

My digestive system—for starving it;

My femininity—for thinking it made me weak;

My endurance—for driving it so;

My body—for criticizing and mistreating it and letting others do the same;

My mind—for allowing it to be manipulated;

My trust—for misplacing it;

My intuition—for not honoring it;

My honor—for disregarding it;

My inner child—for ignoring her pleas and for abandoning her;

My throat—for holding back anger and tears;

My joy—for hiding it and letting fear rule my life;

My respect—for disregarding myself and allowing others to do the same;

My security—for risking it for others;

My finances—for giving them away to the wrong people for the wrong reasons;

My self-worth—for forgetting I had any—for ignoring me and my needs; and,

My daughter—for not being home more, for bringing so much evil into our lives, for disregarding and not caring for myself and as a result in many ways neglecting her.

Then I don't know how long I wrote, but it continued for several days as I took each of these harmed parts of me, and wrote an apology letter. It was cathartic. And when I was done, I wrote a letter to myself. I even wrote a letter to "my" wine, thanking it for carrying me through this hardship and letting it know I no longer needed it for healing; it would now be a healthy part of my life.

Writing those letters to acknowledge my pain and move to forgiveness were healing indeed.

We can't just jump to healing—*just* put a band-aid on it and expect us to hold together. Healing and bandaging is a process we must honor. This action was soulful, in that it recognized and cleaned my wounds through expressing the pain, in both words and emotions. After the expression of the pain, I applied the medicine of forgiveness, and the band-aid of protection, which was the promise to myself to have more regard for my human frailty. I would honor myself, mind, body, and spirit. I would begin to play. I would begin to live free.

I was given yet another assignment to go to the mall and take notes on my experience. This may have been an enjoyable assignment for many people, but I am not a fan of malls.

My healer asked that I write to him about that experience.

Here is an excerpt:

*...Okay, I don't know what I was supposed to experience at the mall...but if it is that who I see in **them** is who I see in **me**, I am in grave trouble!*

I saw people not connected to each other...very involved in the mundane...or should I say simply uninvolved? Overall they looked unhappy...very unhappy. Even when they were with people...they were not together. They would speak to one another, and yet not make eye contact, not even be looking in the general direction of one another. They would walk ahead or behind one another.

...I expected to feel a sense of being overwhelmed in the crowd...instead the place felt vacant and cold. There seemingly was no real life force there...I don't know if I wanted to hug them or get out as fast as I could!

Initially, I felt very sad. The isolation, disconnectedness and mundane being the overall sense.

If that is a reflection of me, that is sad too!

I began walking around. Still observing.

I went into a store. In there I found a long dangling necklace...silver with little rhinestones. On the front were the words, "Smell the Flowers" on the back "What a beautiful day." I decided to purchase this as a reminder to value my existence and the life that is in me and around me.

As I continued to walk I saw the "make a bear store." I had never been in there before. There was this particular bear that seemed to call my name...he

275

was tie dye...pink and yellow and purple...I instantly loved him. Now you know what he was called right? **Endless Hugs.**

It almost made me teary eyed. I thought...that is joy. Endless hugs. So I proceeded to look through every one of the empty bears to find the one that spoke to me above all the others...I picked him out...to bring him to life of course.

Then the woman who was helping me asked me if I wanted a sound in the bear...I am thinking what the hell for? Okay so that doesn't sound like a very cherished moment...but I am a bit out of my element here...and then I tell her "Shhh, don't tell anyone but the bear is for me"...so I picked out a giggle sound...I thought...I need more laughter.

Okay...no really, I am almost done. So then she says, what kind of heart do you want in your bear? One that beats or one that doesn't? I took the beating heart, I wanted a beating heart and she walked me through the process of warming the heart...putting it on my forehead so the heart would know my thoughts...and on my ear so it would hear me and on my heart so it would know love...

Then she stuffs him and asks me if he is over or under stuffed? I make him more mushy by asking that some of the stuffing be taken out...

And then, she tells me to bring the bear to the bathtub and let the air shower (literally air comes out) fluff him up and then brush him out...and I did!

Then I sit at this little computer to name him and create his birth certificate.

I named him **<u>DELIGHT.</u>**

Perhaps in his creation...begins mine.

I actually let myself be the child and I was stunned the sales person encouraged it. She just acted as if I was 10 years old getting this cherished gift...it was really lovely.

That day was truly magical for me because I was playing. I was being silly. I ventured into waters I had never allowed myself to go. After a lifetime of being overly responsible, overly vigilant, overly serious, I was silly. I allowed myself this freedom; that bear reminded me that I needed love, I needed hugs, and I longed to play. I had been missing so many things—love, laughter, and most of all, compassion.

Soon after this trip to the mall, I had written just a brief thought:

Pride is fear in disguise.

If I embrace my fear I will have to acknowledge that I am here.

That I long for an embrace,

That I want there to be a trace,

That…I am alive.

If I embrace my desire, I will have to hold you and more importantly be held.

And at that moment…

Funny that I didn't finish or I couldn't finish. I was really becoming aware of the desire to be held. Like a little girl I wanted someone to tell me it was all going to be okay. I wanted someone to compassionately parent me, and let me know that I would make it through. I also knew that I was that someone, and needed to offer compassion and love to the child inside of me, whose life was so loveless.

As a coach, I have always encouraged utilizing journaling or writing. I believe there is significant power found in seeing our own words on paper. I also was at a phase where I was really looking to awaken that little girl in me, who didn't feel safe to come out and play. She was so tired from carrying me, she was beginning to sense she would be free of her burdens soon.

I believe we should journal and meditate every day. I believe this because I have seen that it keeps us in touch with who we are and where we are. I believe it helps us to lead an aware life. It keeps us from moving so quickly that we forget to make time for us, to stay connected to us, to stay connected to the bigger part of us. There is an old Zen adage, "You should sit in meditation for twenty minutes every day—unless you're too busy, then you should sit for an hour." This idea is not exclusive to any one religion; many religious or spiritual texts present this idea with different wording. The Bible says "Be still and know that I am God." (Psalm 46:10) and "In quietness and trust is your strength," (Isaiah 30:15). These have always been my favorite verses. Now I understand why, they were always calling me to be still, and discover my truth.

We are all connected. Make the time to examine that connection. This one energetic soul connects our many bodies. Our soul, our one source, is God.

Our God is all. We were all given all capacities. The capacity for good, the capacity for evil and we get choose which capacity we live from. We were given free will to do just that.

When I was trained to become a life coach I was taught that when you posed a question to your inner self, you could switch the pen to your non-dominant hand and receive a response, as if your own inner child was speaking. I used this to gain a sense of the well being of my inner child. I was devoted to creating my complete wholeness and announcing that I was ready to Live Free.

I asked for forgiveness, I expressed great gratitude. I promised to nurture and heal and protect all parts of myself. I owned that I would fail at times, and believed that through forgiveness and love, health and joy were possible.

My last words in my letter to myself were:

...release yourself fully, totally, and completely for there is no longer any reason to hide. You are safe; you are a precious, beautiful, joyful, creative, athletic, healthy, lovely, playful child. Behold you are finally safe. You can

trust me now—embrace your life; no more fears, no more tears, for you are free.

Trust me. Perhaps that message was to my inner child to let her know she was safe. Perhaps it was to the grown-up me, the complete woman I had now become. Either way, it was validating that there was wisdom all around me which had always been available. The God in me. As a child our experiences direct us to decide, as an adult we have the power to create any life we so desire.

All of me deserved so much more. I understand that now.

These liberating exercises were clearing the "transitioned me" beyond the point of being awake and led me to the final phase. Being free. As I moved forward, I could feel the darkness of my old life dissipating, and the beauty of my new life beginning.

Living your life in alignment at all levels will create peace and joy for you. This is not just your principles, values, words, actions; it is all of you, your mind, body, and spirit, as one. Open yourself to the larger picture. Take care of yourself, and remember that it is not about perfection, it is about peace. Change starts by embracing where you are. Discovering, and then loving and accepting all of you. Begin to acknowledge the bigger presence of the Universe in your life. God sends you nothing but angels.

Address the beliefs you have and change your thought patterns.

Let us use my beliefs and alter them to a more favorable belief system:

It is not okay to speak of my emotions.

I am free to speak my emotions, as any environment I create will be safe.

Women are weak.

I stand in my own power surrounded in love.

279

Men are authority figures.

No one is my authority. I live by my own guidelines.

It is my job to be sure the man is happy, and, therefore, if the man is unhappy it is my fault.

I am only responsible for my happiness. Our feelings are always our own.

It is up to me to keep the peace.

I am only responsible for my own "piece," so that I might experience peace.

I must do as authority says, no matter what the personal consequences.

I am my own authority and I always honor myself.

I must endure intolerable pain if necessary to please authority.

My "no" cannot be negotiated to a "yes" by pressure from another. I keep myself safe.

If I stand up and speak my emotions, something terrible will happen.

I may speak freely and I trust myself to stay safe.

I do not deserve compassion, only blame.

I do not accept blame for the actions of others.

If someone or something hurts me it is my own fault.

I know I have the power to remove myself from any harmful situation.

If someone or something hurts me there is something wrong with me.

I trust my inner guidance and I am stable and wise.

While I was in the healing process I was beginning to more profoundly recognize my oneness with the Universe. To illustrate this, I would like to share an experience. I have had many experiences like this before this moment, and many more since. I was beginning to embrace that if I was open and ready, everything I needed for a joyful life was available, I decided to honor an intuition. I had always believed that my grandmother was with me. I had actually never met her since she died when my dad was a child.

I chose to speak to my grandmother. First I chose to go through some heritage photos my parents had given me so that I could have a clear image of her in my mind. I placed several photos on display of ancestors I had never known. Not only had I not known these family members, I had never even given most of them an ounce of thought. This is fairly odd given my belief that we can choose to be reincarnated, and we tend to remain in a "family circle" of sorts.

The first thing I asked of her was to help me find something critical I was desperately searching for and could not find. Still with some doubt, I asked my grandmother to help me in my quest. Before I could finish my sentence I saw the missing item I had been frantically looking for. I saw it in the most obscure place. This day, this amazing day, the wonder of our connectedness occurred all day in beautiful synchronicities.

These events were immeasurable in their consistency, multiple moments were occurring seemingly in a direct response to my requests of grandma. I cried out "Oh My God, I am not alone!" as I dropped to my knees. I just stayed in silence and wept. It was a joyful weeping. It was a soulful experience.

281

Then I had to run an errand. I stood from my knees with a sense of awe, and I got in the car and put on the radio as I often do. I was driving up toward the street and I heard these words in that instant:

No more sorrow, no more pain
I will rise on eagles' wings
Before my God, fall on my knees
And rise
I will rise
Words from Chris Tomlin: I will rise

As soon as I heard those words, I knew they were for me, especially having just risen from my knees. I stopped my vehicle in my drive and turned to look at the radio, as if I expected to see God there. The digital dial had the time 3:23. My birthday; March 23rd.

It was as if the Universe wanted me to be absolutely clear that everything was, in fact, connected and that no matter how alone we may feel at times, we are **never** truly alone.

You are here, you are alive. This is testimony to me there is more that your life has to offer to the world, regardless of how big or small that world might be; in your intimate circle, or the bigger Universe as a whole.

I ultimately would decide I was at the "allow" phase of my life. I just needed to stop and be. I needed to "allow" the Universe to flow through me. My river needed boundaries, but only those that allowed a healthy flow. I needed to ebb and flow as directed by my inner knowing. It was time to release control fully; a complete and total surrender. It was time to float peacefully.

Sometimes surrendering allows us to stop fighting long enough to hear the message we need to end the war. In one such instance, in my early stages of healing, I was distraught. My thoughts were racing and I was feeling desperate. I was driving and I screamed out to God, the Universe, anyone who would listen, "What do you want from me? I surrender!" As I spoke those words I heard the resonance of that same word on the radio, in perfect synchronicity to my word—*surrender*. I couldn't miss it. It was a profound experience. I just cried. I found and find that often when I speak to the Universe it responds in measureable and identifiable ways, and if I am open and listen, I will receive that message. Music is often where I hear God's voice; where I get the messages that remind me I am not alone, but the messages can be found anywhere if we are willing to receive them.

Love and honor of myself have replaced my **stamina and endurance**. I have traded those attributes in for ones that offer more regard for me. We must begin to honor all things, including ourselves. This means mercy when you fail to perfectly follow loving treatment of yourself. Embrace everything as it is, with love.

- ❖ **Love yourself fully exactly where you are.**
- ❖ **Always honor yourself.**
- ❖ **Honor others as long as honoring others doesn't cause you to dishonor yourself.**
- ❖ **If someone is asking you to dishonor yourself for them, it is not okay. Say no.**

Honor. I love that word. It is so powerful in depth of meaning. It warms my soul to experience it, both to give it and receive it. What would happen if we all chose to follow that mantra, to love and honor ourselves and others? What would happen in our lives, and in the world at large, if we all chose to live those treasured values, those compelling emotions completely, all of us? If we all look first within, we will change the world. What drives how well we honor ourselves and others? It may have something to do with ego.

Ego

Perhaps you are beginning to see the oneness within yourself, mind, body, and spirit, the connectedness of all parts of you. It may be becoming clear to you why assessing yourself in each of the key areas: Spiritual (Spirit), Financial (Material), Emotional (Heart), Physical (Body), and Mental (Mind) is critical. You can likely see now how the mind, body, spirit, and even your heart, fit into those elements and why once you are whole, the delineation of these parts of you evaporate. You might still be wondering how financial fits into the critical assessment of ourselves, and then wonder how it fits into the oneness of the Universe as well. I believe it all connects in the place of ego.

I hope you will hear the messages that are necessary to assist you in shortening your journey of pain, and enable you to find the life of love you so deserve. The life I believe you are here to have; the life of freedom. No matter how trapped you may feel, no matter how helpless or hopeless, freedom can be yours. Perhaps it is true that we simply have to let go, release all fears, to be truly free.

As you have journeyed on this path to self-awareness, you may have become more intimately aware of your ego. *Ego* is our sense of self. The term "ego" has a long history of being defined and redefined by philosophers, psychologists, and other great thinkers. At the risk of belaboring the subject, I would like to frame this concept a little differently. Most of us consider an ego to be a bad thing. If someone has a large ego, we tend to think of them as conceited. In contrast, I would argue that an ego can be a very good thing. Remember, ego is merely our sense of self, and I think that most people would agree that it is important to have a sense of self.

I do not think that an ego is something that you simply have or don't have. I believe that there are actually two kinds of ego; the **physical ego** and the **Divine ego**. Physical ego is of the *world*, the physical. Divine ego is of the *Universe,* the Spirit; the full power of the God within us. Both egos are our sense of self; our power. Which ego we truly embrace and live from simply directs what we are going to use our power or our sense of self for.

The physical ego has to do with your **attachment** to tangible goods like money or physical possessions or the appearance of such. Money itself is necessary on this planet, but our perceptions of money have a tremendous impact on our life and the lives of those around us. In our society, financial power is perceived as one of the most significant kinds of power. Some people desire to have power over and control of people and things, and money is certainly an effective tool for the manipulations that assist one in achieving those goals. The desire for money can lead to a willingness to deceive; therefore, many deceptions have money at its root.

When you think of *physical*, do not merely think of material possessions as that is an incomplete understanding of this message. The physical, of the world, is where our judgment of others exists. It is where we often use **comparison** to create our sense of self. This ego is held to by anyone that perceives that someone who is different than them is somehow less, or perhaps even more, than they are. People that choose to live under the illusion that they are better than another, or another is less valuable than them, are vested in their image. The physical, is about the "image". The image you are striving to obtain may be one of wealth, power, strength, or maybe an image that evidences you have the perfect family, or you own the nicest cars, or the best business, or are savvy in matters of the financial world. In the "physical" there are a plethora of things one can chose to hide behind, choosing to present to the world the mask of who they want others to believe they are, to cover the truth about who they are afraid they are. You see, but the simplicity of life is to merely embrace all of who we *really* are and present that to the world. Become aware of the truth of our wounds, rather than hide behind them. Look in the mirror of Truth for it will ultimately lead you to stand in the full power of God. There, we easily show up as we really truly are. In that space there is no need to boast of our power and strength. It simply is.

So in summary, in the physical ego we concern ourselves with how we want others to see us, not with who we really truly are. The physical ego is about the "mask" we wear so that we will be perceived in whatever way matters to us most. This "image" could be financial success, being a nice person, or any other characteristic that is presented, merely to feel we fit in and are accepted. The physical ego is about our adapted self.

Think of ego as having a sliding scale. You can be at either side of that scale or anywhere in between, you decide. Those who operate *solely* from their physical ego are more exclusive. They judge people as better than or worse than, based on status. Status here is measured by money, power, and acquisition of those things. People are defined largely by what they have and control, not by who they are as a human *being*. There is a presence of fear and a desire to control. The physical ego is dense, as is its name implies, it is grounded in its physical nature. This density restricts the ability of light to pass through it, and allows for things to be hidden in the shadow. This sense of self, grounded mainly in attachment to things, and therefore on a quest for power over and control of, operates from the shadow side. Just as a physical object casts a shadow, the driving forces of the physical ego come from the shadow. The forces of *fear, power over, and control of.* The more you allow all of these to dictate your life, the larger the shadow that is cast.

In contrast, the Divine ego is full of light, it is translucent.

The Divine ego operates from the **Spirit,** *of the Universe,* from the God within us. People are defined by who they are as human *beings*, not what they have in terms of physical assets or appearances. Those driven by this ego are more inclusive and believe in a connected world. They acknowledge that no one is better or worse. They believe that people and nature are the greatest resources. They embrace the presence of love and a desire to *allow.* This ego is translucent, spreading, connecting, and offers transparency. This translucency allows for the light to dominate the shadow.

Your Divine ego is your total peace. It is Love. It is your oneness with the Universe. It is God operating through you. Our Spirit ego or Divine ego holds in it the power of compassion, love, wisdom, and acceptance. The fullness of the Divine ego is an energetic flow, it has no density. It connects us, moves us, joins us; it is nothing but God. No fear, no desire for power over or control of. It is compassion in motion. Living fully in the Divine ego is the ultimate in being free. Only there will we reach a place where we are not only whole, meaning no longer fragmented, but also free from our wounds and attachments.

The Divine ego is the highest ideal in residing in our true nature, our true self. When you live fully from your true self, your "image" or how others see you is meaningless. Your comfort in your own skin is based on love. Love is the only measure.

Consider that we are born as Divine ego, totally aware of our connection to source, or God…and then once in the physical world we are often moved to the idea of the importance of these physical possessions and confuse them with the sense of love and acceptance. We merely wish to fit into our current environment, which seems to teach us things contrary to our accepted wisdom while we were aware of our connection to source. We shift from what we thought we knew, to what we now are learning from the physical. We depart from our wholeness seeking love and acceptance in the physical world…we begin to lose sight of our connection to source. We then spend most of our life feeling alone and inadequate, and it is *that* which drives us to seek our wholeness once again. Regrettably, we seek it "out there" in the physical, rather than awakening the force of God in our heart. "He" awaits dormant, waiting for us to use our power of free will, to accept the fullness of the gifts "He" has availed to us. Now, in our quest for wholeness we need to begin to release our attachment to things of the physical, allowing us to experience the fullness of our light once again.

The entire Universe is motivated by **love**, and if you are living without a sense of abundance you are motivated by **fear**. Once you decide that love is the core of all things, and apply that knowing to all things, including you, a life of abundance becomes your reality. An abundance of love, joy, peace, health and yes, even money.

You need to assess and understand "financial," your views about money, to understand life on a personal level, as well as the world at large. In becoming more self-aware you will be better prepared to see manipulations. You will recognize as people choose to manipulate and control in their quest for money or power. Those with money often leverage it for power, just as those with power often leverage it for money. A sense that there is not enough, or creation of a scarcity mentality, certainly causes fear. Anything that causes fear can create controlling power if we let it. And anything that causes fear is not from God.

During fragmentation, as I have said, we choose to operate only from our shadow or only from our innocence. In both cases we are absent of the ability to experience the full power of God within us. Even though we may not acknowledge the existence of our opposing side, it is still within us. Fear, for example, comes only from our shadow. This is why acknowledging our fear is such an important part of reaching our wholeness. Even though we may deny the existence of the shadow, the fear penetrates our life in the fragmented state, even if we do not recognize this fear. When we operate only from our innocence, we cannot do harm, and do not know we are supposed to protect ourselves. We see *only* the needs of others and ignore our own presence and power in our life. Even in those who operate solely from their shadow, their childlike innocence may remain, perhaps even a glimmer of love, we can't know for sure. What we do know is they are often so focused on the chess game they are creating, the thought of true love and compassion does not reach the surface. Fragmented, we will never know the joy of wholeness and our full connection to Source, the God within us. God has never abandoned us; in our fragmented state we have chosen to deny the full power and presence of God, leaving that power dormant within us.

Those who operate solely from their shadow will always experience only their physical ego. They cannot experience the Divine as they believe there is no source more powerful than themselves. They deny the existence of the Divine. Their only goal is to obtain *power over* and *control of* things and people; and in the full depth of the shadow they make no distinction between the two. People are merely objects. They believe there is no true love, no true peace, so any reflection of those Divine traits in them are only portrayals in an effort to obtain dominance over the object of their desire. There is no **trust** in the purely physical ego; there is only *fear, power over, and control of.*

Those who operate only from the light of their innocence often believe in the existence of the Divine. They strive for peace, they long for love, they deeply offer compassion. However, time after time they find themselves pulled into the physical ego by fear, fear of losing what they have. They do not see themselves as worthy of the full power of God. They see themselves as not good enough just as they are. They can only keep trying to do better and be better, never fully calling upon the power within them. Like those operating from their shadow, those operating from their innocence have no **trust**. Without trust they cannot experience the fullness of the Divine ego.

The fear in the physical is what drives our *attachment*. When we have attachment, we are bound. We are bound to this physical world. We define ourselves by things that we have or control. We fear that if we lose those things, or lose control over those things, we will lose ourselves. Physical ego is, quite literally, having a physical sense of self.

Once we embrace all parts of ourselves and we are willing to acknowledge our fear of losing our "things," then we can fully shift to the Divine. However, pure acknowledgement is not enough. **We must let go**. We must realize that there is only one thing worth holding on to, and that is love. Love is the Divine. The physical is just that, physical, held to the earth. We will not obtain peace through tangible things, only through love of ourselves and others. When you let go of the *attachment* to the physical, you can truly move to the *Divine* ego. As we release our attachment, we begin to acknowledge **trust**. When we let go of the attachment, our battle to be free is won.

In my life it was my fear of looking bad, losing my assets, losing what I thought defined me, what I deemed as my security; I feared experiencing the shame attached to that loss. These attachments to the physical, this lack of trust, kept me from experiencing the fullness of my Divine ego. The battle we create in our lives is a battle within ourselves, we can release our attachment to the physical, our desire to control, our desire to maintain appearances, for complete and total love and acceptance of ourselves and others; the ultimate experience of God.

In our personal world, like in the world at large, messages of impending doom or danger repeatedly induce massive fear, causing us to act to avoid shame or severe consequences. In fact, these messages are often nothing more than efforts to control us. Those who wish to harm us create whatever illusion is necessary to extract from us or cause us to give, whatever it is that they desire. Yet, now that I see the Truth, the abundance and freedom was with me all the time. I simply had to release my fears and attachments in favor of **trust,** and embrace the full powers available to protect myself from harm. What if this knowledge, the knowledge to release our fears and attachments in exchange for faith and trust, would allow for the world to be at peace? We all are free to live from our Spirit of God, recognizing our oneness with all, and choosing of our own free will, to love and protect.

Just as you must accept and embrace all parts of you to achieve the experience of total inner peace, it is only when we accept and embrace all parts of the world, even those we have rejected in the past, that we can observe world peace. This peace is created through experiencing the full power of the endless source of Love. We are not meant to judge, only to love. Just as all parts of us as individuals are interconnected, mind, body, and spirit, so are all parts of us as a world, as a Universe. We are all connected by that one source that runs through us, should we choose to acknowledge and embrace it, God, the greatest source of Love.

We cannot reject that which is a part of us and be whole and complete at the same time. To experience true peace we must embrace and know our oneness. We must only determine which parts of the Universe in its entirety are wise to allow into our personal lives. Those parts which are not healthy for us we can acknowledge and then dismiss with love. There is an abundance of all the necessary components for peace and comfort in our lives **and** in the world. There is no shortage. This will become more evident as greed and fear are overcome by Love.

Those who live in the shadows hope we never discover our freedom. They hope we never realize the deceit, presented as truth, which hides in their shadow. It is in embracing the fullness of our light, our power of God within, that together, we can reveal all that hides in the shadow. Acknowledging the full capacities within us, we are *awakened*; we enter the **enlightened path**. We must recognize our oneness, and from our awake place we are able to clearly see the deceptions. It is time to distinguish between those in a mere puddle crying for help, and those in the depths of the water about to be drowned in the pull of the undertow, after having willingly treaded water and fought for their breath.

Money and the nice things it can do and buy should carry with it no shame. The imperative assessment is to discover which ego is directing its abilities, how the "tool" of money is being utilized, for *power over* and *control of* or for **Love**. The problem lies in our tendency to become *attached* and to begin to define ourselves by these tangible things. The person at peace does not fear losing any of the things in their possession because they know that "things" are fleeting. Only Love is everlasting.

The attachment to the physical literally binds us in that space. We are unable to move completely to the Divine until we sever all attachments. Release, and let go.

You may be wondering how you can simply let go of that attachment. After all, money is necessary to live in our world today. The idea of releasing the stresses formed by our attachment to money, our *fear* surrounding money, may seem ludicrous and impossible. But as I have said before, **trust** is the antidote to fear. The more you know, the more you discover what you don't know. When you begin to trust in the Universe, and in yourself, you no longer have a need for fear. In fact, when you operate from a place of **trust** to the point that you have reached your Divine ego, you no longer have a need for your shadow at all, although you are aware of its existence.

Understanding that these may seem to be complex notions, allow me to restate these thoughts:

Fragmentation is a result of a childhood experience which led us to decide to disown parts of ourselves. Most specifically, we decided to either operate from the light of our innocence, dropping our sword, unconsciously denying the power of God within us, or operating from our shadow, vowing to only use our sword, unconsciously denying the power of God within us.

Fragmentation makes us vulnerable. Whether or not we believe that we are vulnerable, whether or not we present that we are vulnerable, the vulnerability exists within us. It is only by acknowledging and embracing this vulnerability that we begin to address it. It is only in our wholeness, in the uniting of the power of our shadow and our innocence, that we become safe in our love *and* our power. Power without love is meaningless, love without power is defenseless. Embracing the whole of ourselves allows us to *truly* become invulnerable to those who wish to harm. We can finally find peace in our safety.

Those who only operate from their shadow harm others.

Those who only operate from their innocence, harm themselves, even if only by allowing others to harm them.

For us to be whole we must embrace the fullness of our innocence **and** our shadow. For when our innocence acknowledges and embraces the shadow, the full power of God ignites in us. We now hold our sword and can protect ourselves and others. As we move to heal our wounds, we become *complete*, aware we have everything we need, and all we ever need is Love. We are our Divine ego. In this translucent, connecting space, we know we are all one and our greatest purpose is **only** to Love and Protect. We trust and know, Love is what we are. We are invulnerable, not because no harm can ever come to us, but because nothing can damage or destroy us. We know it is not what happens to us, it is how we respond once it does. We have no fear. We have what we needed to be free, **Trust**. As Divine ego we see the truths and we believe what we see. We are no longer blinded by the shadow of deception. In seeing the Truth we know all is abundant, we are grateful. We are invulnerable because we know only Love is Real. We know Love cannot die, Love cannot be lost. Love is eternal, just as we are. With our trust and our power we create our beautiful life. We trust and know, that no matter what happens, if we stand back far enough, ultimately we will see the good that it brought, even if we are met with apparent tragedy. We know, The Universe is always orchestrating for our highest, greatest good. We live in peace. We know we are safe.

Those who operate only from their shadow would need to embrace the lost light of their innocence to experience the full power of God. However they are often unable to see through the cover of their own darkness to discover the light.

Whatever side we operate from is what we tend to see in others, since we cannot acknowledge in others what we reject in ourselves.

For many of us, this leads us to abusive relationships. You see, by choosing to drop our sword, our full power within us, we embark on a journey unarmed and unarmored. Because of that lack of safety and longing for the "rest of us," we tend to operate from a place of fear, something found in our shadow. Since we do not acknowledge the shadow, we do not see this fear. We tend to be *targets* since we do not see the capacity for evil in others, until we can finally see it in ourselves.

When we acknowledge the existence of the shadow in everyone, including ourselves, we can more easily recognize those who are manipulating us, and those who are filled with love. In the moment we embrace the lost part of us, we Wake Up.

Once Awake, we channel the power of our shadow in order to Stand Up and remove ourselves from abuse. We all have this power to Stand Up against abuses, on a small scale first in our own world, and then in the world at large. We must decide to love and protect as needed in the world.

When we embrace our denied capacity and awaken, we then journey to become complete. At first we may dwell on the things we have lost (physical ego). To reach our whole and complete state we must move away from such attachments to what really matters, Love.

Eventually, we will begin to trust ourselves and that we are part of the larger Universe able to participate in healing on a grander scale. The **trust** allows us to *release* our fear and our attachments and ultimately we no longer live in any form from our physical egos. First we must trust ourselves, and then we can begin to see the higher orchestration of Divine trust from a new level. We will allow our inner knowing to guide us.

From our place of **trust** and **love**, *releasing* all attachments, we reside in the power of the Divine ego. We continue to acknowledge our shadow side, but no longer need to use it. We are safe. Now that we trust ourselves and the power of God within us, we will see the capacity for evil in others. Remember, those who operate from the shadow vow to never be victimized or harmed by another. *No one will have power over me, no one will harm me* is their mantra. This is why when they feel they cannot escape entrapment, they have been known to kill themselves. Should those who wish to harm seek us out, we will intuitively know how to keep ourselves safe, our hands comfortably resting on our swords, prepared to use them if necessary. We will not allow those shadow dwellers into our lives or the lives of the innocents. Our ability to identify these people emanates from us. We present an aura of knowing, which will often scare off the would-be abuser. It is because of this, we will generally no longer *need* to use our sword. We can protect, we have no fear. Our power is felt by those who wish to harm.

When we come together as one to trust in the Divine ego, release all attachments, and acknowledge that there is abundance, there will be healing in the world. Wealth is not bad. Prosperity can provide for the world, if we can choose not to *grip with fear*, but instead *release with trust*. It is our attachment to things, our fear of losing such things, which stops the *flow* and creates scarcity and density, where abundance would otherwise be.

As a light and flowing energy of love and compassion we can see the Universe as more than just what meets the eye, or the bank account of the physical. We see it as an energetic flow that creates abundance in full proportion. If love is at the core, healing occurs. When we are healed, we operate in the world in our fullness of our capacities. We can hold our own piece, and we have the strength, power, and love, to hold the pieces of those who truly can't hold their own, acknowledging and embracing our shadow, we can help protect them.

Our Divine ego is about releasing, trusting, allowing, protecting, and **love**.

Our physical ego is about attachment, **fear**, power over, and control of.

We attract what resonates within us. In our fragmented state we unconsciously attracted to us what we sought in our quest for wholeness. We sought our missing piece outside of *us*. We do not need to journey outside of ourselves to discover our wholeness. It has always been within us. It is our denial of our capacities which causes our harm. The power within us can only be activated by our knowledge and acceptance of its presence.

Fragmentation attracts fragmentation, as we unconsciously seek that which will make us whole. We attract the parts of us we are missing. Once we are whole and complete, there is nothing outside of ourselves that we need. Our wholeness only attracts to us those who are also whole. To illustrate this, consider the tuning fork. If you have two tuning forks that vibrate at the same frequency, and you strike one, then mute it with your hand, seemingly inexplicably you will hear the other untouched tuning fork sound. The frequency of the vibration elicits a response from the other tuning fork. This is called sympathetic resonance. It exists only because the two forks are of the same make up; in essence they are whole and complete. If either tuning fork is broken, fragmented, the sympathetic resonance is no longer observed.

If we are fragmented, we attract those who are also fragmented. Having not embraced our full capacities, we attract what we are seeking for our wholeness—that which we have disowned. That mirror, symbolically held by another, is intended to wake us up to the presence of the parts of ourselves we have rejected. As you will see, we must choose to not be blinded by the mirror that will enlighten us.

You see, when we chose not to awaken, ultimately we may fall apart. With all our pieces on the ground we have the ability to not just pick up all those we have chosen to own in the past, instead, we can choose to pick up all the pieces, even those we previously chose to disown. And from our pain, from our falling to pieces, comes our wholeness.

The critical message is that we don't have to fall to pieces to arrive. We simply need to Back Up, Wake Up, Stand Up and Live Free. Right now, you can be at any phase of this process, evaluate where you are, and just know that living free is available to you any time you decide. You can heal, without falling to pieces.

It was our childhood experiences that led us to disown parts of us. As I said in the beginning, I say in the end. Our stories are not that important, it is what we decided about life because of our stories that is of supreme importance. Our stories can only serve to heal others, once we acknowledge the damaging beliefs we allowed them to create, and change the conditions of our life.

Once we have reclaimed all disowned parts, we will be better able to see the wholeness or fragmentation of others. Even if this is not immediately visible, we will know as we observe.

Imagery tends to have a lasting impact. To better understand ego and the battle created to achieve wholeness and peace, picture a person standing alone in a room.

Those with a dense ego do not recognize the presence of the light in this room. Those that operate from their darkness, refuse to regard and honor the light of their innocence and goodness. They utilize the capacity they embrace; power over and control of; they cling to their power of deception as their most envied tool. They will not *allow* the light to be the power, as they wish to hold *all* the power. They have cast the light aside in favor of their physical ego, attachment to things, power over and control of. The light they have ignored is now behind them, idle at their feet. However, the power of the light cannot be fully hidden. The power of that light still shines. There is no way to turn off the light of our innocence, but from being cast aside, being tossed to the earth behind them and left unacknowledged, it shines up, casting the huge shadow in front of them. This shadow is powerless against those standing in the fullness of the light, those who have embraced the fullness of their capacities, and terrifying to those who have not embraced their own power; even if those people cannot see their own fear. Those operating from their darkness, manipulate others by using the threat of the power of their shadow. They go through life dominating and controlling through deception.

Less dense are those who value people over things and are unwilling to harm another, even to protect. These people only operate from their innocence and goodness, not realizing the full power of the light. These people are often aware of the light, but see it in front of them, casting a beam down upon them from above. They see this light, but not the shadow. They refuse to see the shadow that is cast behind them from that light, the shadow that would give them the full power of God if they would only embrace it in union with their light. The shadow is small, because the light is so high to them, out of full reach, and because their physical ego isn't as dense, it has some translucency. They want peace, but find fear, because they feel they are alone, the unconscious feeling created by being unarmored and unprotected without their shadow. Those with this kind of fear see themselves as insignificant. They are often the abused, as without a shadow they cannot protect, nor harm. They will allow harm only unto themselves. They grip what they have in fear of losing it. They cling to anything or anyone that might give them a sense of worth. Perhaps they think these "things" will give them the density, the sense or worth they feel they lack. They seek the strength of the shadow, but seek it outside themselves, in others, and in the attachment to things. They cannot find it there, they must look within.

In essence, while standing only in the light of our innocence and goodness, we feel the presence of that light "out there" being cast upon us, but we believe we are powerless to direct it. We are aware of the Divine, but refuse to embrace the full power of God that resides within us. We accept the light, we do not consider the light is given to us to use as free will allows, in all its power.

Each of us has the capacity to embrace both the light of our innocence **and** the darkness of our shadow. Once we do so, once we embrace all the capacities, from this merging we now operate in the full Power of God. Once we heal our wounds and release attachments, we occupy only our **Divine ego**. At this time we realize that we have merged with the fullest power of the light. Only then will we finally experience our Divine peace; then we will be whole and complete. You see, in the precise moment we acknowledge all the power that was always within us, when we allow that power to operate fully through us, we have joined with the greatest co-creator of the Universe; the greatest source: God. Until that moment, this power, this omnipotent source, often had to sit idly by, as we were given free will and our choices often held this power at bay. If we refuse to allow the full power of the light...it cannot shine in all its glory. We are the directors of the light. We must allow the light to operate through us fully, then, we become **enlightened**.

God was always our co-creator; however, that source is limited by what we will allow. Our effort to do it alone, to believe we should never ask for help, to decide we are not worthy, left us without the benefit of the full power available. Our belief that we should not be protected if it means someone may be harmed, often left us powerless; when in fact the greatest source of compassion, love, and protection, was waiting for us to honor the fullness of the power available. In the moment we embrace fully this Truth we allow the occurrence of the greatest miracle for the highest, greatest good; Abundant Love.

I invite each of us to reclaim our power and allow the power of God to ignite the world in peace. For this purpose, God gave us free will; we must allow this will. People often say, *Where is God?* I believe God, as Love, asks, *Where are we?* "He" longs for us to embrace and allow the power that can be bestowed through us, the greatest gift, the full power of God within us. We must allow this power to be utilized for the good of all humanity. Collectively this power intensifies. Awake and whole, we can always prevail over those who are fragmented, living from their shadow, refusing to see the power of God within them, clinging only to their power of deception that while we sleep, controls us. We also can allow this power to protect those who operate only from the light of their innocence. Together, we can help them heal their fragmentation and embrace their full power. The deception that surrounds us is only hidden from us in our innocence. In the full Power of God, all is visible.

The entirety of us, standing as one in the room, embracing the power of our light, can insure the whole room is lit, and then keep the entire world illuminated. We simply must choose to stand in our full power of God. We can direct the power of this light to insure that things cannot stay in the shadows. We can Stand Up and insure that no one can use deception and fear, power over and control of. We must choose to no longer dim the light of truth in favor of our fear. With the light shining from directly above us and all around us, we know there is a shadow cast directly beneath us. The power of the shadow is ours to use as we will, and in the Power of God, it will only be used to protect and serve. Being aware of the presence of the shadow, and standing in the completeness of our light, allows us to rest assured that we can trust what we see, and use our power to protect and love wisely. In our wholeness, we are now able to heal our wounds and live in our Divine peace. We may do so in our personal world, and as we unify, in the world at large.

We are the directors of the light. Which way will you choose to *allow* the light to be directed?

We have always had free will. We always get to decide.

The Mirror

You might be asking yourself how to find your way to this wholeness, how to discover the pieces of yourself you have denied. I have given you several tools that may bring you to your self-awareness through introspection. I have also suggested that we need to recognize the parts of us that we have rejected so we may reclaim them. The question you may be asking is how will you know what the rejected pieces of yourself are, what parts of yourself you have denied, and how do you then reclaim them?

I have mentioned that God has sent you nothing but angels. All those who have entered your life have been intended to awaken you to the missing pieces of yourself. If we are willing to be open to our healing, seeking it, all those who cross our path can awaken us.

I have discussed the idea that we were unable to see the truth about those looking to manipulate us, and now that you understand the concept of the scale of ego, it should be easier to understand why. Our own ego, our attachment to things, was part of what blinded us to the truth. We feared losing what we had, we feared that loss would be the loss of us, but you see in our pain we were not yet "found." We were attracting the pieces we were missing, the pieces that we needed to become whole and complete. In our fragmented state, we attracted one who dwells in the shadow, the shadow we denied in ourselves.

Our kind Universe supplied us with that which we sought. All those who enter our life are symbolically holding a mirror so that we might see the truth about our missing pieces; first, so we can restore our fragmentation to wholeness, and then use the future reflections to recognize those wounds we must choose to heal to regain our complete wholeness.

I remember once learning that when I was being abused, treated with cruelty, to make eye contact with the abuser to attempt to remind him I was real. Now I realize we all need to make eye contact with our abuser, we need to see ourselves, all parts of ourselves in that mirror, even the parts of us we denied. It is our own distorted image that keeps us from being free.

As I look closely now, I see that those things that I judged others for, such as being irresponsible and careless, being cruel and unkind, those things that I thought were just a result of their injuries, were really my soul asking me to look at myself. Wasn't I being irresponsible and careless? Wasn't I being cruel and unkind—**to myself**? What if the way we judge another is often a reflection of ourselves? As I was judging their incongruence wasn't I ignoring my own? I saw them as the injured soul, but if I would have looked more closely in the mirror, if I would have paused and looked into my own eyes, my own window to my soul, I would have seen the injured soul was me—these promptings are to awaken us to see ourselves. The deep and painful truth in the mirror, what we judge, we often are. Even if we are not those things, the feelings of judgment must prompt a look inward, to examine something unresolved within ourselves.

To illustrate this concept, consider this; perhaps you find you are irritated by those around you for being irresponsible at work or calling in sick. Whether or not their behavior is in fact irresponsible is irrelevant. Know that all people are acting within the confines of what they deem acceptable behavior. The person calling in sick for example, has determined that this action is acceptable to them. The important question to ask yourself is, *Why does it bother you?* Look inward to discover what the irritation you feel about *them* is telling you, about **you**. This is how we begin to learn who we truly are. Are you bothered because you feel you need to carry more of the weight as a result of their behavior? Is it that you have always needed to carry the weight at home, and now you feel burdened by having to carry it in the office as well? Are you intolerant of ineptness because you feel you are more capable, and, therefore, those individuals are not? Is it that perhaps you are irresponsible in other areas of your life; at home for instance? What you need to undoubtedly know is seeking to understand the emotion you feel will lead you to better know *your* truth. Perhaps this circumstance is simply reflecting an unresolved issue of the family dynamics of your childhood. When as a child, did you feel this same feeling of frustration, anger, disgust? There is no absolute in revealing the message, except to say if it is bothering you, then there is a message in it, for you. Seek it. The behavior of others is not about you, if you feel that it is, look in your own eyes in the mirror to answer the question, *Why?*

It is imperative to look for incongruence, in others. It is at least equally imperative to look for it in ourselves.

Because I refused to see these truths about myself, they were showing up more boldly every day. This is why I mentioned to be careful about how you judge another, because it just may be that your own lesson is hiding in that judgment. What we judge we may be confronted with at a very personal level. Knowing the truth of the mirror, now as I feel inclined to "judge" another, I ask instead, why does this elicit such a reaction from me? What is this telling me about myself?

And so it is, that all our peace rests "back there" in the places we refuse to look buried deep within us. Perhaps the truth is hidden by the density of our ego…we must be willing to look.

Isn't all that controls our life, all that inflicts our pain, grounded in our fear of loss? In our fear of losing our assets, our "image," our relationship, or whatever we perceive we need to obtain love and acceptance? All the control that I allowed others to have over me was grounded in my attachment to things, to my "image" of being the "strong one," being the "capable provider." My suffering was caused by choosing to believe I was nothing or less without those things, or I was a failure if I could not achieve the goal, never really looking at me and the value I had by just being *me*.

When we are "wounded" we hide the parts of us we think are unacceptable...those parts also lurk in the darkness of the shadow.

When we are "fragmented" we hide the fullness of our shadow, our power, our ability to protect, our capacity for evil. We commit to ourselves we cannot harm, we cannot lie and we do not protect ourselves...the inverse is true of those that refuse to see their innocence and goodness.

The truth is all visible in the mirror, if we just look.

Previously I shared an image to help you visualize how the shadow is cast. Now, let us use that image to solidify our blindness, and how accessible the truth was all along.

We allowed ourselves to stay blinded, and see only the parts of us we were willing to see. We lived in delusion, refusing to embrace the parts of ourselves that would make us whole and complete. You see, as these men in my life were holding up their mirror so that I might see the darkness of my shadow being cast behind me, I refused to look in that mirror. I saw only the light emanating from *around* the mirror, this was all I was willing to see. This light was shining upon me from above, casting a shadow behind me, a shadow which I refused to see. Because these men stood in front of me, I mistakenly thought the light I saw was theirs. I believed it to be their innocence, but this was merely an illusion. This was my light, the light that seemed so out of reach, but still I reached for it, and thus I reached for them. I refused to acknowledge the pain inflicted on me so I could not see the contradiction. I did not have self-love, I did not honor my right to exist, which is why I would not see or acknowledge my pain. All the *judgments* I cast on them were reflections of the parts of me I refused to see. All that I *embraced* in them was all I was willing to accept about me, it was all I could see.

To them, as I stood in front of them holding my mirror so that they might see their innocence, the projection of the light behind them, which they had cast aside, allowed them to see only their own shadow which was cast upon me. My abusers and I could each only see what we were willing to see, the part of ourselves we were willing to accept. If only we chose to look directly into the mirror at our own reflection, we could have seen the truth. We could have seen the fullness of ourselves, even those parts we refused to see, the parts that were hidden "back there." If we were willing to deal with the truth that we saw, then we would have entered our paths to freedom. If I looked more closely at myself in the mirror, I could have seen in my reflection the shadow behind me, and in embracing that shadow instantly healed my fragmentation. Now whole, I would have seen their shadow cast upon me and know that I was allowing it to effectively bury my light. This is true of all those living from their innocence. We must turn our eyes away from them and onto ourselves to have the whole truth revealed to us.

Our "missing piece" was right there behind us, had we used the mirror to see. If only we would have chosen to stay focused on seeing ourselves in the mirror, rather than looking everywhere else, focusing on trying to see them and their pain behind their mirror. We focused only on the external, never recognizing the role we played in all our pain. That is, until we allowed our eyes to focus on the mirror that was in front of us all along. They too had the chance to see the light of innocence that was shining behind them, but they too did not seek the truth.

In our wholeness, we no longer allow others to abuse us. We no longer tolerate the intolerable, for we know now our Divine presence, our fullness of love, and our deservingness of honor. When we can stand comfortably in our full power, we have found our wholeness. When our wounds are healed we will no longer feel the need to judge another, or have a defensive reaction…this is how we know, we have found our way to being whole and complete. Total acceptance of ourselves in all our capacities, in the fullness of who we are, allows us to embrace others with eyes wide open and accept them as they are. We need not fix them, only observe who they are. We believe what we see, as they show themselves to us. We recognize those who are directly inflicting harm, and that ignites our power to protect. We know we have our sword and are clear on when and how to use it, but often our presence of power is enough. Once whole, we can more easily see the truth before us. As we continue on this path and heal our wounds, the clearer and more peaceful our lives and the lives of those around us become. We will not only be whole, we will be complete. Aware we need nothing outside of ourselves. Love is in fact, all we need. When something is trying to awaken you, I believe now you will know. Always keep your eyes on the mirror. Peace and happiness come only from within.

You see, I now understand the wisdom of the mirror. It is the tool to help us find our wholeness, which was available to us all along.

Renowned Psychotherapist, Carl Jung says, "Everything that irritates us about others can lead us to an understanding of ourselves."

Everyone in your life is there for a reason, holding the mirror up so you will see. When you feel the discomfort of irritation, when you are bothered by others or experiencing what you will now recognize as misalignment, pain, or lack of peace, ask yourself what you are not willing to embrace or accept about yourself. Do not be afraid to look directly in the mirror. Without looking in the mirror, you cannot look into your own eyes and see the whole of your existence.

I am hoping this message will be forever a part of you. A part that can simplify what seems like our complex world, all we need to do is look within. We need to no longer judge, but instead observe, and acknowledge our oneness. Be awakened to harm, but do not become so cynical that you perceive that harm exists where there is none. The truth is always inside of us, if only we would quiet our minds from the chaos, embrace our hearts, and look fully into the mirror.

What if even those who are evil to us, are unconsciously on a quest to help us heal? Our abuser holding up the mirror is perhaps saying to us, *See your darkness, the fullness of yourself, so you might heal, it is right behind you.* But because we are unwilling to accept our darkness, our shadow, since we have long ago disowned that part of ourselves, we cannot see the darkness, not in them and not in ourselves. Their darkness bothers us, but we excuse it away instead of looking directly at it. We distract our eyes from the mirror of truth, the shadow that lurks behind us longing to be reclaimed; we focus only on the light that blinds us. The light we think emanates from them.

As we are holding up the mirror perhaps we are saying to them, *See your light, the fullness of yourself so you might heal.* But because they are unwilling to accept their innocence, their goodness, since they have long ago disowned that part of themselves, they cannot see the innocence, not in themselves and not in us. Our innocence bothers them, and so they accuse us of not being so. They distract their eyes from the mirror of truth; they cannot see the light that lurks behind them longing to be reclaimed. They can see only the blinding shadow that falls over the mirror. The shadow they think is us.

As long and hard as we have tried to show them the light in the mirror, they too have been trying to show us the shadow in the mirror. We have each unconsciously been trying to make the other aware of their wholeness. However, recall that no one can be forced to embrace the fullness of the power of God, we must each choose it for ourselves. Only through consciously engaging in self-reflection can we move from fragmentation to wholeness. We believe that we can make people see the light, but only people who are looking for the light, can see it.

When we accept the light and the dark within ourselves, we have acknowledged all the capacities we possess. We now have the eyes to see deceptions and truth. We have the eyes to see evil, and we have the power to Stand Up against it. We have eyes to see the bountiful genuine love and we choose to surround ourselves in it.

Once whole, we operate at such a high resonance that we attract to us more goodness and light. In our wholeness we have a balance in our energies; we know we can swing the sword. We have no desire to do harm; instead, we have a desire to love and protect; and this includes ourselves.

In all areas we seek and acknowledge our connectedness so that all things may operate together as intended: **In harmony.**

When we are truly filling the needs of ourselves and others, there is gratitude. Gratitude is a sign of all things being in balance. **Gratitude creates abundance.**

When the blessings you are bestowing on others have you feeling resentment and pain, instead of compassion and joy, you must acknowledge that you are out of alignment. Any time you are not at peace, there is a misalignment.

Give freely, without expectation. When the blessings you give are being received with claims of your inadequacy and insufficiency, recognize this as a sense of entitlement, which is in opposition to gratitude. Give expecting nothing in return, but know that if you do receive a response, it should come in the form of gratitude and grace, not criticism and contempt. Be wary of greed masked with words of love. Be aware of misalignment.

Our assessment of our position about money, image, and ego reveal the circumstances of our personal world and also the world at large. On the physical plane, if the focus is only on power over and control of, with an increasing blatant disregard for people and the planet—the world will not be able to sustain itself. Just as in our own world, this desire to control can destroy us; the same is true in the world at large. We must stand in the light, in our goodness, without forgetting our shadow, thereby never allowing ourselves or others to be diminished in our presence. If we embrace all parts of us, we can shine the full power of our light on all deceptions, and free ourselves from our pain.

It is through honoring ourselves and others, that both our personal world and the world at large will experience abundance, an abundance founded in generosity and giving, not power over and control of. The more others try to control us, the tighter we often grip what we have. As we grip, we create scarcity. Abundance can't be regulated, it must be *allowed.* We mustn't stop the Divine flow that is available. We must love ourselves and each other enough to trust and know when it is time to protect. No longer can we be blinded by the shadow of darkness that wishes to harm.

Imagine a world in which we honored one another and valued each person regardless of our differences. Imagine a world in which we only took a stand when we were truly being harmed, and allowed all of us to be loved and accepted as we are…imagine the flame of light that would be lit in the soul of all of us as we felt valued and validated, no longer willing to allow anyone to diminish our light. We must awaken inside ourselves so that we may stand strong together and help the world awaken.

Those who are grateful will always have abundance.

In the end, I have nothing but gratitude. God truly sent me nothing but angels, who were trying to awaken me from my slumber.

I believe complete wholeness, or better stated, "oneness" is the purpose of all life. Complete wholeness is not merely reparation of our fragmented selves, it goes further than that. Complete wholeness is healing of all the wounds left from the injuries of the past. It is embracing the interconnectedness of all things. It is the ongoing journey of enlightenment. Without attachment, without wounds, we may discover the depths of our own Divine selves, as we venture on a path to uncover the vastness of Divinity.

We must find our complete wholeness in ourselves first, and then use the powers we have discovered in ourselves, to heal the Universe as a whole. Just as we cannot reject, hate, or deny any part of ourselves, any part of our mind, body, or spirit, we too must accept that we are one with all that until now, we perceived was "out there." It is internally, through each breath we take, and the love we give, that we join together the external as one. As more of us begin to honor our connectedness, our strength and power offer love and acceptance to overshadow the fear. As more people move toward complete wholeness, the illumination of those living from their shadow will be inevitable. Illuminated by the power of our light, they will stand powerless. It is only under the shadow of darkness that they can prevail. Eventually, there will no longer be a need to swing the swords that hang powerfully at our sides, as all will be illuminated and there will be nowhere to hide.

There will be peace.

I am grateful for my wholeness and I wish the same for you.

We must look closely in the mirror, only to see the fullness of ourselves. Embrace those parts that are behind us and reclaim them. In our wholeness we can clearly see our wounds. The mirror is a powerful tool. Remember to look in it closely when you feel defensive or irritated. You may find another unaddressed wound staring back at you.

We must not create a life of only doing. We must have moments to just *be*. We are human *beings*. We must release our compulsion to have a life of only doing. It is only in *being* that we can reflect. In *constantly* doing we miss the whole connected Universe that is all around us. We must stop judging externally and see the truth within ourselves.

Know that God, the Universe, Love, has no limits. When we begin to appreciate our oneness with everything, we begin to sit in silent wonder at the world around us. Know that the messages that you are intended to receive can come from any source. Do not overlook the flower, the sunset, even the dirt beneath your toes. You are a part of all these things. Contemplate their meaning, appreciate their beauty.

<u>Living Free</u>

How did I come to understand the binding that occurs with attachment, and the full freedom that comes from releasing and allowing? How did I come to embrace that our sense of self, our ego, can be grounded in fear and control or trust and allowing? What gave me my conviction that we can choose to act from the physical or the Divine space?

To share my moment of enlightenment, we must step back to when I first reentered the "real" world with my new found sense of freedom. It was once I was free and awake, and willing to always look internally for the answers, that the rest of the truth was beautifully revealed. I was always able to live free. All I had to do was let go. We are the creators, the constructors of our life, and we have the full power of God within us when we are ready to experience it. At the moment we truly let go, we realize we have a loving co-creator easily manifesting through us all the many wondrous desires of our hearts.

The most arduous part of my journey had come to an end, and I felt whole and complete. Not only was I free from abuse, but I had picked up all the pieces of my life and felt joyful. I was finally fully feeling and experiencing my life and I loved it, I loved me. I had not been working much during my healing and growth, but I knew it was time to start again.

Having no other promptings, I felt led to return to my roots in financial services. I felt it would fulfill my desire to serve, and it would use my vast bank of experience and knowledge. However, I would approach my career on my terms, my hours, my way. I finally decided authority had no power in my life whatsoever, not even in the business arena. As I began my new position, I had far more peace than I had all my life. I was looking to make a living, but I did not feel like I had to be the best, rise to the top, or get validation from authority. I was happy to be my own validation. It was a completely new experience for me.

As I journeyed through that first year in that new position, I focused on the aspect of this job that I had always loved, serving others. I quickly rose to amongst the top "first year" income earners in my role, but I was no longer succeeding in search of praise, it was simply the result of operating from my heart. I offered my clients the best products and services available, and the money seemed to follow. As much as I enjoyed my interactions with the people in my work, I rather quickly found myself unfulfilled. I sensed an incongruence, I felt an inner prompting. I recognized a lack of peace stirring. I looked inside of myself to discover what that incongruence was. I realized that I felt a misalignment between my values and those of my "leaders." I realized I was entrenched in the physical ego of others. A place I no longer wished to be.

This time, when I felt the incongruence, I listened. I recognized I was not at peace, and I was no longer willing to settle for a life void of peace. I needed to make a change. Without hesitation, I decided to downsize my home so that my financial needs would be reduced, and my life simplified. I thought that might be a first step toward being able to leave my job, and return to full alignment with myself. My large acreage and the vast investment in extensive improvements, byproducts of the previous manipulations I

312

allowed, were a big monthly nut to crack. I had thought about selling my home for some time, but frankly I felt trapped by the money I believed I needed to obtain from this property in such a soft market. I wanted to simplify, but feared that I couldn't survive financially without recovering my investment. I was beginning to release that fear, and I considered that if I did downsize, perhaps I wouldn't need to work at all. I wanted to serve my purpose, not simply earn a paycheck. However, how to go about serving my purpose still seemed unclear to me.

For now, I just knew that I needed to honor the incongruence I felt, by taking action. It was a very quick decision. I wanted my home on the market. I finally knew that it was the right thing. It was a deep absolute knowing. I loved my place, it had become my sanctuary. On the weekends I would just go outside and connect with nature. I was learning to take nature photographs and I would take photos of the dogs, horses, the sunrise, and sunsets. My favorite healing place was on the patio out by my pond. I loved it there. I loved listening to the sound of the water on the falls. I felt so connected to the whole. My home may have started out as a burden I took on to appease a man, yet in the end, as everything is, it was a gift.

I had grown with my home. When my world fell apart, at first I felt so burdened with all I had to do to keep that place together. Soon she, my home, became so worth it. She became part of me. I wanted to release her to sacred hands, and yet, I felt I needed a certain value, given all that I had invested in her building, and expansion. As you can see, some fear still lingered. How would I sell her, how could I get my price? The market was not favorable for selling a home and I perceived I needed more than double what I paid to restore all I put in. My home was an oasis. There were very few homes around her with great worth, so in the physical world it would seem her price was unachievable. However, I was finding my peace and beginning to fully have a willingness to **trust**.

I had found so much of myself on my journey to healing. Healing is simply finding our spiritual wholeness. As I assessed who I really was at the core of my being in all areas, I learned what I loved to do and what made me happy. I also learned what I valued most. I spent so much time getting to know myself. I was more open and less fearful; I was *releasing* completely my desire to *control*. I was deeply beginning to **trust**. I just knew the right support would come to help this downsizing come to pass. Immediately, a friend introduced me to someone who understood what my home had been to me and agreed to help me sell. I knew she understood the whole picture of my experience of my home and I knew she was the right person to assist me in moving forward. I knew. Within days of our meeting, I had signed the papers agreeing to sell my home through her.

I was making good money at my job, but I was incessantly feeling the incongruence of the values of my immediate company leaders and my own. Three months had elapsed since my home went on the market and I had no idea how long it would take for it to sell. The incongruence I was experiencing daily at work was beginning to weigh heavily on me. I also had no idea where I was going to move when my home finally did sell. I could see many aspects of how the Universe was lining up to free me, and yet I still wondered how I could possibly leave my job before my home sold, and survive financially. At this point in time I still was holding to a bit of the physical, the image, the attachment, the fear.

For a moment, for several moments, I felt trapped.

I was frustrated by my sense of entrapment. I was going through the cycles of the box, murder/suicide (which I quickly left), geographic cure, get sick go crazy. I felt momentary anger that I allowed myself to be manipulated into buying this big property. I dwelled upon all the money I had invested in this home, and felt that because of those decisions, I was unable to move on. As I entered the get sick, go crazy wall, feeling stuck in the seeming confinement "of the world," I remembered, I had to *Change*.

I knew I could not, and should not, endure this incongruence.

I went to one of the mirrors in my home. I was crying. I looked in my eyes as if I could connect with my soul, and shouted that I didn't want to live a life that someone created for me anymore. I wanted to live my life and I didn't want to feel trapped. I remember screaming and crying and I remember, adamantly believing, *knowing*, I would get an answer.

314

I had become so aware of all my feelings. I was so connected to the idea of a bigger Universe than just the physical, a spiritual world that was available and desiring to help, and all we need do is ask and believe. Within moments after my emotional experience, I was sitting in my home office and I instinctively looked up at my computer screen. On the page I had left my computer open to, there now appeared a quote. I didn't look for it, it just happened to be there, revealing itself to me as I raised my gaze.

"Your time is limited, so don't waste it living someone else's life. Don't be trapped by dogma – which is living with the results of other people's thinking. Don't let the noise of other's opinions drown out your own inner voice. And most important, have the courage to follow your heart and intuition. They somehow already know what you truly want to become. Everything else is secondary." Steve Jobs

I was awed that the profound Universe showed me these words, words largely of my own choosing; words I had never seen or heard before, but it was obvious I would hear them and know them, and know all was being orchestrated for my highest, greatest good. I read the words, *have the courage to follow your heart and intuition*, and I asked myself, *where am I not listening to myself?* I knew instantly.

My awareness elevated once again. I had released my desire to control in so many areas of my life, but I was becoming aware of my attachment to the idea that money still, in some measure, defined who I was. I had loosened my grip on the tangible, but I had not yet completely released it. I now knew as long as that belief lingered, I would not be fully free. To live free, I had to accept that the biggest roadblock in my own path to freedom came in the form of releasing my remaining attachment to the physical ego. The cord that kept me tied to the physical, unable to fully experience the Divine.

The last piece of the physical world that I clung to, the last piece I feared releasing was so ingrained that it had lingered on. I had a fear, that somehow if my financials were diminished, I was diminished. The *image* of who I was would be gone. In that moment, I released the last thing that kept me in chains; I chose *Love* over *Fear*, I chose *Allow* over *Control* and I was about to embark in a moment by moment endless experience of total freedom. I could **Trust**; just **Know**.

I would no longer be driven by the physical, my money or fear of losing it. I would be driven by my heart, love. I would truly be free. Literally at that precise moment, I called my realtor and told her to drop my price by $75,000. I had never felt right about what I was asking for my home, my intuition had been prompting me all along, but instead, I had taken advice from well-meaning friends who wanted to see me with the financial security I had once had. I remembered that I am my own authority. I was certain that this was the precise message, the precise release, and now my home would sell. I eagerly anticipated the immediate unfolding, as I continued drudging to my job feeling the incongruence.

As if in direct response to my faith, within mere weeks of finally letting go and reducing my sales price, I received a call from my daughter. She was wondering what I was doing in mid May, and if I might like to come and join her and her husband as they welcomed their baby into the world. My baby was pregnant. Love was prevailing.

I had planned on downsizing and likely staying where I was, yet suddenly I was aware I needed to move back to where my life began, Long Island, New York. My daughter was living out east on the island and I knew I was being called home. I finally accepted all that had shattered was becoming whole again.

It had now been nearly eight months since I placed my home on the market. With each passing day there was an opportunity for me to lose faith, for me to decide that all I thought was unfolding was nothing more than my imagination. I could have decided that all the lessons I learned were not real, that life wasn't what I was beginning to believe. I was just waiting; frankly, I didn't understand, why hadn't it happened? Four months had gone by since I dropped my price, and not only were there no offers, there was no activity. Where had I gone wrong? I started to doubt my certainty.

And then, looking within once again, I realized a great truth about me. I was still lacking in faith. I did not have total trust. I reduced my price in alignment with my intuition, but I held on to my safety net. I kept my job. I stayed in the incongruence, living outside of peace. I had to do that didn't I? Who would quit their job without a plan? My logic, my mind, told me to fear. My mind told me I had to stay in the incongruence. I had no concrete plan, but I now considered the reality that I had enough funds to survive for a while. I knew I wouldn't starve.

I assessed all I thought I understood; I investigated my incongruence, my lack of peace. I resolved that I did not have to ever live outside of my integrity. And then, I finally moved to the last step. I released ALL attachments to the physical. I released them all in favor of my heart, my inner knowing, the place where the full power of God resides. I released them all in favor of *faith*, which allows things to happen. I felt total **Trust**. I decided I would just quit my job. I knew with everything in me, all my heart, it was this, my final release that would set me free. In leaving my job, my perceived security, I made my announcement to the Universe that I would no longer live in incongruence. I decided the "how" was not up to me, all that mattered was that I act on my knowing. Just **trust**. I did not have a single **worry**. I had no **fear**. **I was not vested in any outcome.** I was only vested in living in alignment with my true self. I had complete and total conviction. I released my grip.

Professionally, I was unsure of what I would do next. During the early stages of my healing I had completed writing a book that I thought was my life's purpose, yet I had no inclination to publish. The coaching I thought I was born to do was on hold, with no sense of wisdom if this was still my purpose. I previously had allowed this to have a hold on me as well; this sense of barrenness, the emptiness of dreams unfulfilled, but in this moment I just knew everything was playing out as it should. Once I released my grip, once I fully *Let Go*, these thoughts and fears surrounding my lack of clarity simply vanished.

I had no prompting of how my financials would work themselves out, but I had something more, I had **trust**. In total faith I knew, there was no doubt, only knowing. I, perhaps for the first time, was experiencing total peace. Suddenly I considered that in the limbo, the Universe was preparing me. In that place that we often feel lost and abandoned, in that place where clarity is not present, I realized *that* is when the Universe is orchestrating for our highest, greatest good. In that limbo where we start doubting, or start giving up faith, is the precise moment the pivotal reality of all you have moved toward is about to come to fruition. What if I recoiled to my fear as the signs seemed to indicate my *knowing* was wrong? How often do we do that, while right on the cusp of all things we desire? Instead I chose to recognize my lack of peace; I assessed where I wasn't in alignment with what I claimed to believe, and trusted my *knowing*.

I needed to move forward and allow things to play out, with **trust**. I felt I knew the direction I was feeling led and I acted. I just needed to know, I was following my inner knowing. And I did, boldly and completely in total **faith**. I trusted that more would be revealed, and all was being arranged for my highest, greatest good.

I gave my notice to work. I revealed the truth about my observations regarding their operations and asserted that I felt incongruent with their values. I felt no need to force change or to make them hear me, only my desire to hold up the mirror so they might see. I need not control. I embraced my clients, feeling great integrity for the work we had done together and had certainty in my step.

The Universe's response to my **faith**, to my **conviction**, to my **absolute trust and knowing**, was swift.

Months ago, when I had first put my home on the market, prompted by a friend I wrote an invitation to the Universe. I asked for precisely what I desired relative to my beautiful home and its transition. I wrote asking for the perfect buyers to appear.

It was a detailed note filled with emotions that I had finally learned to feel again. Here is an excerpt expressing a sense of my message:

This home deserves to be filled with people that appreciate all she has become. People who have lived enough to really value her for the gift she is...not for her presence that can be felt by the [physical] ego, but for her presence that can be felt by the spirit. She provides great protection but she is love...bold yet gentle, elegant yet simple. I invite those that understand her and love her for what she is...those that don't wish to show her off; instead they wish to share her.

Best of all, at night, they dance on the back patio...with the water gently falling and the lights as bright as they desire, as they cherish the moments this home brings them...as it did me. God's space.

I understand now, the Universe did not respond to my invitation until I truly stood in my trust, my full freedom, my knowing. All would not come to fruition until I released everything that had a hold on me, and walked in full integrity, in alignment with all of me, free from all attachments. I had to allow my highest, greatest good to happen. I had to be willing to trust. I had to allow the full power of God to operate through me.

Coming home that day after quitting my job, I looked around my home; I realized that the *physical* suddenly had little importance to me. I was so content with releasing it all. It didn't matter if I had none of these things. I wanted only love. I felt myself breathe, my first breath of true freedom. My first breath of my new life.

I decided, when the buyers came, they could have it all. Every bit of furniture, anything they wanted.

And I knew they would come.

As I walked around the home, I realized the heart of the home was the only challenge, my cherished *"LA MADONNA IN PREGHIERA" "Sorrowful Mary"* original artist *"SALVI GIOVANNI BATTISTA" (1609-1685).*

Over this time of healing, I spent many a night tearfully speaking to her. She knew of so much pain and I felt her understanding. I felt her acceptance of me in my sorrow. I felt her strength. I felt her presence. Who could know more pain than her? How could I not feel understood in her presence? Her meaning in my life was not measurable in the physical. What would I do with Mary? I didn't see Her as something I owned, She was not an object, She was so much more to me. I loved Her. She had breathed life in me, kept me alive when I felt like dying. She was my confidant and my friend, my warrior and my spirit, when I couldn't find any of those pieces in me; She somehow instilled them and carried me.

Many years earlier I had traveled to Italy and was captivated by Her beauty as I gazed upon Her in a church in Florence. I found an artist willing to create a replica of Her. He poured his heart into Her creation. She truly was a masterpiece and I knew She would be the focal point of the magnificent room I had constructed to hold Her. She was the *heart* of my home and over time, She had helped me find, and open, my own heart.

To me, She was no longer a work of art, She was my friend. In all my tearful nights healing and looking for wholeness, She was there. I couldn't in my heart sell Her, and I knew I could not keep Her. I was downsizing and no home I would now have could hold Her.

I spoke to Her and asked for wisdom. I shared with Her my heart.

I decided all would be revealed to me in its proper timing, not my timing.

And so, I **trusted**.

I had total faith. I had absolutely no fear. Not a morsel of desire to control. I did not vest myself in any outcome. I only vested in **love**. I embraced the freedom of this experience, the presence of love, and the absence of fear. I cherished this feeling of **peace**, of total **trust** and **faith**. I embodied this sense of **absolute knowing**. For the first time, I was willing to admit what I had always at some level known. I had allowed external forces to create my doubt. Not now, not ever again. Now I knew. I had total faith that I could just allow. The spirit of God would allow my river to peacefully flow, all I ever had to do was simply **allow** and **trust**.

The **very day** after giving my notice to work, my realtor told me someone wanted to see my home and they felt confident this couple would make a cash offer. A cash offer would eliminate any challenges of the physical and allow the transaction to be blessed in the spirit, not the bureaucracy and red tape that comes from the regulative control I had always lived in.

The following day when this newly married couple joyfully stepped into my home, the woman began to share, that eight years prior she had a desire to buy this home but a situation in her life made that impossible. Now she had a new life and she reveled at all the changes that had been made to my home. She was in awe over all the improvements and expansion. She shared that she felt she had transformed so much in all those years, and so had the home she desired. She felt bonded, connected and grateful. Now she knew that perfect synchronicity brought her to this place in this perfect timing.

As she walked into the room where Mary was waiting, she looked up in joy and amazement and spoke the most beautiful words, "She is the heart and soul of the room." She turned to her husband, "We have to make sure Mary stays." Hearing these words graced my soul, they loved Her as much as I did.

The agreement in every part of this transaction was made so easily, so beautifully and the very next day we were in contract. I was at perfect peace with every aspect of the transaction. My home was sold within 48 hours of my leaving my job. When I showed true faith and conviction; when I believed my intuition in my heart, over the logic and fear of my mind, the Universe provided immediately. The value of honoring our feeling of incongruence, and getting into alignment is immeasurable. Once we release all our attachments, we move to live in the full spirit of God and all that has always been available to us.

To ensure that Mary's presence would still be with me, this generous couple arrived at my home and presented to me a painting of Mary, beautifully adorned with beads carefully placed on Her one by one, a reflection of the love that went into Her creation. This Mary was a work of art that her sister had made. In her heart she knew, she had to give Her to me to remind me that Mary would always have Her arms around our homes.

You see, I had finally fully transitioned. My ego now was translucent. I no longer had a grip on things. I released all my attachments. I simply had to allow and trust. I fully released the physical. I transitioned to the Divine ego, the enlightened path.

For the first time in my life I did not define success in tangible terms. I knew I was successful because I felt love and peace. I could simply sit, and joyfully reflect upon my life. I did not need to *do* or to *have*. I could just *love* and *be*. *My success is now defined by who I am and how I love. Things are perishable, love is not. I rejoice in finally finding The Truth.*

I had to *allow* the Universe to give me all that awaited me. I had to **trust** that the full spirit of God would operate through me to make all things possible. At the core of my being, I simply had to *know* that I was deserving of all the blessings, and they would come in droves. God gives us the desires of our heart.

I found the perfect home nestled in some trees, just moments from my daughter near the ocean. I was finally just the river ebbing and flowing, enjoying all the scenery. After nearly three decades of treading water, I was now peacefully and simply in the joyful flow of life. *My willingness to Allow, replaced my compulsion to control. Deep penetrating Love and Trust replaced my fear; Behold I am finally free.*

I moved from fear and control, to Love and Freedom.

When I was 10 years old, I remember a moment when I determined that there was something bigger. Something I could not understand, something that no adult had ever been able to explain to me. I hoped to someday get some understanding of this feeling. In that moment I vowed that if I ever did, I would write a book. I would share it with the world. I have grasped pieces of this "something" throughout my life. I have written many books, but none of them ended in peace. Once settled in my new home, the cloud of uncertainty lifted. The wisdom for my book's completion came streaming through. In addition to the peace I found in writing my book, miraculously clients appeared. My coaching business reignited. It simply came to life. These two happenings allowed me to do what brings me the most joy, enjoying countless love filled moments with my family and helping others Live Free.

I now realize I don't have to surround myself with people who choose not to accept me as I am; in the fullness of who I am, inclusive of my imperfections. I have chosen instead to only allow people who are kind to me in my life, people who value the sanctity of all of me.

I am looking to invite each of you to live a transparent life. Just stand in who you are. Be your truth. If there are parts of you that you want to disown, then you can never be whole. I embrace all of me precisely as I am. I apply new "*knowings*" that are revealed to me, enhancing the joy in my life moment by moment. My mission is to grow from every experience and continue a life with only love. I choose to only be surrounded by those who I can trust with my intimacies. I proclaim, "This is me; all of me, transparent me. I love me".

When you believe something down to your core as I did, then your outer world will prove to you that your belief is true, by constantly reflecting this truth in your outer world. You will find yourself met with experiences that illustrate the truth you are holding onto in your inner belief system. If you want your life to change, you must release those beliefs that are creating pain in your life, in favor of the knowing that you are loved and supported by the full power of God, and if you choose to allow it, together you will create a life of endless joy. There may still be bad "out there" in the world, but focusing on the good draws that good to us. As more of us focus on that good, the good in the world will triumph.

Today I am free. I no longer feel a constant feeling of guilt or a feeling that I am bad. I love who I am and every day I make healthy choices for my life. What makes them healthy is they honor me. Freely now and easily, I do as I please. On those rare moments I want an indulgence or I feel I didn't make the healthiest choice; I still celebrate me. It is okay. I am okay.

Know too, that as we close out each and every chapter of our lives that holds in it that deception, as we break free from all delusion, we create life anew. We create a life that invites in people who will treat us with love and honor, as we have finally learned to give that blessing to ourselves. In doing so, we announce to the world it is all we know, and all we will allow. We choose to no longer tolerate the intolerable in our personal lives or in the world at large.

Once we have fully focused on holding our own piece of the jigsaw puzzle and achieved the peace that comes with that focus, when we understand and embrace all our powers, we then have the awareness that together we can allow the full power of God to flow through us, to help and protect those truly in need. Our light reveals all that lurks and hides in the shadows. We see The Truth, and will join to protect those who need our protection, those who long to hold their piece and are willing, but in this moment are unable. Once we are truly holding our own piece, we have the strength, power, and awareness to know which pieces need to be held and protected, to have a world at peace. Our jigsaw puzzle can be held in our strength. Imagine if we could all find our own peace. The puzzle of the world would become peacefully whole and complete.

As I was writing the final pages of this book, I was having breakfast with my daughter and her then two month old son. She seemingly, out of nowhere, shared that she remembered something I had told her when I ended one of my relationships many years ago. She said that I had come home and told her that the reason I ended the relationship was, "He was a bad man who did some good things and he wasn't healthy for us to live with anymore." She and I had never spoken of that moment, and unbeknownst to her, I had shared that story in the pages of this book. As my daughter recalled that memory she said to me, "I never forgot that, I think that is why I was intolerant to any form of abuse all my life." By grand design, in synchronistic beauty, my grandson laughed and allowed his smile to linger as he gazed upon us. My daughter and I looked in each other's eyes, and we knew, the cycle of abuse had been broken.

I had finally found my peace. I found my peace within me, and that peace and trust allowed me the freedom to be here, watching my daughter enjoy her peace, as I float down my river in total tranquility. I am whole, I am complete, and for the first time in my life I am experiencing the true happiness that comes with peace. My daughter had been peacefully floating down her river for years. Eventually, she had found another who was also floating peacefully along in his. They chose to merge their rivers and create a meaningful, beautiful life together. They have gratitude for one another, and all that is in their life, individually and together they have peace. They have faith in the abundance of their love and the rest just seems to fall into place. Born from that love is my grandson. I see evidence that every step of my journey has been worth it in the light of his smile, and the fact that I am alive, and here to see it. Now *that*, is a sight worth Waking Up for.

As all the great prophets and leaders have taught; awareness is the key. I hope I have helped you to find yours. In our humble awareness, we can change the world. Simply love and trust yourself. Choose to embrace the full power of the loving Universe, and know that all the pieces will fall perfectly in place. I vest not in any outcome of this journey of life, it is the moment by moment flow that I rejoice in, and so it is. I choose to relish in the knowledge that I am in communion with a powerful co-creator who is conspiring for a world filled with Divine Love, where we embrace one another with compassion and exist as a world—at peace. If we can simply choose to **trust** our *inner knowing* and love all our capacities, we will **allow** all things to happen for the highest, greatest good. This power has been with us always, if only we would **awaken**.

"Success is not final, failure is not fatal: It is the courage to continue that counts."

-Winston Churchill

"Character: *In the great scheme of things, what matters is not how long you live, but why you live; what you stand for; and what you are willing to die for."*

-Paul Watson

Acknowledgements

I would like to thank all of the participants in my life, for without them I would not have had the necessary experiences, and gained the knowledge that I needed to synthesize and build upon, to create the message held within these pages. In one sweeping motion I would also like to thank my abusers, those that most dedicatedly held the mirror up so that I might see the pieces of me I refused to embrace.

I would like to express my gratitude, first to my professional teachers and then those who joined me in my personal circle, relentlessly providing love and acceptance, strength and support.

MaryAnn Kilmartin Thrush

It was more than 20 years ago that I first stepped into your office asking for emotional therapy and guidance about my life, and the relationships in it. Today as I write, I see your lessons in the fabric of all that I have written. You took me on a unique journey to learn and fully absorb human behavior, and the emotions and response of such. You laid the foundation for me about holding only my own piece, to experience peace, and the concept of boundaries and how to set them and live them. Coming to you with a distorted sense of self and a desire for external validation, you taught me how to be a parent to myself and begin to discover how to find who I really truly am. For your countless responses to my cries for help, and your constant desire to teach me to get out of my box of frustration through *the change wall*, I thank you.

Doug Lennick

In nearly the same timing I entered my career in full force, I met you, one of my strongest teachers; my leader, my mentor, but perhaps most importantly, my friend. You confirmed for me my internal belief that leading with compassion for people was at the core of success, and that bottom line results were achieved through helping those you lead find their power. You believed in the inner flame of all people. Your belief in my inner flame, kept me always striving to be in alignment with who I really was at my core to achieve meaningful results. I believe you were the heart of the company I grew up in, and your influence led me to understand that alignment between principles, values, beliefs, actions, and words would yield positive results. You taught me that people persevere for leaders who believe in them, embrace and value the essence of who they are. I cherish your wisdom and your heart. You pushed for me to understand my moral compass, and that its power was more powerful than rules. My integration was slow, but I arrived and I am grateful.

Dr. Jayne Gardner

It would not be until hiring you as a coach that a tiny little off the cuff comment you made would begin to awaken me to my truth. The truth I never wanted to face. I was afraid of my intimate partner. We never spoke of this in any detail as the purpose of our relationship was business, but the subtle message that *I chose to whisper as he entered the room* and suggesting that just might be a sign of my fear, unconsciously began to awaken me. Thank you for your subtle nudge that began to move me toward freedom and for coaching me to realize, I was not my job.

Doug Carter

I can't know if you consciously or unconsciously knew that your decision to invite me to one of your events would in essence, allow my life to be saved. Who could have known that I would awaken the day before boarding that plane? I arrived in perfect synchronicity, to be introduced to those who could provide the wisdom to begin to strengthen me enough for the remainder of my journey to wholeness.

On that trip there were many who availed themselves for my healing, some preferring to be nameless, although in no way does that lessen their power in my life.

328

John Cunningam

During Doug Carter's event, you introduced me to the concept of sociopath, an integral part of my life that I had no familiarity with. You further helped me see the truth about my circumstances. The healing exercises that you took me through were paramount in my finding the fullness of my power. I have never looked back. Your support, heart and devotion, will always joyfully be remembered by me.

Timothy Trujillo

As my world had fully crashed and I found myself in a tug-of-war, longing to live and wanting to die; longing to be free, but confused on the path, a God moment brought me to you. With your loving and gentle healing style, you helped me embrace where I was so that I could be free. Accepting me as I was every step of the way, moment by moment and teaching me to do the same. You strengthened me and helped me discover, and later define, a path to wholeness. I am no longer, a "self-sociopath."

Clients

Thank you to my many clients for revealing their truths, helping me to see pieces that I had missed. In my effort to help you, I had more truths revealed to me. You helped me paint the picture so that my teachings could be seen by all who choose to look.

Friends

In my pain and development I have had many supporters, countless lifelong friends, Debbie Kitson, Donna Sutton, and Alice Riviezzo, and Arlene, to name a few. You allowed me to lean on you, and always offered to guide and support. Your love has been my lighthouse. And then there are those friends who appeared at the most challenging time in my life and directed and carried me, Terri Lindley, Jennifer Rae Borné, Jan and Gary Allison, Donna and Mike Cunningham and Chris Steels, who likely saved my life. Each of your appearances in my life clearly was by grand design and I cherish all you are to me. A special thanks to Lori Pescatore. I have known you nearly all my life, and certainly called you friend. However, at my time of crisis, you came through for me in immeasurable ways, and I thank you. Thanks too to Lynne Hardin, Freda Deskin, Sharon Boykin and Rhonda Keison, for pieces of wisdom, guidance, and power along the way. Special thanks to Matt Pryor for your devotion supporting me in spite of how my story must have sounded. Thank you as well, Kerry Blackburn. A debt of gratitude to Susan Conway who made it possible for me to be here in NY, surrounded in love, by leading me to John and Andi Sheperd, who catapulted me home, by answering my prayer for the perfect buyer for my treasured home and the perfect souls to love my cherished Mary. Lastly, special thanks to Dana Rose, Sarah Steels, and Peter Haas for your enthusiasm and insights.

My Parents–Albert and Lillian Iannarone

Mom and Dad, you were always such loyal supporters of my goals. Attending all my events and always responsibly caring for me. Mom, you helped me believe that I could do anything I set my mind to, and Dad, you taught me it was important to succeed. You both were and are unwavering in your care and feeding of my confidence and for that I am grateful. Perhaps most importantly, Mom and Dad, when I finally realized I was vulnerable and my world fell apart, you showed up no questions asked, and stayed and endured much of the fear and danger I was finally awakened to. There was never a time you were not there for me, and I am grateful, for your love, for your knowledge, and for who you are. Our close bond, our joyful shared experiences, for these I am grateful. Mom, I want to thank you specifically for our meaningful, deep conversations about the world, about our lives, about our love and connection. You are my friend. I Love you Mom and Dad.

My daughter–Ashleigh Gardner

Nothing can surpass the power and force of your love, of your acceptance, of your belief in me, and your ability to see the truth.

In all the twists and turns of my life you were there. In every journey you endured with me, you held on knowing the one thing I never wanted you to miss. I loved you and always would and that no matter what we encountered that would never change. That was one message I thankfully know I never failed to send you.

In my quest for wholeness, I had a distorted view of priorities and couldn't see that who I was had value, the value of my life as just me. I could only see my value as what I did, how I provided. Your eyes always could see the truth I was missing, if only I could have embraced your wisdom sooner.

You were there for me as my child offering unconditional love, smiles, and joy beyond measure. You gave me a reason to keep moving forward.

At times you were there as my parent. I remember one such time as I sat on the floor in tears, you screamed at me, "You claim you believe in God, and yet you crumble in fear." Such wisdom, if only I heard you then. Time and time again, you would attempt to shake me awake to what you could see. I am only grateful that your life is a testimony of your awakeness.

And now I am grateful to call you friend.

After more than 20 years of effort in the creation of this book, with absolute knowing I presented to you, my finally finished product knowing you would use your knowledge of me, your knowledge of my intention, your brilliance, and your love and translate for me some of my more intangible thoughts into powerful words. I knew you were the right person to help me draw a compelling and clear picture to the reader. Because of you, your wisdom, and ability to communicate powerfully, I believe this book will be more powerful, and have a positive impact in changing the world.

I commit to you, that without you, my daughter, these words would never be in print as they are, and the messages would not fall together as beautifully as I believe they have. No one understands me, knows me and loves me as you do. Not a day goes by that I am not proud to call you daughter, for all you do, for all your successes, but more than anything for who you are. I love you and with gratitude for our entire journey thus far, I thank you.

Love to you Todd for the greatest gift of loving my daughter as life intended. And of course my deepest love to my beautiful grandson Finn who adds joy and laughter beyond measure.

References

De Becker, Gavin (1997). *The Gift of Fear*.
New York, NY: Dell Publishing.

Hay, Louise L. (1999). *You Can Heal Your Life*.
London: Hay House Lifestyles.

Ruiz, Don Miguel (1997) *The Four Agreements*.
San Rafael, CA: Amber-Allen Publishing, Inc.

Ruiz, Don Miguel (1999) *The Mastery of Love*.
San Rafael, CA: Amber-Allen Publishing, Inc.

Walsch, Neale Donald (1995) *Conversations with God* (Book 1).
Charlottesville, VA: Hampton Roads Publishing Company, Inc.